PRAISE FOR
SO YOU MARRIED A NARCISSIST

"I would have been spared years of anguish, bewilderment and trauma had I read Freya's book while I walked that path. She puts names and structures to my experiences and brings reason and logic into an otherwise unreasonable and illogical journey. She lays out a path to hope, recovery, and freedom."

—Calli J. Linwood,
author of *Walking Tall: Healing from Domestic Violence,
Abuse and Trauma, Break Forth: Becoming Victorious over
a past of Abuse, Trauma and Domestic Violence* and
Coming Through the Fire: Preparing for Battle

"Like arrows to the heart, the reader is hit with the stark, malevolent reality of life with a narcissist as they read Freya Strom's book. Seeing their realities in black and white helps those ensnared understand and trust what their instincts are telling them, helping them evade the pitfalls and traps set to snare and consume them. This book is a stunning exposé of the narcissistic world, interspersed with personal testimonies displaying how the different aspects manifest in real-time. Infused with statements of humour, hope, and encouragement, the reader is strengthened for the battle before them."

—Jocelyn A. Drozda,
author of *Invisible No More: Personal Identity Restored,*
facilitator of Healing Identity Seminars

"*So You Married A Narcissist* is a well-articulated, fully researched, and convincing case designed to help those of us who have had an unfortunate encounter with this type of manipulation and abuse. She offers steps to take when we have failed to tend to our boundaries, self-love, and self-worth in any relationship—the intelligence that supports healthy relating abounds here!"

—Christine Patton,
author of *Showing Up: Becoming the Me I Want to Be*

"If you've ever stayed up late at night researching the topic of narcissism, you likely have a deep knowledge of the pain and destruction narcissists cause. This book combines research, real-life experiences, and a practical guide to identifying, dealing with, and escaping relationships with narcissists. Her clearly constructed inventory of narcissistic traits and their accompanying behaviours are particularly helpful as they provide an objective checklist for those trying to determine whether they're in a relationship with a narcissist and, if so, how they got there. This book confirms whether you've been sucked in by someone with NPD and offers understanding and healing once you've set boundaries or left the relationship."

—Jill Wilson,
Coordinator of Continuing Education
at Concordia Seminary, St. Louis

"Freya's book is a candid description of the painful reality of a relationship with someone with narcissistic personality disorder. *So You Married a Narcissist* will be especially helpful to those who are just becoming aware of these dynamics in a relationship, who need to be validated and empowered, or who are looking for strength to get out. So often we blame ourselves when our relationships do not go well; this book shifts that perspective away from self-blame to acknowledging that while we are powerless to change the relationship, we are indeed empowered to do something about it."

—Rebecca Berghorn, M.S.Edu,
licensed marriage and family therapist

"Although I did not marry a narcissist, I have worked for two. I wish I'd had this knowledge and the strategies from this book back then."

—Lauren Duncan, Ph.D.,
screenwriter

"*So You Married a Narcissist* is packed with information, anecdotal stories, and practical advice. The author explains how to identify narcissistic abuse by defining the characteristics of a narcissist and by laying out what it looks like in everyday interactions. Freya shares stories from people who have lived with it and through it. She shares her personal story of her life with a narcissist and encourages the reader not to be afraid or ashamed of reaching out for help. Freya ends the book with well-laid-out practical steps on how to heal and gives a strong message of hope to help you move forward with your life after narcissistic abuse. This book lets you know that you are not alone, and there is help and healing that can be yours."

—Carmel Hoyer,
massage therapist

"Freya Strom takes us into the world of women who are stuck in narcissistic abuse. So many of my clients failed to see what was happening until caught in the web. This book is written from first-hand experience along with well-researched material. A must-read for women who want to find their better life but need things explained in layman's terms."

—Julie Starr,
life coach and author of *Your Husband Left:*
Now What?! How to Be Your Own Hero and
Live Your Better Life After Divorce

SO YOU MARRIED A NARCISSIST

SO YOU MARRIED A NARCISSIST

An Empath's Guide to Healing and Empowerment

FREYA STROM

SO YOU MARRIED A NARCISSIST

Editor: Nina Shoroplova—ninashoroplova.ca
Cover Designer: Pagatana Design Service—pagatana.com
Book Interior and E-book Designer: Amit Dey—amitdey2528@gmail.com
Production & Publishing Consultant: Geoff Affleck—geoffaffleck.com

ISBN: 978-1-7782296-0-2 (Paperback)
ISBN: 978-1-7782296-1-9 (eBook)
ISBN: 978-1-7782296-2-6 (Audiobook)

PSY022080 PSYCHOLOGY / Psychopathology / Personality Disorders
PSY003000 PSYCHOLOGY / Applied Psychology
SEL008000 SELF-HELP / Codependency

CONTENTS

LETTER FROM THE AUTHOR

Perhaps you have picked up this book because you are wondering if you are in a relationship with a narcissist. I get it! I was unknowingly in a relationship with a narcissist for almost six years. I did not truly understand what a narcissist was until several months after I was out the door of my marriage. Sure, I had heard the word "narcissist" before but I didn't understand what it really meant. Toward the end of my marriage, I was in a perpetual state of shell shock and I didn't know what was happening. I didn't understand how my husband could turn on a dime to be so cold, callous, and abusive, whirling on me with such rage, and creating strange accusations out of nowhere. I wanted our marriage to work and was pleading with him to listen, to hear me, and to care. Instead of trying to work things out, I was stonewalled with such a strong contempt. Along with the other psychological mind games, I felt like I was going crazy (I later discovered that this is what *gaslighting* is.) I was desperate. I didn't want to end my marriage; however, I could *not* continue to live with the way things were.

When we finally went to counselling, I was thinking there were two possibilities: that our counselling would either provide a miracle from God, or it would be confirmation that I needed to get out. During our sessions, things went downhill with lightning speed. In a matter of weeks, I felt that our relationship drove off a cliff the size of the

Grand Canyon. (As I would later discover, these drastic turnabouts are called the "devaluation" and "discard" phases in the narcissistic cycle. These are inevitable, textbook moves and behaviours associated with the narcissistic personality disorder.)

I continued with counselling long after he stopped going and after our marriage had ended. In the beginning the counsellor never said anything about narcissism but she did talk about "contempt." And when *contempt* enters a marriage, it's pretty much game over. I began to research everything. I looked up articles on contempt. Which lead me to abusive personality disorder (APD). This led me to researching more about emotional abuse, where I learned about sociopaths, borderline personality, and Narcissistic Personality Disorder (NPD). I began to slowly understand what I had been living with, and what I was experiencing. I dove headfirst into books, blogs, articles, YouTube videos, and anything that could explain what had happened. I began to truly understand about narcissists, who they are, and how they operate.

In my research, I also wanted to understand how I wound up with a narcissist and what I needed to learn and do differently in my own life so that this would *never* happen again. It takes two to tango and this drastic wake-up call clearly demonstrated that I had a lot of *my own* personal work to do. I searched for the ways where I needed to change and grow. *We can never truly change another person; we can only change ourselves.* This is a huge theme throughout this book, and when you embrace it, it is very empowering! I kept up with my counselling, and was finally attending to the deep and hidden wounds that had been covered over for decades and were in desperate need of healing.

Yes, I have *many* imperfections, and I am constantly continuing to learn and grow in my own journey. I am writing this book not as an expert, but as someone who has been there, who understands, and who has lived the journey of wholeness after separating from a narcissist.

It is my desire to encourage you in your own process of awareness, healing, and empowerment.

You are certainly not alone.

Through this book, it is my desire to

- educate and bring to you a greater understanding of what narcissism is.
- enlighten you to the short-term and long-term effects that can take place in your life if you are in a relationship with a narcissist.
- explore possibilities as to why you may have a narcissist in your life, or perhaps why they are allowed to continue to exist in your life.
- give you greater insight and understanding into your own story.
- reveal some of my own blind spots (and the blind spots from others) and see if you can relate to or learn from any of these stories.
- give you some strategies to deal with narcissists.
- show you how to make a few personal shifts so that you can "narcissist-proof" your life.
- help you to reprogram your brain and your heart.
- give you encouragement, through the many experiences in this book, to know that you are not alone.
- provide you with hope and empowerment to step into the amazing life that you most certainly deserve!

This book is designed to give awareness and bring hope, healing, and empowerment to those who are currently in, or who have previously been in a relationship with a narcissist. Know that in whatever you have gone through, there is meaning in your pain. You can come out of this experience with a healing that goes even deeper than what has happened during this relationship. This experience does not have to paralyse you. Instead, it can lead you to greater strength, wisdom, power, and love. I invite you to join with me on this journey of healing, freedom, and empowerment. You too can not only survive, but *THRIVE* after being with a narcissist!

Wishing you the very best in your journey,

Freya Strom

DISCLAIMER FROM THE AUTHOR

First of all, let me say that I am not a psychologist, psychiatrist, or a counsellor. This book is not designed to diagnose Narcissistic Personality Disorder (NPD) or to give professional advice to the reader. My knowledge base comes from firsthand experiences of being in relationships with narcissists, in my capacity both as a friend and life coach, through listening to the stories of others, and through researching what the experts have to say. During my investigation, I learned the professional terminology for what people experience in narcissistic relationships, including "gaslighting," "triangulation," "word salad," "love bombing," "devaluation," "hoovering," "the discard phase," "split personalities," "stonewalling," and countless other terms. These are all part and parcel of being in a relationship with a narcissist.

Although narcissism does occur across the gender board, for the most part, in this book I often refer to a narcissist in the masculine form. This personality disorder is more prevalent among men, whereas other personality disorders are more common among women.

I am writing this book to share my experiences and the experiences of some dear friends who have dealt with narcissists, in order to give you, the reader, some insights. This book is designed to take you on a journey of learning what happened, to give insight as to why you got into a relationship with a narcissist (or why they continue to show up in your life), and how you can heal and move on to a fulfilling and beautiful life. This book is sprinkled with quotes to give you snippets of wisdom and sometimes a much-needed laugh. You are not alone in your journey of recovery and returning to the best parts of yourself. It is my hope that these lessons and insights will give you awareness, healing, and growth in your own journey after the narcissist.

DEFINITIONS AND HISTORY OF NARCISSISM

No doubt you have heard the word "narcissism" or you have heard of someone described as a "narcissist." This term has been thrown around quite loosely in our society, particularly when it comes to entertainers, politicians, and self-centred or egotistical people. However, a narcissist is much more than an arrogant, self-absorbed person. The term describes a very dangerous and destructive personality disorder. When this disorder is taken to the extreme, there will be inevitable and devastating consequences for anyone who remains in a relationship with that person.

Former FBI Special Agent, Joe Navarro, author of *Dangerous Personalities: An FBI Profiler Shows You How to Identify and Protect Yourself from Harmful People,* scales the Narcissistic Personality Disorder (NPD). When a person is at the low end of the narcissistic scale, they will take an emotional toll on others and they will be difficult to work with. At the higher end of the scale, a person who has NPD will be "an emotional, psychological, financial, or physical danger to himself or herself or to others."[1]

Personally, I compare narcissism to cancer cells. We all have a bit of narcissism or narcissistic traits within ourselves, just like we all have cancer cells within our bodies. There's nothing we can do to completely eradicate cancer cells from our bodies. That being said, although everyone does have some cancer cells, the majority of people have not crossed over to "being diagnosed with cancer."

In the same way that we all have cancer cells, we can never truly be without some degree of narcissism in our lives. Although we can all be selfish at times, the majority of people have not crossed over to the extreme level of being branded with NPD. Small doses of either cancer or narcissism are not ideal; however, we are all human. Regardless of whether you are talking about diseased cells in the body or a personality disorder, when certain negative traits multiply and grow to the point where a person officially crosses over to being diagnosed, this is when you have a really destructive problem.

In the same way that cancer has degrees and stages of severity (stage four being the most dangerous), narcissism also has a scale of treachery. The more narcissistic traits a person has, the more dangerous they become. For more information from the professionals, I encourage you to read Joe Navarro's book, *Dangerous Personalities: An FBI Profiler Shows You How to Identify and Protect Yourself from Harmful People*.

Throughout this book we are going to explore narcissism in more depth. For now, here are a few definitions to help you understand the Narcissistic Personality Disorder.

Psychology Today's Definition

The hallmarks of narcissistic personality disorder (NPD) are grandiosity, a lack of empathy for other people, and a need for admiration. People with this condition are frequently described as arrogant, self-centered, manipulative, and demanding. They may also concentrate on grandiose fantasies and may be convinced that they deserve special treatment. These characteristics typically begin in early adulthood and must be consistently evident in multiple contexts, such as at work and in relationships.

People with NPD often try to associate with other people they believe are unique or gifted in some way, which can enhance their own self-esteem. They tend to seek excessive admiration and attention and have difficulty tolerating criticism or defeat.[2]

Wikipedia's Definition

Narcissistic personality disorder (NPD) is a personality disorder in which there is a long-term pattern of abnormal behavior characterized by exaggerated feelings of self-importance, an excessive need for admiration, and a lack of understanding of others' feelings. People affected by it often spend a lot of time thinking about achieving power or success, or about their appearance. They often take advantage of the people around them. The behavior typically begins by early adulthood, and occurs across a variety of situations.[3]

Other Less Clinical Definitions

Narcissistic Personality Disorder:

One of the few conditions where the patient is left alone and everyone else is treated.[4]

—Gail Meyers

Narcissist (n): A more polite term for a self-serving, manipulative, evil asshole with no soul.[5]

—Narcissist Meme

The History of Narcissus

According to Greek mythology, Narcissus was a hunter who was known for his beauty. He was also known for his exorbitant amount of self-love, and for how much he disdained and mistreated the people in his life who loved him. Nemesis was the goddess who was responsible for giving out divine punishment to those who yielded to their fatal flaws. Nemesis paid close attention to how horrifically Narcissus treated other people, especially the ones who loved him the most. One day, Nemesis brought Narcissus to a crystal clear pool where he was stunned by the beautiful reflection that he saw of himself. He fell head over heels in love with his own reflection.

From this point, there are a few variations as to how the story ends. One version of this myth tells that Narcissus, being so completely mesmerized with his own image, was unable to move away from it. He stared at his reflection until he died of starvation and thirst.[6] Another version conveys that when Narcissus's image was not able to reciprocate the love back to him (since it was just a reflection), out of disdain for not being sought after as he "deserved," he committed suicide.[7]

Regardless of the details of the endings, the core of the message remains the same. Narcissus was driven mad by the love of the *image* of himself, and was sentenced to die alone. After rejecting and mistreating everyone who loved him, Narcissus was never able to give or to find true love outside himself. He was consumed only with the love of himself and was forced to die miserable and alone.

These days, a narcissist is also someone who is completely fixated on the *image* of him or herself. This obsession can revolve around their own physical appearance, the image they have of their false self, and the public's perception of who they are. Indeed, at the core, it is the *IMAGE* of *themselves* that the narcissist is truly in love with. This image has been a lifelong project that they have carefully crafted and will protect at all costs. This image is perfect, unrealistic, fraudulent, and delusional.

There are no flaws in the image they have created of themselves. Therefore, a narcissist is someone who is not able to love and accept their true self, which of course is imperfect and does have shortcomings. They only love this "false" image that they reflect to others and to themselves. Truly, no one is as wonderful, deserving, or as all-important as the *image* that a narcissist has of themselves. Much like Narcissus, many narcissists will treat those who are the closest to them with cruelty and disdain.

I wonder if the course of narcissism through the ages would have been different had Narcissus peered into a cesspool. He probably did.[8]

—Frank O'Hara

What Is Narcissistic Abuse?

Whenever you are in close relationship with a narcissist, inevitably you will suffer from narcissistic abuse. The effects are devastating and it is almost inconceivable as to how they can treat you with such inhumanity and cruelty. Narcissistic abuse can cause victims to feel anxious, worthless, and even suicidal due to the chronic devaluation and manipulation they experience. Unfortunately many narcissists are not held accountable for their cruelty because of their deceptive and charming mask that the rest of the world sees.

So You Married A Narcissist is designed to educate you about narcissists, to give you ways to heal from the experience of being in a close relationship with one, and how to live an empowered life long after they are out of your life.

PART I

Twenty-One Characteristics of a Narcissist

Countless books, blogs, and articles have been written by experts to pinpoint traits, signs, and symptoms of the Narcissistic Personality Disorder (NPD). No doubt you have picked up this book because you are shell-shocked by the devastating cruelty and have been blindsided by a narcissist in your life. Things were *not* as they appeared! Although this is not designed to diagnose NPD, nor is it an exhaustive list of narcissistic traits, Part I of this book describes twenty-one characteristics of a narcissist to give you greater clarity in knowing and understanding what a narcissist is.

CHAPTER 1

WHAT ROLES DOES
A NARCISSIST PLAY?

Narcissistic Traits 1 to 5

How do you know when you are dealing with a narcissist? Narcissistic Personality Disorder (NPD) involves so much more than an arrogant person who is full of themselves. A narcissist is not a person who is merely in love with themselves; they are in love with the *image* of themselves. This image is perfect and covers up all of their flaws and insecurities. If you ever threaten, challenge, disbelieve, or attempt to expose their false image, they will try to destroy you in the end. However, it is surprisingly easy to get sucked into the absolute charm of their wonderful false self. And why wouldn't you believe that the person being presented to you is the real person?

The first five traits as listed in this chapter deal with the different roles a narcissist plays. You may have seen a few or all of these roles play out in front of you—The Charmer; Dr. Jekyll and Mr. Hyde; The Image Driver; The Critic; and The Martyr and Victim.

Trait 1. The Charmer—Their False Self

The role of the Charmer is that highly enchanting, magnetic, kind person who is so quick to help others and is often considered to be a pillar of society. Unfortunately, this is the false self and not the real person. Since narcissists are so dependent on the love and attention they get from others, they will go to any lengths to make sure that they portray a persona that others will admire and seek out. The narcissist creates a magnificent image and hides their true self behind this mask. You will probably recall that this simulated charmer is the person you first met and were completely captivated with. However, beware, as this is their *false* self.

The expression "what you see is what you get" does not apply to a narcissist. What you initially see will not operate in the long run. Eventually and inevitably, you will begin to see another completely different person emerge; that person will seem diametrically opposed to the person you originally fell in love with. It is confusing, exhausting, heartbreaking, and bewildering when their mask comes off and they start to reveal their true self. It is difficult to know what to believe about this person and it is particularly challenging when you are the only person who sees their mask slip off. Only those closest to the narcissist will ever see their true self emerge. While the rest of the world sees the false charmer, only the most intimate partner, spouse, family members, and close associates will ever see the cruel, selfish, raging, abusive person who is devoid of empathy. Unfortunately, this is the narcissist's *true* self.

Be careful ... not all are what they seem. Some people pretend to be the beach, but they're actually quicksand.[1]

—Steve Maraboli

Much like the historical Narcissus, the present day narcissist is madly in love with the false self or image that he portrays to the world. It is through presenting this persona that the narcissist is able to gain their desired status and to fill their deep need, whether that need is for attention, admiration, love, respect, awe, or fear. However, the more their false image is fed with their deep need (attention, admiration, love, respect, awe, or fear), the more removed the narcissist becomes from recognizing their "true" self. In turn, the more pronounced their projected false image becomes. The narcissist only truly loves his image and lives to impress others with this charming persona.

Narcissists are actually not capable of loving anyone, not even themself (at least, not their true self). Rather, a narcissist falls in love with the impression they make on others. The narcissist may, however, feel a shallow form of false love toward those who are the most in awe of the image they portray. That is simply because in that moment the admirer is feeding the narcissist's need for their supply of attention. The admirer now becomes an object and not a person to the narcissist. They become a mere "supply" of attention to the narcissist and nothing more. However, if and when that "supply" suddenly sees through this fake image and finds any faults or flaws with the narcissist's "true" self, the Charmer vanishes.

When this happens, you can expect to see the narcissistic rage that erupts from the true person. They have an intense contempt for anyone who discovers their true self and they will treat you with utter disrespect. In a lightning flash, you will experience the radical change from the superficial love that the narcissist has for you, their "supply", to a loathsome disgust for you because you have either discovered or revealed their true self. Most narcissists will either run away as fast as they can or they will attack the person who has discovered their true identity and has seen behind their mask. The narcissist cannot risk acknowledging, even to themselves, that their image is false.

> *The first thing you must know about a narcissist is that you will truly never know anything about the narcissist.*[2]
>
> —Shahida Arabi

Melanie Tonia Evans is a narcissistic abuse recovery expert, healer, author, and radio host. She writes,

> *The narcissist can't create any real relationship with his or her False Self—because it's NOT real. The only relationship the narcissist could ever have with him or herself is with the true inner being—and that's been killed off and replaced....*
>
> *Because the narcissist does not have a healthy relationship with "self" (there is no "self" to have a relationship with), there is no ability to trust anyone else either. For this reason narcissists feel terribly vulnerable and controlled by others when forced to operate like a decent / honest person. The narcissist feels it makes him or her inferior, "like everyone else," and causes him or her to lose superiority and a vital upper hand.[3]*

The University of Oxford-supported dictionary Lexico definition of *fraud* is "a person or thing intended to deceive others, typically by unjustifiably claiming or being credited with accomplishments or qualities."[4] Narcissists are classic frauds—at loving, parenting, befriending, and creating any other important relationship in life. Their intention is to not be transparent, honest, or vulnerable in their relationships. They desire to deceive you in order for you to admire them so that they will have control over you. It all starts with a charming mask.

Trait 2. Dr. Jekyll and Mr. Hyde—Split Personalities

Narcissists have contrasting dual, or split, personalities. You will inevitably experience their extreme hot and cold behaviours at some point. One minute they are sweet, generous, romantic, and charming the socks off you; the next moment they can be angry, selfish, sullen, cruel, and abusive. For this very reason, narcissists are often referred to as being Dr. Jekyll and Mr. Hyde. This concept is based on Robert

Louis Stevenson's classic novel, *Strange Case of Dr. Jekyll and Mr. Hyde,* which was later made into a horror film in 1941 starring Spencer Tracy and Ingrid Bergman.

This story centres around a character who has a dual or split personality. The honourable, esteemed Dr. Henry Jekyll has an alternate and dark personality, Edward Hyde. Mr. Hyde is a hideous creature devoid of any compassion or remorse for the cruelty he inflicts upon others. Throughout the book and the movie, we see that Dr. Jekyll has a solid character and he has many friends. He is professional in his demeanor, respected wherever he goes, and many people would refer to him as a pillar of society.

The sharp contrast comes when he transforms into Mr. Hyde. Mr. Hyde is a sociopath who is mysterious, self-indulgent, violent, and evil. The more that time passes, the greater Dr. Jekyll's alter ego, Mr. Hyde, grows in power. People see less and less of the upstanding Dr. Jekyll and more of the evil Mr. Hyde. Eventually, Hyde grows to be stronger than Jekyll. In the end, the hideous, soulless creature overpowers the good Dr. Jekyll and murders him.[5]

In the same way, the narcissist contains these two contrasting personalities. The narcissist is often esteemed as the giving, serving, honourable Dr. Jekyll to his friends and the rest of society (this includes you in the beginning!). This mask is carefully constructed and will not slip. Only those who are in a close relationship with a narcissist will ever see Mr. Hyde. Fast forward to later in the relationship. When Mr. Hyde shows up on a consistent basis, all you can expect now are cycles of being treated horrendously cruelly with a cold indifference. This is followed by acts of service or affection when the narcissist transforms back into Dr. Jekyll. When the transformation back to the good soul occurs, the narcissist will act like Mr. Hyde's actions never happened.

In this way, they will expect that all of their cruelty, abuse, and threats should just be swept under the rug and forgotten. They will say that those events "never happened" and you are "crazy" to believe they did. This type of denial can cause you to think that you must be imagining their bad behaviour. Naturally you second guess yourself when you see the wonderful Dr. Jekyll. This could *not* be the same person! It may also cause you to believe that *you* are reading the situation wrongly or perhaps your abuser was just having a rough day. After this consistent hot and cold treatment, you actually get used to the unpredictability in your relationship. It becomes your new normal and you unconsciously brace yourself for the next unsuspecting time that you will need to walk on eggshells.

In these crazy cycles, the shift to Mr. Hyde often occurs when the relationship is solid, and when trust is being restored from the last "incident." When things are going well, beware of Mr. Hyde. However, when you see the mask slip and you call the narcissist on it, he will attack you and, like a cornered tiger, he will shred you to pieces. At this point, you are now experiencing what is known as narcissistic rage. After such an episode, the narcissist will go into complete denial of their rage and desperately attempt to regain control of your perception of them by playing the good Dr. Jekyll.

As you can imagine, with a split personality at play, it is very difficult to discern *who* the narcissist actually is because you experience them as being two completely different people. On one hand you have the charming, doting, upstanding pillar of society who is crazy about you; and on the other hand you have the abusive person who lies to you, belittles you, disrespects you, negates you, and is ultimately out to destroy you.

This type of split personality can also be seen in the 2009 film, *Dorian Gray*. Dorian Gray was a young and stunningly handsome man. People everywhere admired his good looks and his magnetic charm. To ensure that he would always have an attractive and eternally youthful external image, Dorian sold his soul to the devil. In exchange for his soul, Dorian had his portrait painted. This painting would bear all the ugly effects of aging and any scars from the consequences of his wild living, rather than them showing up on him directly. After it was completed, his body was transformed into perfection, devoid of any blemish. The split between his body and his soul into two separate entities began.

Dorian Gray's perfect body and darkened soul were quite the dichotomy. Two entirely different beings. His physical embodiment was an attractive, flawless image that the masses flocked to. However, his portrait contained the true state of his soul. If an individual would ever see the true portrait of his soul (that selfish, evil, cruel person), they would run. Dorian went on to pursue a hedonistic lifestyle of amoral experiences and extreme cruelty at the expense of others. All the while, the only thing people saw for decades was the embodiment of a striking, flawless man who never aged. As the years passed, the portrait constantly morphed into something more hideous. It showed the effects of his hard lifestyle and the ugly sins of his inner soul. The painting grew extremely grotesque. Dorian became fearful that someone would discover the truth of his soul so he kept the portrait carefully locked up. He even murdered a close friend for discovering the truth. Eventually he despised the painting so much that he stabbed it in the heart. In doing so, Dorian's body immediately became the grotesque figure in the painting, and he died with a sword in his heart. The truth ultimately came out. Dorian's soul and body become one again and the painting is restored to the original portrait.[6]

Dionne, a close friend in my support group, depicted the similarities between her narcissistic husband and this film. She wrote this in her journal:

Other people saw my husband as the embodiment of Dorian Grey—very attractive, eternally youthful, and a wonderful man! However, I lived with the portrait. At first it was just the ugly marks of selfishness that I noticed, but over time the maggots of his soul started to gnaw at the beautiful portrait. The painting was being transformed right before my eyes; however, I was the only one who saw it. The destruction of his toxic lies darkened the portrait further and damaged his eyes until he was blind to his own wretchedness and destruction. After a time, his lies, cheating and cruelty unleashed the real demon. Those eyes were now blazing, hell-bent on destroying me because I saw the true portrait of his soul instead of the flattering embodiment that everyone else saw: the image of Dorian Grey.

Trait 3. The Image Driver

The most important purpose in a narcissist's life is about maintaining the image they portray to make the world buy into their incredible false self. They take note of what society values and admires. The more signs of success they have and the more ways they have to attract others to give them attention, the better it is. Due to the fact that much of western society highly values appearances, narcissists will often take great pains to be very physically attractive. They also have a superficial, magnetic charm that many people are drawn toward. You know this because you have experienced this personally! You too were sucked in by their irresistible charm and charisma. Narcissists will find out what other people like (especially their targets), and they will wear whatever mask it takes for others to give them the admiration and attention that they so crave.

Narcissists are notorious for treating the general public much better than the people closest to them. Why is this? Narcissists are intensely concerned with the quality of their public image or "Billboard."[7]

—Shannon Thomas

You will find that the narcissist will do whatever it takes to impress others at an external level. For men, it's often the sports car, the stunning home, the big boat, the extraordinary bank account, and the impressive watches. For women, it's the designer clothes, the high-end purses, and the glamorous jewelry. They are fixated on maintaining a beautiful body, which they make sure you see by their revealing clothing choices. Female narcissists often dress very provocatively and are obsessed with maintaining their youthful looks.

However, it is not only their exterior image that narcissists are concerned with. They are also focused on protecting their false internal qualities. They crave to be seen as a great leader or that upstanding person in society. Narcissists are often the ones who will serve and help out, as long as others see that they are doing it. While they may be completely generous to perfect strangers, they can also be the biggest scrooge with their family. In public, the narcissist can have a larger than life personality but at home they can be moody, sullen, childish, and raging. The world knows the narcissist as one person and their family experiences them as the complete opposite.

The narcissist would rather impress a stranger than be loved by his own wife and children.

Narcissists will do whatever it takes for the world to fall in love with them. As for family members who have seen the mask slip and who know the truth, at some point, the narcissist will no longer feel the need to impress their family by keeping up with the façade. Unfortunately, they become their true self at home. Then the family (mostly the spouse) gets the brunt of their callousness, raging, and other forms of abuse. There are of course times when the family will get a break. Especially when the narcissist needs to maintain their family image for a public appearance such as a wedding, a business deal, or a political campaign.

It's amazing how a narcissist can be such a "man of the people" in public and such a bigoted prick in private!

The ex-spouse of a narcissist

It should also be noted that the narcissist did indeed choose you, not only because you admired him, but because you specifically enhanced his image in some advantageous way. Perhaps you were extremely good looking, you had youth, business skills, intelligence, money, athleticism, artistic or musical talents, a wide circle of social "capital," popularity, or most likely, you were a combination of several of these traits. For whatever the reason (and don't bother trying to figure out which one), they chose you because you enhanced their image. They used you to bolster their persona and image to the world.

Your only role is to meet THEIR needs and make them look good.

Trait 4. The Critic—Hypercritical Yet Hypersensitive to Criticism

Narcissists are hypercritical. They love to find faults with everyone and everything. Their intense self-loathing and self-rejection extends to everyone around them. Whether this debasing and demeaning of other people is conscious or subconscious, narcissists are overly critical with others in order to feel better about themselves. They always have to maintain a sense of superiority with whomever they are talking to. In most things they say, they will often nonchalantly and subtly belittle the other person no matter how discrete or harmless it may seem. Their intent to remain superior to others is always present.

These scenes would bring to my mind one of Master's inimitable observations: "Some people try to be tall by cutting off the heads of others!"[8]

—Paramahansa Yogananda

Conversely, when other people give constructive criticism to them, even when it is a well-intentioned suggestion, a narcissist can't take it. Narcissists can dish out criticism by the truckloads but they can't take a grain of it for themselves. They are not even able to receive positive criticism, be grateful for it, or want to grow from it. You will find that narcissists are overly defensive and have over-the-top reactions to being criticized. When it comes to being on the receiving end of criticism, narcissists lack any poise and will lash out at you. They can become indignant, aggressive, and cold, perceiving and interpreting criticism as though you are directly threatening either them or their image. They fear that you will injure their carefully crafted mask, and they will defend that mask at all cost! Whoever makes a critical remark to them will be held in contempt and devalued. By further diminishing you, the narcissist minimizes the impact of the criticism on himself.

Trait 5. The Victim and Martyr

Narcissists often play the perpetual victim or the martyr. When they play the victim they are more likely to win over your empathetic heart. They can create their own book of martyr stories about the sacrifices that they made for you and for others, and tell the grandiose tales of the horrible things they've had to endure. They will lead you to believe that they always drew the short end of the stick in life. However, many people who have endured worse circumstances in life do not constantly give excuses and demand a free pass to treat others with cruelty.

They play the victim and the martyr to obtain their supply of other people's attention and to escape any guilt and responsibility for the actions they have done or will do to you. They cannot deal with the reality of their actions and how they have treated people because it would place *them* in a bad light. Instead, they deceive you and flip the switch by playing the victim in their own game of cruelty. In playing these roles, they actually start believing their own lies and tales of woe.

Narcissists are delusional and are not willing to accept any consequences for the things they have done. When you point out something hurtful they have done, they will start talking about their abusive childhood or their evil ex. Before you know what's happening, you're consoling them, even though they were completely disrespectful and intentionally hurtful toward you just moments earlier. How are you supposed to be mad at someone when they open up to you about traumatic events in their life? Unfortunately, this is not a plea for help in order to change; rather it is their way of further manipulating you.

In another instance, you might ask your partner to stop humiliating or ridiculing you. However, since being humiliated and ridiculed paints *you* as a victim, they are quick to flip around the situation since they must always be the biggest victim. Instead of addressing your legitimate concerns, they will bring up (or make up) something completely unrelated from the past where they claim that you have hurt them. Or perhaps they may switch topics to tell of the sacrifices they have made for you and how you have been so ungrateful for all that they have done for you. Again, this is to point out their continual victim-and-martyr role and how they do not respect or listen to your concerns. It is how they get you to excuse their bad behaviour. Do not be fooled by their manipulation and how they turn the tables. They will twist it to how they have been deeply wronged by you and therefore it must be *you* who apologizes to them.

The terms "victim complex" and "martyr complex" can often be interchangeably used. The person who has such complexes greatly desires empathy as someone who is innocently wronged. Narcissists desire to be seen as someone who has suffered injustices and oppression. *Merriam Webster's* dictionary defines a true victim as, "one that is injured, destroyed, or sacrificed under any of various conditions; one that is subjected to oppression, hardship, or mistreatment; a person who is tricked or duped."[9] Alas, the perpetrator does not fit the victim's bill. When a person deliberately plays the victim, it is usually a fabrication to seek attention, evade responsibility, manipulate others, or justify abusive behaviour.

A true martyr is typically someone of exceptional leadership and heroism who displays great courage and is willing to suffer in the face of extremely difficult circumstances. A martyr *complex* is when a person routinely emphasizes, exaggerates, and creates a negative suffering experience, in order to place blame and guilt on another person. Having a martyr complex involves pointing the finger at other people or situations in your life and blaming them for all of your disappointments, emotional turmoil, crushed dreams, and even illnesses. It is the source of passive-aggressive behaviour and can be considered a form of masochism. Narcissists love the martyr position, because by seeking out suffering or persecution, they will garner pity, empathy, and attention, while evading any responsibility.

Some martyr statements include "Because of you I have endured this." "Because of you this happened to me." "Because of you I suffered this" or "I missed out on that." One middle-aged narcissist (still dodging any onus for his life) victimized his story to the world after three rapid-fire divorces. He lamented, "I was threatened into every one of my marriages!" I'm quite sure that none of these three women put a gun to this grown man's head as he bought them their engagement rings, as he walked down the aisle, and as he said his vows to them in front of his family and friends.

Narcissists will amplify the victim and martyr roles when they are under pressure, such as when you have decided to divorce them and are moving toward a settlement. This is when they will play the victim role to the hilt. Family members, friends, and everyone within earshot will hear about how badly you have treated them, about your monstrous cruelties, your insensitivity, your lack of empathy, and your emotional coldness. Beware, as this martyr role can be very convincing to the people in your social circles. A narcissist will essentially play the victimized saint who has been emotionally harmed by you. Especially when it comes to divorce, do not be surprised at the lengths a narcissist will go to convince others how you are the villain and you have "broken up" the family (while they are allowed to continue scot-free with their own threats, affairs, and gaslighting).

Tamara had been meeting different men in the online dating world. On her first date with a narcissist, she asked why he was divorced. With tears in his eyes, he explained how his first wife had an exorbitant number of affairs with numerous doctors. This man had tried everything he could to hold his marriage together. He told heroic tales of how he made sacrifices for his children and tried to keep the family together even though he was the sole person working on the marriage. Unfortunately, between his ex-wife's "deteriorating mental health" (she was "going crazy" and was "abusive") and with all of her "affairs," he could no longer be in a marriage like that. Tamara bought his sad tale hook, line, and sinker. Eventually the two got married. As she was later to find out, the reality of that story was that *HE* was having affairs all over North America, while his first wife suffered the traumatizing effects of his lies, his gaslighting, and his emotional, financial, and psychological abuse.

When Tamara finally left him after going through her own cycle of his abuse and affairs, he had a new martyr tale to tell. He told all their friends about how Tamara abandoned him out of the blue for no good reason. He didn't understand how she could leave him after he had tried so hard and made numerous sacrifices. When Tamara heard this, she assumed that his interpretation of "try" was to give out threats, gaslight, stonewall, and continue in his affairs.

Unfortunately, many of their friends were sucked into his tragic story of brokenness as she had once been. Tamara experienced not only the harsh reality of his betrayal in their marriage, of having to leave her home, of enduring the smear-campaigns against her reputation, but also of having lost long-term friends who would no longer speak to her because they bought into his martyr story. She recognizes that she probably doesn't even know the half of what he said. However, Tamara continues to walk in confidence and freedom as she knows that the truth eventually comes out.

A narcissist paints a picture of themselves as being the victim or innocent in all aspects. They will be OFFENDED by the TRUTH. But what is done in the dark will come to light. Time has a way of showing people's true colours.[10]

—Karla Grimes

Regrettably, it is almost too easy for narcissists to play the martyr. They are also able to effortlessly and shamelessly turn the tables upside down on you and claim that they were the ones who have been cheated on, abused, and chronically abandoned despite their attempts to "sacrifice everything" to hold the relationship together. As the narcissist recounts their sad fabricated stories, they will cast themselves as the victim and you as the villain. However, know that the inverse is the truth, and the way they depict you is more often an accurate description of themselves.

CHAPTER 2

WHAT DRIVES A NARCISSIST?

Narcissistic Traits 6 to 10

Now that you have discovered a few of the various roles that narcissists play, we are going to delve into five traits that drive a narcissist to do what they do. Whether they are conscious of it or not, a narcissist has certain drivers behind their behaviours. These drivers include being self-centred and egocentric; being motivated by fears of rejection, abandonment, and loss of their image; the need to never be wrong; black-and-white thinking patterns (things can only be either all good or all bad); and the tendency toward addictions (their addiction to attention being only one of them).

In continuation of the twenty-one narcissistic traits ...

Trait 6. Self-Centred and/or Egocentric

Narcissists fantasize about themselves with a sense of grandeur. They have larger than life illusions of who they are and what they have achieved. Many times, they obsess over how brilliant, attractive, and powerful they are. With their grandiose sense of self-importance, the narcissist believes that they are unique and "special" and that everyone else is not. They can become absolutely fixated on this amazing image they feel they are portraying to the world. This explains why narcissists can often only associate with elite, higher status people. They are convinced that rubbing shoulders with such people will increase their own image.

In contrast, it would be devastating to have their image tainted by associating with anyone they perceive as being less than their great selves. In their mind, the majority of people suck! The narcissist considers most people to be stupid, incompetent, ugly, pathetic, and moronic. It is for this reason that they do indeed feel entitled to use anyone they want, at any time, to further their own purposes.

> *Don't ever forget that a narcissist is, first and foremost, an opportunist who feels falsely entitled to do whatever he wants, whenever he wants, with whomever he wants, at anyone's expense.[1]*
>
> —Zari Ballard

Since the only person who really matters to a narcissist is themself, you will very rarely hear them inquiring about other people. Narcissists can become bored very quickly when the focus is not on them. Or they can grow distant and sulky if the conversation does not include them. In social settings, they might turn every discussion into one that highlights their own talents and achievements, whether these achievements are real or imagined. Many times you will find that a narcissist will take credit for things they never actually did.

In other contexts, since they believe the world actually does revolve around them, others must always wait on their behalf. They often arrive late to business meetings, family functions, and important dinners, considering only their own schedule. After all, they are arrogant enough to believe it is truly only their time that matters.

Due to their extremely selfish nature, narcissists require an excessive amount of admiration. Relationships, for them, are not meant to be a two-way street of mutual give and take. When you fail to give them all the attention they desire (which is a bottomless pit), they will immediately start to seek other sources of "supply." Any perceived loyalties that they had are quickly discarded in lieu of pursuing the new supply.

> *These are people who live selfishly at others' expense.*[2]
>
> —Joe Navarro

Learn to readjust your expectations! You simply cannot have a healthy, thriving relationship with a narcissist, as a narcissist will never be able to see beyond their own image. A narcissist's hollow, decaying soul is not capable of empathizing with others as they never look beyond their own interests. No matter how much you give, or how many sacrifices you make, in the end, this one-way street is all about them. You have to remember that you are not, and will never truly be, part of the narcissist's equation. You never have been. They were using you for a specific purpose. In their eyes, you are not a real person with needs, dreams, and value. You are not a person who fully deserves to be heard, honoured, and thanked. In a close relationship with a narcissist, you can forget about being appreciated for what you do and for who you are.

Trait 7. Motivated by Fear of Rejection, Abandonment, and Maintaining Their Image

In order to begin to understand a narcissist, it is best to recognize what motivates them. The instances of love bombing and re-love bombing you are when they treat you amazingly (more about this in chapter 5). They are often motivated to do so out of their deepest fears combined with their need for adoration. Do not be fooled! This wonderful treatment of you is not because they adore you and appreciate you. They treat you amazingly in order to avoid their deepest fears of being alone, or being rejected and abandoned by you. Narcissists intensely fear rejection and abandonment more than most people. It becomes vital for them to have their supply of attention from you, or from others, in order for them to survive. In fact, there is a strong and complete dependency on attaining this supply. Without their narcissistic "supply" (your attention, adoration, and later on, your submission), the narcissist becomes incapacitated, and their personality starts to break down. Just like a drug addict, they will do anything in order to obtain their drug of choice: the adoration and attention of other people.

When it finally got to the point where Amber had to leave for her own safety and sanity, she discovered her narcissist's true motives for wanting her to stay. Even in his most frantic attempts to get Amber back, the only words she heard from him were ignited by a desperate fear of abandonment. He told her, "I'm afraid you're going to leave." "I'm scared you're going to leave." "I don't want to be alone." There was no actual apology for any of the lying, cheating, threats, or emotional and psychological abuse that he inflicted.

Amber reflected, "Apparently these were his best attempts at bringing restitution to our marriage. Or of trying to win me back and convince me of his love. It was strange that never once in his weak attempts to get me to stay did I ever hear the words, 'I love you.' 'I'm sorry.' 'Let's try to work this out.' 'How can we make this work?' 'What can I do?' Wouldn't any of those have seemed the obvious thing to say at some point? In the end, I'd say that it was really all about him not being alone and there was nothing about restoring the relationship. After I left, it was interesting that his story to the world was, 'She abandoned me. She just left me for no good reason. I have no idea why she left.' He claimed to be absolutely 'blindsided' by my leaving despite the abuse, cheating, and my pleas for us to continue with counselling and to work things out. It's amazing that he was also 'blindsided' when his first wife left him for the exact same reasons (which I later found out to be the truth). Clearly he was not desperate enough to change his character. I found it very insightful that his story to the world was only and all about me 'abandoning' him rather than any of the real reasons as to why I was leaving."

The moments of *re*-love bombing and the seemingly *nice* treatment you experience from a narcissist periodically, after you have been in a relationship with them for a longer period of time, is because they fear you will reject or abandon them. In these moments, if a narcissist *does* suddenly make a grand gesture or faux-pologizes to you, rest assured it is not because they regret what they have done or that they feel any remorse for the pain they have caused you. It is because they fear you will abandon them and they have not yet secured their back-up narcissistic supply of attention from someone else. In such moments of re-love bombing, remember that a true and sincere apology will involve actual remorse, admitting the wrongs that have been done, and taking responsibility for their actions. You know someone is really serious when they take it a step further by actually *CHANGING* and showing the fruit of their sorrow.

Since narcissists are so dependent upon the praise of others, they cannot be alone. Being in between, or without supply, is unbearable to them. When Victoria was dating her narcissist, she remembers telling him about how she went on a two-week solo excursion to Europe and it turned out to be one of the most amazing trips of her life. She shared about her adventures of kayaking, hiking, going to museums, art galleries, concerts, exploring different foods, and also meeting some fabulous people with whom she still kept in contact. Her narcissist responded with, "That sounds like pure hell! I would never do that! How can anyone be alone like that?" At the time she was taken aback by his strong response. Victoria didn't understand what he meant, especially since he was supposed to be the introverted one out of the two of them. Now she recognizes that narcissists need the constant infusion of other people to make themselves feel okay. They *cannot* be by themselves as they might have to face their true self. And being with their true self is … pure hell! When it comes down to it, they do not like being in their own company.

Narcissists can avoid their true self by being with others and maintaining their grandiose false image; this is of the utmost importance. Paradoxically, although narcissists feel superior to others, they are dependent upon others to reflect back to them this positive self-image. This is why most narcissists are also codependent. They need buy-in from others for this grandiose image to exist and they need continual positive reinforcement in the form of adoration.

In emotionally healthy people, self-esteem is obtained internally. However, the narcissistic personality needs adoration and attention reflected back to them externally from others in order to regulate their self-esteem. Ironically, this makes the narcissist very needy of others, which also explains their need to control others.

Trait 8. They Are Never Wrong

When Susan was bombarded with accusations for being the sole contributor to her divorce, she confronted her soon to be ex, "Considering that this is your third divorce, I'm just curious, *who* do you think is the common factor in all of this?" Her narcissist raged back, "I HAVE *NOTHING* TO DO WITH ANY OF MY THREE DIVORCES!!"

> *There's a reason narcissists don't learn from mistakes and that's because they never get past the first step which is admitting that they made one.*[3]
>
> —Jeffrey Kluger

As long as you are in a relationship with a narcissist, you will be the object of their blame. They cannot be seen as being wrong or at fault in any way. They take zero responsibility for their actions. Mindy remembers how her narcissist claimed that she was solely at fault for their marriage ending. When she inquired further about that, he came up with some pretty flimsy ideas since he couldn't actually find any concrete reason. He argued that their marriage was over because she wasn't riding bikes with him. Their marriage was over because his running times had slowed down and she probably didn't like that. Their marriage was over because he didn't make enough money for her (although they never blended their finances). While Mindy knew she needed to explore her own contributions to their divorce, her perspective as to why she was leaving had more to do with the abuse, the pathological lying, and the revolving door of affairs, and less to do with hobbies, non-competitive running times, and their always separate bank accounts.

After Mindy confronted him about his abuse and cheating, Mindy's narcissist ignored what she said and replied with, "I'm sorry I wasn't good enough for you. I tried to provide a nice home for us, but I guess that's just not good enough for you because you're so demanding." Notice that what followed after "I'm sorry," revolved around attempting to gain sympathy from a victimized position (not being good enough for her). It told of his heroic ways of providing (a nice home), followed by an insult ("You're so demanding").

Can you see what else is happening here? He avoided the issues of cheating and abuse along with his behaviour and responsibility for doing those things. Instead of owning his behaviour, he accused her of being demanding, all while claiming the title of being the shining provider who could never meet her impossible standards. Narcissists love to deflect any accusations of being in the wrong while thrusting blame back onto the other person as they play the victim and the hero.

The narcissist never genuinely apologizes because they believe they are exceptional individuals who never do *anything* wrong. The only type of apology you may ever get from them is a *"faux*-pology." These fake apologies may start off sounding like apologies but they are devoid of remorse while they shift the blame to you and attempt to wiggle out of any responsibility that they might have.

Faux-pologies are designed to belittle you and to deflect any wrongdoing that they have done back onto *you*. Most often the person making the fake apology paints themselves either in a brilliant light, as the tragic victim, or as both. A few examples of faux-pologies are, "I'm sorry you are so sensitive and can't handle real life." "I'm sorry you get so angry with me." "I'm sorry you took that wrongly and overreacted." "I'm sorry you have no sense of humour and can't take my jokes."

Due to the fact that narcissists see themselves as perfect and above reproach, their sense of superiority reinforces their belief that they are always right. Although the narcissist may be responsible for a certain incident, it is all of the other "inferior beings" who are to blame when anything goes awry. Narcissists can't accept the fact that they did something wrong, even if deep down they know it's true. They will lie and twist the situation until they somehow have flipped it around so you are the one who is at fault and they are the victim who is suffering.

Trait 9. Black-and-White Thinking

Engaging in black-and-white thinking is another common trait among narcissists. This is when a person thinks in the extremes such as something being *either* all black *or* all white. There are no shades of grey. There are no other possibilities or outcomes. Something or someone is judged either one way or its opposite. Period. A person is either all bad or all good. It is either one hundred percent or zero. There is nothing in between. From a narcissist's perspective, the narcissist is always all good and you are always all bad. There can only be *one* way.

Therefore, if they are always right, then you are always wrong. Since you are always wrong, then naturally you are also wrong regarding your concerns about them. To go further down that slippery slope, your thoughts and feelings are therefore erroneous and meaningless. Your emotions and point of view are judged to be "bad" and "wrong."

Have you ever tried to explain how you felt to a narcissist and noticed what happens? Yes, even then, you are wrong. You are incorrect either for feeling the way you do, or it is assumed that you don't really know how you feel. Of course they know better what you are feeling and they will explain what your feelings are to you. Essentially everything about you is wrong and everything about them is right.

Another facet of black-and-white thinking is the inability to accept the dichotomy of another person. After all, every person has both positive and negative traits. We are neither all good nor all bad. In reality, we are fallible human beings. We all have weaknesses, inconsistencies, quirks, and we all fail at times. No person can live up to such an idealized image that the narcissist conjures up.

Black-and-white thinking combined with idealism leads toward perfectionism, and setting unrealistic, impossible-to-reach expectations. Attempting to reach a narcissist's flawless goal of one hundred percent perfection is impossible. This is how relationships are sabotaged. However, for a short period of time in the beginning of your relationship, you were idealized. For a very brief time, you were, in the narcissist's book, "all good." Unfortunately, after seeing some of your natural human flaws, and after you disagreed with them or stood up to them, you are now in the "all bad" category and you are no longer idealized.

You are not the only person that a narcissist puts into these two categories. They also do this to themselves. The narcissist will deny and defend themselves (sometimes by way of narcissistic rage) to make sure they are not put in that horrific "all-bad" classification where you and all other people belong. They fear any exposure of their bad self, and having any human flaws means they will be one hundred percent "all-bad."

While narcissists believe they are special and superior to others, they also have an extremely fragile self-esteem and can be exceptionally touchy. This causes them to end up turning on you when you are not in agreement with them or when you question their behaviour or character. In doing so, you will become public enemy number one.

It is due to all these traits that they obviously have trouble forming and keeping relationships. When it comes to black-and-white thinking, how can anyone be in a relationship with another person when they are always in the wrong? How is a relationship supposed to work when a person is not allowed to be human, when their feelings are disregarded, and when they are constantly treated with contempt?

Trait 10. Prone to Other Addictions

While not all addicts are narcissists, all narcissists are addicts. For narcissists, their number one drug is a need for attention and adoration from others. A narcissist needs their hit of approval and admiration just like a heroin addict needs their fix. The people who give them attention are known as the "narcissistic supply." (Note—these people are "supply." They are no longer viewed as people; they are a thing and a means to an end.)

Like a drug addict, a narcissist's whole day can revolve around devising strategies of how to get more supply to feed their addiction. "The Hit" or the high they receive is the attention they get from various sources. They can gain attention through their grandiose claims, their Facebook posts (which attempt to earn sympathy or garner attention), through their charming gestures, their sexual encounters, their wealth, their intelligence, or their power. All of these things can be real, exaggerated, or fabricated.

A narcissist needs their source from the outside, from someone else, to confirm that he or she is worthy. As their addiction progresses, the need is satisfied in more debasing ways. A need for love often manifests in unfaithfulness. A desire for achievement may make false claims or steal credit from someone else in order to be admired. A need for power can lead to embezzlement, white collar crimes, or other corrupt means.

Narcissists and addicts are absorbed both with themselves and with how to get their next fix, all while being completely oblivious of, and callous toward the needs of those around them. Both addicts and narcissists have a hidden sense of shame and denial that are deeply intertwined within their fractured self. The narcissist often lives in conflict between deflection—"I haven't got a problem, it's your fault!" and the deep-seated truth of how they feel—"I am not good enough."

Besides the addiction to attention, narcissists are prone to other obsessions and addictions such as pornography, sex, work, power, money, gambling, alcohol, and drugs. People trapped in addictions turn to substances rather than people for love, connection, comfort, and fulfillment. When addicts do not trust people or relationships, they turn to things they can control. Narcissists use both people and substances to soothe and numb themselves and to maintain some form of control. In turn, the narcissistic-addiction cycle is vicious because addictions can cause people to become more narcissistic. When you are addicted, you will do whatever it takes to get your high even if it means lying, cheating, stealing, or exploiting others. Although it is true that not all addicts have crossed over to being a narcissist, I have yet to hear of a narcissist who is also not also addicted to something (or to many other things), besides attention. Through feeding their addictions of sex, work, money, gambling, alcohol, or drugs, they become more narcissistic and abusive toward others, which tends to cause more distress and the need to further feed their addictions by numbing themselves.

CHAPTER 3

HOW COLD CAN A NARCISSIST BE?

Narcissistic Traits 11 to 15

This chapter outlines five relational sabotaging traits that narcissists carry with them into their relationships. These traits shut off growth, safety, and intimacy in any close relationship. When these traits are present, it is impossible for a relationship to be secure and to thrive. These traits include being devoid of empathy, showing contempt and arrogance toward those they are in relationship with, devaluing others, being unable to bond, and resorting to stonewalling when they are upset.

Trait 11. Devoid of Empathy

Empathy involves caring for others, their feelings, concerns, and points of view. Empathy gives you the ability to understand another person, to put yourself in their shoes, and to see things from their perspective rather than your own. True narcissists are completely devoid of empathy. They can neither see things from another's point of view by understanding their perspective, nor do they care to.

The first truth that survivors must accept is that narcissists do not feel authentic empathy for their victims' emotions. The closest narcissists get to feeling anything is a "narcissistic injury," which is the rage and despair they feel when a person "critiques" them or poses a real or even false threat to their excessive sense of superiority and entitlement.[1]

—Shahida Arabi

Narcissists are completely unable to recognize and identify with the feelings of others. Emily recounts after a marriage counselling session with her narcissist, how he said with absolute indifference, "Huh, I never actually thought once about how you felt in any of this." Then he casually shrugged his shoulders. It was as if he said, "huh, I didn't think it was going to rain today. Oh well." After this interaction, it was obvious to her that he was still not willing to waste one of his precious minutes to consider her thoughts, feelings, or perspectives. She knew there was no desire or intention to consider her feelings, either now or in the future.

Months later Emily had severe pneumonia. She was having trouble breathing after a prolonged period of coughing up bloody phlegm. Her husband was sitting right beside her on the couch and didn't flinch. When she could finally talk, Emily said, "Thanks for caring." He responded by looking straight ahead without a glance her way, "Oh, are you talking to me?" She was stunned by his cold, callous, inhumane response. Zero empathy.

Malignant narcissists and psychopaths do not have empathy, remorse, reciprocity, accountability, integrity, authenticity, honesty, compromise, trust or respect — all essential elements of healthy relationships.[2]

—Shahida Arabi

Due to a narcissist's lack of empathy, they can also rage at you, stonewall you, and be abusive toward you without any remorse whatsoever. A narcissist may even tell you that you shouldn't feel a certain way, or that your feelings are "wrong" or "stupid."

> *Sometimes you have to give up on people, not because you don't care, but because they don't.*

Narcissists are often intentionally harmful to you and they have no remorse for what they've done, or any empathy for how you may feel. They intentionally manipulate you, mislead you, use and abuse you to get what they want. They can be deliberately mean-spirited toward you and shrug it off as they were "only joking" and you are "too sensitive." A narcissist can pillage your finances, sabotage you and your work, "lie," and cheat on you without giving it a second thought. To them you are not a real person with real feelings.

> *They have no empathy for the hurt they caused, just a complete sense of entitlement, a complete lack of insight, and a complete lack of courage to face what they have done.*

Be aware though, that they can "fake" emotions extremely well and they can become what they believe others need and want from them. At least … for a time. Being expert chameleons, they can muster up fake empathy when they want to. This is when you see their crocodile tears. "Crocodile tears" is an ancient phrase used to describe hypocrites displaying fake grief toward others. The phrase comes from the age-old belief that crocodiles shed their tears even while consuming their prey. Perhaps this metaphor foreshadows how a narcissist can shed his false tears all while he is devising a plan to consume you.

Trait 12. Contempt and Arrogance

Narcissists exhibit a great deal of contempt for others on a regular basis. Contempt is a feeling that someone or something is not worthy of respect or approval. Contempt is always directed toward a "lower status" individual. Narcissists live out and embody this contempt in their attitude toward others and in how they treat people. It is as if to infer that others are beneath their consideration, that they are worthless, or only deserving of scorn. A demonstration of contempt, where your feelings are actively disregarded and dismissed, may sound something like this: "That's stupid of you to feel that"; "Your thoughts are wrong"; "Your opinion doesn't count"; or "Whatever that is, it's not what you are feeling."

When you are with a narcissist for a prolonged period of time, you will inevitably end up on the receiving end of their contempt. Eventually everything you do, think, and feel is dismissed, wrong, and stupid. To a true narcissist, NOTHING about you counts. Their attitude is, "I matter and you don't. You are beneath me." Other physical and verbal signs of contempt include eye-rolling and sarcastic remarks whenever you have something to say.

> *Invalidation is about dismissing your experiences, thoughts, and above all, your emotions. Indeed, the intention is to not even allow you to have those thoughts, experiences, and emotions. It's a way of invading your head and reprograming it. It's psychological abuse (messing with your thoughts) and emotional abuse (messing with your feelings).*[3]
>
> —Danu Morrigan

Obviously when one person's words are constantly dismissed, their input is discarded, and their opinions are either invalid or wrong, the connection between people becomes completely severed. When you have experienced contempt, it can give you overwhelming feelings of hopelessness and the belief that this relationship is desperately unfixable. In most cases this is true. Renowned relationship expert John Gottman says that contempt is the single greatest predictor of divorce.[4]

> *The way to be really despicable is to be contemptuous of other people's pain.*[5]
>
> —James Baldwin

You may notice that your narcissist also has contempt for other people. Contempt goes hand in hand with their arrogance and air of superiority. After all, narcissists will not want their image to be tainted by associating with people who are less "worthy" than themselves. Neva distinctly recalls being part of two different church groups with her narcissistic husband. It didn't take long before he wanted certain people out of the group because he looked at them with great disdain. "Those people" were not at the same perceived level as he was (intellectually and financially) and he thought they should be kicked out of the group. "Those people" did not or should never belong in his circle. After all, his association with them might taint the perfect image he had of himself and he disdained them for that.

Trait 13. Devalue You

Devaluing you is the second phase of narcissistic treatment. The narcissist often goes back and forth between the two stages of *love bombing* and *devaluing*. This can be extremely confusing. One moment they treat you like gold, then in an instant, they say derogatory, intentionally hurtful things to you. Naturally you want to give the person you are in a relationship with the benefit of the doubt. After all, maybe they were just having a bad day, or perhaps you misinterpreted them. Maybe they didn't mean it. Surely the wonderful moments you've experienced with this person are genuine and *that* is who they truly are. This cruelty must be a "misunderstanding." Unfortunately, it may take years to realize that the wonderful treatment was *love bombing* and only a façade so that you would give them attention. And the person who actually intends to devalue and hurt you is the real person.

When narcissists devalue you with their words, they attempt to strip you of your self-esteem. What are you insecure about? Is it your love handles, a low bank account, your lack of higher education, or your shyness? Narcissists will pick out those traits and prey upon you with sometimes subtle, and other times outright, denigration.

What are your past hurts and wounds? Jeremy shared his abusive past with his narcissistic wife. When he was in the devaluation stage with his wife, she ended up verbally assaulting him and intentionally using the same specific language that his childhood abuser used. She knew his triggers and what specific words would wound him and she used that arsenal against him.

What are you the most proud of in your life? A narcissist wants to tear down your strengths because you might look better than him. Or they resent you for being happy about living in your strengths. When you are being devalued, narcissists will discount, discredit, and belittle all of your best accomplishments. Melanie was a budding real estate investor. Before they married, her husband had previously lost around $100K through real estate investing on his own. After investing with Melanie, he made over $300K in a few short years. Rather than praise his wife to the world, he told people she was "incompetent" and "didn't have a clue what she was doing." Even though at times narcissists may benefit from your success, their goal is to tear you down.

What do you love about yourself? Narcissists will be sure to twist the specific traits that you love and are loved for by others to mock, belittle, and degrade you. This type of devaluation is the complete opposite of being loved, cherished, honoured, and respected. They do this to discredit, discount, and disrespect all of the amazing things within you.

When someone disrespects you, beware the impulse to win their respect. For disrespect is not a valuation of your worth, but a signal of their character.[6]

—Brendon Burchard

Narcissists have a sadistic way when it comes to devaluing and dehumanizing their victims. Toward the end of the relationship, they actually enjoy making their victims feel worthless and anxious. In a sick and twisted way, this satisfies their own need to be in control and to make themselves superior to those around them. In the end, you must realize that you were not a person of value to them (because they cannot truly value any person). You were merely "supply." You were a source of attention for them. You enhanced their image, provided them with money, status, social capital, or whatever else they may have been craving at the time. You helped to cover up their abusive lifestyle. In the end, their pathological treatment of you was downright inhumane, emotionally violent, and psychologically abusive. Let's call it for what it really is.

Their devaluation begins when you have criticized them, ignored them, or failed to adore them in the way they want to be idolized. Just so that you know and that you are clear, it is ***impossible*** for a person to meet the demands of a narcissist. Narcissists are deeply unhappy people who, if they remain unchanged, are doomed to live in eternal discontentment and misery. Even the most compliant partner will fail to meet the endless, ongoing requirements of a narcissist. Devaluing you is an inescapable part of being in a close relationship with a narcissist.

Trait 14. Inability to Authentically Bond with Other People

How does narcissism develop? Psychologists have no concrete answer. However, they have two different theories about how narcissists grew up. The first is that as a child the narcissist had excessive praise and was constantly told that they were special, in fact *more* special than other people. They weren't given strict boundaries or rules and they were very much indulged in whatever their heart desired. This theory fits in with their grandiose sense of self. On the flipside, the second theory is that as a child they were neglected, undervalued, overly criticized, and abused. Most narcissists have a very low self-esteem and are trying to avoid any type of shame and humiliation. This helps to explain why narcissists will avoid like the plague anything that will paint them in a bad light. In either theory, most psychologists believe that many narcissists also had a parent who was a narcissist and that they unconsciously learned many behavioural patterns from this parent or from a significant role model in their life. Whatever the roots of narcissism, a narcissist remains both as an emotionally stunted child who is unable to authentically bond with others and as someone who has the adult abilities to manipulate others and be ruthless.

It is impossible for narcissists to bond with other people when they constantly see others as "beneath" them. They never view the majority of people as equal. Other people's thoughts, feelings, needs, concerns, and hurts truly mean *nothing* to them. The fact that there could be such inconvenient things going on in another's soul detracts from the fact that the sun was meant to rise and set on them alone. And this, is very problematic.

A narcissist will use the phrase "get over it" because, to them, your concerns are trivial and if it's not about them, then they're not interested.

Narcissists, sociopaths, and psychopaths all share the same relational bonding problems that include an absence of empathy, a lack of mutual respect, poor problem-solving patterns, a deficiency in coping, a high level of inconsistency, and very poor communication skills. A true narcissist can never genuinely care for and love another person. Their reality consists of fulfilling the demands of their ego. They are unable to bond with people because they see the people closest to them as objects for their own means. Other people are merely a means to their ends. Narcissists will get all they can from their "supply," suck them dry, then resent them and promptly discard them. How is any type of relationship or bonding ever supposed to occur in such an atmosphere?

Trait 15. Stonewalling

Stonewalling is essentially when the narcissist erects a solid, emotional stone wall between themselves and you. In fact communicating with them is as effective as talking to a stone wall, expecting it to listen to you, and wanting that stone wall to speak back to you with kindness and understanding. Stonewalling can be described as emotional abandonment. It manifests as acting with incredible coldness, indifference, and a lack of caring in the relationship. In the end, there is an outright refusal to communicate or cooperate.

Stonewalling can also show up in the form of silent treatments or by shutting down physically and/or emotionally. Physically, the stonewaller may turn away from you, cross their arms, or leave the room. One woman told how her stonewaller husband actually erected a pillow barrier between them while they were sitting on the couch watching TV. When I heard this, it reminded me of when my sister and I, as children, would draw that invisible "line" while we rode in the car together. This line was our barrier and the other person absolutely could not cross it. Of course we were three and six at the time and not in an adult martial relationship ...

Emotionally, stonewalling is the absolute refusal to consider anyone else's concerns, perspectives, or any other side of the argument. If the narcissist ever does listen, they do so dismissively, mockingly, or with contempt. When you are being stonewalled, it is impossible to communicate with the stonewaller. Without communication how can there conceivably be any conflict resolution or any type of relationship for that matter? It is extremely stressful to be on the receiving end of stonewalling. As best-selling author Steve Becker says, there are very common feelings among those who have been stonewalled: anger, shame, helplessness, and even feeling unhinged. These people share a need to be heard.

Victims can actually obtain physical symptoms from being stonewalled. The heart rate and amount of adrenaline increase in your body when you are being stonewalled. As the recipient of stonewalling, you feel ignored, misunderstood, invalidated, and deeply hurt. There is a chronic sense of uneasiness and insecurity in your relationship. You always feel you have to walk on eggshells around the narcissist if you don't want him or her to shut down.

> *In aggressive stonewalling, a stonewaller knows that the silence, cold shoulder, and emotional isolation hurt his partner. He stonewalls to gain leverage or power.[7]*
>
> —Steven Stosny

According to world-renowned therapist, Dr. John Gottman, founder of the Gottman Institute, stonewalling is one of the Four Horsemen of the Apocalypse when it comes to relationships. Stonewalling is one of the four behaviours that predicts divorce with over 90 percent accuracy.[8] You know you are being stonewalled when the other person is completely cold to you, and dismissive of your feelings. This can manifest through being passive-aggressive or by showing blatant contempt toward the other person. Stonewalling and a complete lack of empathy is common among both sociopaths and narcissists. This bone-chilling indifference to your pain is not something you can change. For your own sanity and dignity, the best thing you can do is to leave such destructive relationships.

This chapter has highlighted five sabotaging interpersonal traits that are consistent in a narcissist's close relationships. You will inevitably experience their void of empathy, receive their contempt and arrogance, be familiar with their devaluation of you, grasp their inability to bond, and eventually experience how they resort to stonewalling you when they are upset with you.

CHAPTER 4

WHAT WAYS ARE NARCISSISTS ABUSIVE?

Narcissistic Traits 16 to 21

Hold onto your hats! This chapter dives into the darkest and most destructive traits of narcissism. Narcissists have many abusive games that can be extremely confusing until you understand what they really are. At this point you may still be questioning whether your situation is abusive or not. You may ask yourself, "Am I just reading things wrong?" "Am I responsible for their abuse?" Rest assured that you are NEVER responsible for another person's abuse. This is a testimony as to how powerful their manipulation, lying, and mind games actually are. Their crafty control can make you feel as though you are in psychological warfare, or that you are going crazy. This chapter will tackle the various forms of abuse that a narcissist dishes out: blaming and word salad; manipulation and gaslighting; pathological lying; numerous affairs; and abuse.

Trait 16. Blaming and Word Salad

Narcissists blame others so that they will not be held responsible for their actions. Any lies they have told, any wrongs they have committed, any betrayals or malicious acts, are always caused by someone else or something outside themselves. Blaming helps narcissists to avoid looking within themselves or admitting that they have done something wrong and might need to change their behaviour.

Blaming is a self-sabotaging behaviour and it never serves anyone. Blaming is an attempt to escape any form of accountability, and to cast a negative light on the person being blamed. It allows a person to stay in the same destructive patterns and never lets them fix their blind spots or grow to the next level. (This is why you also will never want to allow blame into *your* life. Moving away from blame leads toward empowerment.)

Unfortunately, many people who are targets of the narcissist's blame actually buy into what the narcissist is saying about them. Don't fall for their trap. It is their own unconscious guilt or fear that they are projecting onto you. Pay attention to what they are accusing you of— they are often confessing. When you hear strange accusations out of the blue, they are probably engaging in that very behaviour. They could charge you of being greedy for money (while they are scheming to clean you out). They could accuse you of making them look bad in public (when they have recently ridiculed or mocked you in front of friends, family, or business colleagues). They might say you are turning friends against them (which they are actively trying to do to you) or that you must be cheating on them (whereas they have several secret lovers).

> *A narcissist will always have someone they accuse of ruining their life. It is invariably the same person the narcissist is trying to destroy.*

Elaine had been a devoted wife to her husband but could no longer take the narcissistic abuse from him. Elaine and her husband were still living together but were now in separate rooms. All of a sudden, out of the blue, he charged her with having *multiple* boyfriends. Elaine was shocked by these crazy accusations as she had always been unquestionably loyal to her husband, even during the most horrendous times in their marriage. During the season of these flying accusations, she was also having severe health issues and was living in survival mode on every front. For goodness' sake! Even if she was so inclined, when would she even have the time or energy for an affair, let alone multiple affairs? Who would want to pursue another relationship when you can't make sense of the craziness happening around you and when you are reeling in so many directions anyway? She would later discover that during the same time her husband was accusing her of having multiple boyfriends, he was about to enter into his third affair for the past few months (at least … the third affair that she found out about).

In another strange incident, Jenna was aimlessly accused of having secret money deals with her business partners. Baffled, she asked her husband who she had these deals with and what were they about. He couldn't answer her, of course, because there were in fact no secret deals. Nor were there were any grounds for this sudden, random charge against her. However, Jenna was later to find out that he had given his mistress $50K a few weeks prior to the accusation. In a matter of a couple of weeks he had also been hiding several hundred thousand dollars by buying undisclosed properties. The moral of the story is, pay attention when you are harshly accused of something for which there is absolutely no basis. The narcissist is unintentionally projecting onto you a confession of their actions.

Miranda remembered hearing her narcissist husband tell her, before she married him, about how his first wife had had "multiple affairs" and that this was what tragically ended his marriage. He had done "everything possible" to save the marriage. Despite the counselling they went through, his first wife kept having "numerous" affairs.

Looking back, Miranda says that the crocodile tears that flowed from this martyr's performance were Oscar worthy. Of course, not knowing who he *really* was at the time, she was easily sucked into his lies and her heart went out to him. He also said that his second wife ended up trying to take him for all his money. However, it did seem as though he wound up with everything. Hmmm ...

At the end of Miranda's marriage, she discovered documents that went back decades. She read about the dozens of affairs he had had when he was married to his first wife, and of the numerous affairs that he had on his second wife. He also tauntingly wrote how he got the house out from under his second wife. Ironically what had finished Miranda's own marriage was that her narcissist had multiple affairs and tried to wipe her off the title of their home for his own financial gain. This was a very insightful discovery—everything that he said had happened *to* him was in fact what *he* had done. If a narcissist accuses you or someone else of some horrible behaviour, most likely they are currently engaging in it and/or they have done it in the past.

What is baffling is that a narcissist will throw these wild accusations at you even if you have proof and evidence of their own destructive behaviour. Any of your attempts at trying to get the narcissist to take responsibility for their abusive actions will put them on a path to destroy you.

Narcissists use this targeted blaming strategy to throw you off kilter and put the focus on you defending yourself. After all, the things that they say and the attacks on your character and integrity can be so infuriating that you feel you *have* to say something. The point of their blame is to deflect the attention away from themselves and to make you feel as though *you* are the one in hot water. They accuse you because they want you to be so focused on defending, explaining, and justifying yourself that you forget about what they have done. As they feed off your frantic energy and watch you self-destruct, they will use your *reactions* to prove their victimization. "Look at how ... (angry, bitter, crazy, or fill in the blank) you are!" When narcissists see you unhinged like this it feeds into their own feelings of supremacy.

In their blaming, narcissists also use "word salad." This comes in the form of distraction, circular reasoning, and illogical arguments. The key intention with all of these word salad ingredients is to lead you to nowhere, to frustrate you into submission, and to prevent any further attempts to resolve the matter at hand. You will recognize word salad, when you are feeling utterly confused and have no idea what has just happened in the conversation. When you feel that logic, rationale, and relevance to what you are speaking about has been thrown out the door, you, my friend, have been served a bowl of narcissistic word salad. After you have been dished up any type of word salad, just know beyond a shadow of a doubt that your discussion will go ... nowhere.

There are clinical references to word salad when it comes to mental health disorders. These are traditionally for people who have schizophrenia, autism, bipolar disorder, and dementia. Word salad in these cases includes a lack of logic, circular repetitions, and disjointed words that are unrelated in context. In such cases as these clinical disorders, word salad is involuntary. However, with a narcissist, a sociopath, or a psychopath, it IS voluntary and intentional in order to manipulate you; to evade responsibility; to frustrate, confuse, and ultimately to control you.

The common ingredients in a word salad are blame, shame, projection, confusion, and control. Part of word salad involves bringing up any slight wrongs that you have done, while *completely* dismissing the horrific things that they have done to you. Did you do the unspeakable to them and "raise your voice" when you discovered the evidence of their affair? They will use crazy talk to make it seem like you were completely in the wrong because you raised your voice and got angry about their cheating and betrayal. Now, all they can talk about is what an angry person you are. (They conveniently forget about their own abuse, lying, and cheating.)

Did they clean out your bank account and now you are the worst person in the world because you don't trust them and you are being "petty"? It is absolutely absurd that they make you out to be the bad person because you don't trust a thief! Maybe they have been completely cruel to you, emotionally dismissive, and tear you down in underhanded, humiliating ways in front of others, but you are to be shamed and labelled as "insecure" because you can't "take a joke." Whatever attempts you make to confront a narcissist or to keep them accountable for their actions, they will label *you* as "abusive." The whole point of word salad is to make you feel unsettled and unhinged as you attempt to defend yourself. Word salad allows them to put you in that state so that their feelings of power and control are accentuated.

Erica has a great example of word salad in a conversation with her narcissist, where basic human logic and reasoning were completely thrown out the window. Erica had moved out of the family home and her husband was supposed to have transferred her portion of the funds for their home to her lawyer. He kept failing to meet the dates he had guaranteed. Four promised deadlines came and went.

The conversation between Erica and her husband (not a six-year-old child as you might assume) went like this ...

ERICA: I really need you to pay the settlement like you promised. The lawyer was to receive the money at the very latest twenty-four days ago. Four of your promised dates have now come and gone. I am asking you to simply do what you said you would do, and pay the money. Stop lying to me about saying you will pay the money and please just do it.

NARCISSIST: I'm not lying.

ERICA: Ah, you assured me multiple times over the last month that the money would be paid to the lawyers and on time. It is now twenty-four days late. You haven't paid it. You also promised me four times over the last three weeks that you would go in and pay it and you still haven't done it.

NARCISSIST: That's not a lie.

ERICA: Yes, it is. When you promise to do something, you don't do it, and you actually have no intention of doing it, that is called lying.

NARCISSIST: No, it's not.

ERICA: What would you call *lying* then?

NARCISSIST: *You're* a liar!

ERICA: When are you going to pay?

NARCISSIST: You are so petty! You never trust me! How did I manage to survive in this marriage for so long?

And that's how the charade goes. It is actually impossible to communicate the basic foundations of a relationship, logic, or human behaviour to a narcissist. They will never understand about honesty, respect, kindness, and empathy. In this case, it is wise not to be trapped into defending yourself as to why you are not a liar and why you are not petty. Also, don't allow your thoughts to go in the direction of the narcissist's blame and shame regarding how they could have "survived" in this marriage with you. After all, you are the one who has lived with the word salad, blaming, manipulation, and crazy making for years.

If you find yourself trying to explain the basic concepts of human behaviour in attempts to get them to see your point, don't waste your breath. These are things you should never have to explain to an adult. A true narcissist will never get what kindness, respect, and basic human decency are.

Here are some clear signs that you have been served a pile of "word salad":

- The conversation ends up being focused on *you,* not the issue or problem you were trying to resolve.

- You repeatedly attempt to explain basic human experiences and emotions to this grown adult, to no avail.

- Instead of accomplishing any resolution or getting some accountability from the narcissist, they will jumble the conversation to make personal attacks against you. This is when you will likely find yourself backpedalling to defend and explain yourself.

- You end up being extremely confused and somehow can still end up trying to seek their validation.

- You leave conversations feeling drained and as if nothing was accomplished.

- Out of frustration, you end up accepting a mediocre answer.

- You feel diminished over time as you are never heard and nothing gets resolved.

- You dread asking about anything because you know it will open up one of these confusing and attacking conversations.

The motivation of a word salad strategy is to demonstrate that there is no solution. At least, no solution that they can be a part of since *you* are entirely the problem. Word salad is designed to destabilize you into hopelessness, frustration, and submissiveness, and to prevent you from making further attempts of resolve. Remember that YOU DESERVE BETTER! So don't waste your precious time and energy on someone who treats you this way.

Trait 17. Manipulation and Gaslighting

Narcissists use manipulation in order to control another person, to get what they want, and to further their own goals. They are the invisible puppet master who guides you in the direction they want you to think and behave so that they can use you for their own purposes. Who they appear to be is drastically different from who they truly are, as they embody the classic "wolf in sheep's clothing." On the surface, their words seem harmless, sometimes even complimentary; however, underneath you feel demeaned or you even sense a hostile intent. They manipulate you to provoke doubt within you and to subtly cause you to feel fear, obligation, and/or guilt. Various forms of manipulation include shaming, guilt-tripping, and emotional blackmail that may involve threats, bouts of anger, warnings, intimidation, or punishment.

One manipulative tactic is to always remind you that the narcissist understands you like no one else ever can or ever will. It is essential for them to make you believe that they are the *only* one who can truly understand you. Part of this manipulation is designed to isolate you from others and to make you dependent upon the narcissist. Also by constantly telling you that they are the only one who could ever truly accept you with all of your flaws, problems, and quirks, the narcissist is subtly belittling you and planting the seeds of self-doubt within you.

In a healthy relationship, you are loved unconditionally. However, with a narcissist there is always a hidden agenda and ulterior motives. Through them telling you they love you *despite* your flaws, their actual goal here is to highlight and condemn you *for* your flaws. By constantly bringing up your shortcomings, in some strange paranoid way, the narcissist wants you to feel unlovable. It is another way of developing control to ensure that you will never leave them. This is narcissistic manipulation at its finest and it is very important that you recognize it for what it is.

Gaslighting is a specific form of manipulation and control. It is defined at *PsychCentral* as "Intentionally making you distrust your perceptions of reality or causing you to believe that you are mentally incompetent."[1]

The Oxford dictionary definition of *gaslighting* is "to manipulate someone by psychological means into questioning their own sanity."[2] Wikipedia goes into further detail to explain how the psychological manipulation of gaslighting can cause a person or even an entire targeted group to question their perceptions, memories, and even their own sanity. It is accomplished by persistent denial, misdirection, and lying to intentionally delegitimize the person or group.

The term "Gaslighting" originally comes from a 1930s play called, *Gaslight*. The expression was made even more popular by the 1944 academy-award-winning movie, *Gaslight*, starring Ingrid Bergman. The plot portrays Gregory (Charles Boyer) trying to convince his wife Paula (Ingrid Bergman) and the other people throughout the city that she is crazy. Gregory does this by causing Paula to believe that the incidents happening around her aren't actually happening and that she isn't remembering or perceiving things correctly. For example, Gregory hides an expensive brooch that he previously gave Paula as a gift. Later when she can't find it, he is upset and tells her how she is constantly misplacing things. He hides paintings and other objects around the house and later on "discovers" them in front of Paula. He convinces her that she is the one who has been hiding the objects in odd places around the house and indeed, she is not "mentally well" and must stay inside their home and away from others. Gregory tells stories to the people in the neighbourhood about how his wife is mentally very ill and he must dutifully take care of her.

Toward the end of the movie, each night the gaslights dim shortly after he leaves the house and has gone to "work." The fact is Gregory has not gone to work. He is up in the attic looking for Paula's expensive heirloom jewels with the intention of stealing them. In the process, he has dimmed the gaslights and is making all kinds of noise. When he "returns home," Paula tells her husband how the gaslights turned down and how she heard noises such as footsteps directly above her. This continues night after night. He repeatedly tells her that she is really going crazy and that it is time to lock her away in a mental asylum for her own safety. She is starting to believe that he is correct. She feels as though she IS actually going crazy! Does he end up being successful? I HIGHLY recommend that you see this movie![3]

Narcissists are adept in manipulating and brainwashing people close to them so that the victims will take on the guilt.[4]

—Rokelle Lerner

Gaslighting is a technique that narcissists, abusers, sociopaths, psychopaths, cult leaders, and evil dictators use in order to convince you that the abuse you are experiencing from them is not real, that it is all in your head, and/or that it is all your fault. It is a form of slow brainwashing and anyone can be susceptible to it. Gaslighting is intentional, malicious mental and emotional abuse used to plant seeds of self-doubt regarding the abusive situations that occur. Its purpose is to make you question your own reality and sanity.

Narcissists may make a bold statement in one breath and in the next breath proclaim, "I never said that." You could be showing them a document that is in their own handwriting or play back to them a video of something they did and they will adamantly refute it: "That wasn't me." Repeatedly denying these facts gives them great pleasure because they know that they are frustrating you, defying you, making you question both your take on reality and whether indeed it is *you* who is the problem.

Gaslighting is a classic manoeuvre of a narcissist to attempt (and often they are successful over time), to convince their victims that the victim's perception of reality is completely off. They repeatedly and deliberately endeavour to make you doubt yourself and cause you to feel like your thoughts, feelings, perceptions, and experiences aren't valid. This unquestionably becomes emotional abuse.

A Narcissist's Prayer:
That didn't happen.
And if it did, it wasn't that bad.
And if it was, that's not a big deal.
And if it is, that's not my fault.

And if it was, I didn't mean it.
And if I did, you deserved it![5]

—Supriya McKenna

Narcissists gaslight so that they can engage in any type of behaviour they want to. Such behaviours include cheating on you, cleaning out your bank account, lying to win court cases or custody, and ultimately to beat you down. Their denial is all about protecting themselves from reality because they cannot cope with who they really are. It is also about them remaining superior and in control of you.

After months of being bombarded that you are "losing it" or "going crazy," even the strong spirited begin to question their own sanity. Narcissists also work very hard at persuading your family, social circles, and society in general that you are crazy.

Pathological narcissists enjoy calling anyone who challenges their self-perception "crazy." It's the word they'll use to describe any valid emotional reaction victims have to their shady and inconsistent behavior.[6]

—Shahida Arabi

With gaslighting, narcissists invalidate your emotions and have their own convenient form of "abuse amnesia" where they "forget" and deny all of the abusive incidents they have put you through. Not only does gaslighting allow them to escape accountability and responsibility for their cruel actions toward you but it also invalidates your reality and makes you feel unbelievably crazy. When the narcissist chronically invalidates you and denies your feelings, needs, and perceptions, you begin to doubt yourself and mistrust your own interpretations and instincts. You are no longer the owner of your perceptions; the narcissist is.

Some examples of gaslighting are these:

- "I never said that."
- "That never happened!"
- "You are overly sensitive."
- "You're imagining things!"
- "I was just joking."
- "You are taking things too seriously."
- "You're silly. I can't believe that's how you interpreted that!"
- "Okay, now you're really losing it!"
- "I don't understand why you sabotage our relationship when everything is going so well."
- "You're such a drama queen."
- "Your feelings are wrong."
- "No, you are not remembering things right."
- "Is that another crazy idea you got from your (friend or family member)?"
- "That is not a lie."
- "You're imagining things."
- "You are mentally unstable."
- "I don't know what you're talking about."
- "You are going crazy."

Gaslighters will invalidate your experiences, criticize your emotions, put the blame on you, and deny that anything has happened. By refusing to acknowledge your feelings and thoughts, the gaslighter causes you increasingly to doubt yourself. Their manipulation of your reality is designed to control you and to make them (the narcissist) your go-to person for reality, a reality that ends up being their delusional lies.

If they are questioned or challenged, the narcissist may act as though you hurt them. How could you possibly question their "loyalty" and "wonderful" treatment of you? Haven't they done X, Y, and Z for you? You may begin to feel guilty for doubting the very person who is manipulating you and has boldfaced lied to you. Little do you know they are only trying to control and destroy you. Using gaslighting, the narcissist may feign concern that they are only acting in your "best interests." Meanwhile your feelings, thoughts, and perceptions are crushed and minimized.

Signs that someone has been gaslighting you:

- You feel confused and off-kilter.
- You second guess your perceptions and abilities.
- You feel minimized—your feelings, perceptions, and thoughts are denied and crushed.
- A part of you does feel like you are going crazy.
- You feel the need to always apologize for your actions and for who you are.
- You feel as though you are too sensitive and are overreacting.
- You feel isolated, depressed, misunderstood, and hopeless.
- You are not as happy as you used to be.
- It's harder to make decisions because you don't trust yourself.
- You feel like you are a weaker version of yourself.
- You stay silent because you are afraid of speaking up about your opinions and emotions.
- You feel threatened and on edge with this person.
- They publicly discredit you and tell others that you are irrational, crazy, and unstable.
- Their strong confidence in reciting what happened mixed with a fake compassion for you cause you to believe that you have it

all wrong. They do this so that you start to believe their version of recounting the "facts."

- They minimize or deny what you think and feel.
- They reframe everything that you say so that it puts them in a good light and makes you look evil or crazy.

At the heart of gaslighting is a powerful form of emotional abuse that slowly eats away at your ability to make judgements. The narcissist will tell blatant lies to keep you questioning and unbalanced. They will deny having said or done something, even though you have proof of it.

Charen had physical proof of her husband's affair: his journal, which blatantly stated numerous times that he was having an affair, and a copy of a bank draft that he gave to his mistress for an exorbitant amount of money. She also found a love letter that he was intending to give to yet another of his girlfriends. He denied everything even though she physically showed him his own writing in both his journal and the letter, plus a copy of the bank draft for the funds he had given his mistress. Despite all of the evidence, she was the "crazy" one. She was "making stuff up." She was "going insane"! Charen thought of how ironic his statements were because those were the exact same words she always heard him use to describe his former wife. He branded his ex-wife as having mental problems and constantly stated that his ex-wife had clearly gone "crazy" and was "insane."

And she was made to appear crazy by the man who drove her there.

Projecting their faults onto you and denying their part in the events is another form of gaslighting. They accuse you of the very things they are doing—such as lying, cheating, or stealing. You become so distracted at defending yourself that you stop paying attention to their behaviour. This is intentional, as everything they do is intended to distract, confuse, and control you. They try to convince you that you are crazy and that everyone else is a liar. Everything they did they now flip and deflect onto you. They will accuse you and blame you for all the things they have done and for the abuses you have suffered. Then watch how they turn the tables to play the victim and the martyr and label you as the abusive one.

> *Beware the person who STABS you and then tells the world they're the one who's BLEEDING.*[7]
>
> —Jill Blakeway

Trait 18. Intentional Cruelty

Narcissists have a deliberate cruelty. Their cruelty comes out in various ways. Many times their harsh or sarcastic digs are disguised as "jests." Other times they will insult you directly but then will cover it up by saying, "I was only joking!" or "Can't you take a joke?" Brutal name-calling, debasing, and humiliating you are common forms of their verbal cruelty.

They intentionally provoke you where it hurts and then feed off your pain. Their cruelty is indeed calculating, deliberate, and intended to harm and/or to devastate you. Oftentimes when you are experiencing such brutality, you may plead with the narcissist to treat you with more kindness. Yet the narcissist will continue in their ruthless behaviour. Sam Vaknin, a professor of psychology and a self-admitted narcissist, describes how narcissists are aware of the damage and hurt that they cause others, and they blatantly do not care. They can consume another person and then offhandedly cast them aside.

Narcissists can demean anything about you. Nothing is off the table. They can degrade your greatest accomplishments, your line of work, your values, your friends and family, your appearance, your intellect, or your lifestyle. Without empathy and compassion, there is no filter for their cruelty and the continual bombardment of it can be completely demoralizing. This cruelty, however, is usually hidden to the public under a mask of charm and service. You can count on the fact that most people will *NEVER* see this side of the narcissist. Although the narcissist would like to escape accountability for their actions (and they do so by playing the denial or blame game), the narcissist fully knows what they are doing to you. Remember, with a narcissist, it is deliberate, intentional, and they feel no guilt.

Narcissists do not feel guilt or remorse for what they have done. Since a narcissist has no conscience, there are no limits to the pain and destruction they can cause. Not only will they not feel guilty for what they have done to you, they will most likely blame YOU for it!

Trait 19. Pathological Lying

I'm sorry, what language are you speaking? It sounds like Bullshit.

What will narcissists lie about? Anything and everything. They do this to escape accountability for their actions. After all, if they *"actually"* did do all of these horrible and abusive things they would also have to be responsible for the consequences. "Deny and lie" becomes their way of life.

Normal people feel guilty when they lie. They feel bad that they are not telling you the truth so they actually feel relieved when you stop asking questions or when the subject is changed. Sometimes you can note the lack of eye contact or uncomfortable physical shifts when a normal person is being dishonest. However, a pathological liar will show no emotions or uncomfortable physical shifts when they are lying. They can look you directly in the eye, lie to your face, and be completely unfazed without any guilt. It is shocking and chilling how narcissists deny their lies, make up excuses, and then project their horrific behaviour onto you (as if *you* had performed their actions) without even flinching. Expert liars such as these have been perfecting their dishonest craft over a lifetime and it can be *extremely* difficult to tell when they are lying.

The most dangerous liars actually fully believe they are telling you the truth.

Narcissists must lie because there is a perpetual need to keep up the façade of their perfect image. In the false narrative that the narcissist tells themselves, they are always the star of the show and the hero in any story. They will go to amazing lengths to exaggerate what they have done or to take credit for the work and skills of others.

Narcissists also lie to gain empathy from you so that they can further manipulate you in the future. Both narcissists and psychopaths lie to make others feel sorry for them. These two personality disorders know exactly how to elicit sympathy from their targets. They exploit and take advantage of the natural desire most people have to extend compassion and to help their fellow human beings. Since they want you to have sympathy for all their problems, injustices and woes in life, it is very common to hear about the "crazy" exes, unjust court battles, what others have "stolen" from them, and about appalling, biased treatment against them throughout their entire lives. Their ability to lie pathologically, easily, and confidently makes it possible for them to convince others of their sob stories (whether exaggerated or pretend), and to further draw others into their manipulation and exploitations.

Let's play truth or dare! Oh wait! We can only play dare. You don't know how to tell the truth.

Living a lifetime of creating lies, excuses and cover-ups, the narcissist is used to completely detaching from reality. They are no longer able to even discern what the truth actually is. After nearly two decades into a marriage, in what must have been an incoherent moment, one narcissist finally confessed to his wife that he had lied so much to her that he no longer knew what the truth about anything was anymore. Pathological liars can eventually be unequivocally convinced of their own deceptions.

Never argue with someone who believes their own lies.

What Will Narcissists Lie About?

In actual fact, you will likely never be able to find out the reality of *all* the lies narcissists tell. However, when it comes to their big lies (such as the ones below), the truth is often eventually exposed. Since you have been fed their lies for so long, it is always beneficial for you to verify their information with reliable parties outside your relationship.

Here are some things narcissists are likely to lie about.

Past Relationships and Their History

Check into the *real* reason why their last several relationships or marriages have failed. Yvette's narcissist told her that his ex-wife had many "mental illnesses," she had "various affairs" during the marriage, and she was also "physically abusive" toward him. His ex-wife had been incredibly "manipulative" with him and had "turned his children against him." Yvette bought his sad story completely. (They met online and she never had any other outside information to confirm or contradict what he had to say.) Yvette was *NOT* looking forward to the day when she might meet this woman. A month after Yvette and her narcissist were married, she did meet the ex-wife. Ironically, Yvette's initial impression of this woman was that she was a sweet, kind, gracious woman and a good mother. It was hard for Yvette to reconcile her initial impression of this person with the stories she had heard over the past two years.

Fast forward to a few years later when the narcissist showed his true colours and Yvette could no longer take it. After Yvette's own inevitable divorce, she eventually got to know this woman. Of course

Yvette now knows that her narcissist didn't tell one word of truth about his ex-wife. Yvette discovered this woman was truly the salt of the earth.

This woman would never hurt a fly, let alone be physically abusive, and oh yeah, it was actually the narcissist who had the serial affairs on her, tried to turn his children against her, and he was the one capable of being the "master manipulator."

Remember, narcissists project their faults and horrific deeds onto others. He did all of the things he accused his ex-wife of doing while she was completely innocent of his smear campaign.

Their Love For You

Narcissists will make great confessions of their love for you. They will declare they have never had such a soul connection with anyone before in their life like the one they are currently having with you. Christine bought this one—lock, stock and barrel! After five months of dating, her narcissist was telling people that he never had such an incredible relationship like this in his life, including any of his past marriages. It was only at the end of their marriage that Christine discovered that their *entire* relationship was fake (at least on his part).

The truth is narcissists aren't capable of genuinely loving you. They charm, love-bomb, and re-love-bomb you to lure you in until they have gotten everything they want from you. What narcissists *are* in love with is how they feel around you. The attention you give them is the "hit" they receive for their addiction. After they have sucked you dry, be ready for the prompt "discard."

By the way, when you are in the "discard" stage, although you may still be together, your narcissist is already in pursuit of, or actually has, a new lover in place. At this time, they will tell their new prize that their current relationship is over, or that they are about to break up, get separated, or be divorced (if they haven't already said that they are). Most likely you, the unsuspecting party, have not even had a conversation about this.

To their new lover, they will expound the exact tales of love that you once heard in the beginning of your relationship. Their words, like a broken record, will once again say that they have never felt as "in love" with anyone else as they are currently feeling with their new lover. Beware, the narcissist is extraordinarily skilled at getting you or a new person (or any number of persons at the same time) to believe that you (or all of you) are their "one and only."

When people lie to you, their actions are saying that deep down they either don't value you or the relationship enough to be honest with you.

What They Have Done for You

Narcissists love to play the victim and martyr so they can talk about all the sacrifices they have made. They lie, typically with a dash of truth sprinkled in to make it believable. You can be sure that they will take credit where credit is not due them. They are all about reaping where they have not sown and taking all the glory, credit, and attention they can. Reflect back on the early stages of your relationship. You have likely heard them taking all kinds of exaggerated or false credit from the people in their past. Be assured that they will be doing the same with you.

Diana battled for months in the process of her divorce to get a small settlement from her money-hungry narcissist. She was willing to leave their home just to get away from his extortions and abuse. After being threatened that she would walk out of their marriage with the clothes on her back and that would be it!, he finally gave her a tiny percentage of the money that she had put into their home. The money was barely enough for a down payment on another condo. However, Diana was thankful simply to be away from him even though it meant taking quite a financial hit in mid-life. Years later she discovered how her ex told tales to his family and their friends that he generously paid for her *entire* townhouse in full while she raked him over the coals and left him with the scraps.

You cannot expect honesty from a narcissist. Most likely you will get a fabricated story that either make them the victim or the hero. They never cast themselves as the villain.

Their Cheating and Secret Affairs

Sandy found out about her husband's affairs through finding his journals (plural), where he wrote about all of his affairs. The first affair that he had in their marriage was actually with the woman who broke up his second marriage. (Sandy was his third wife.) He wrote all about the day he and his mistress were reunited, their rendezvous, and about twenty pages of his undying love for her. After finding the journals it was all starting to make sense. His horrendous abuse began the day that he got back together with his ex-mistress. (Sudden and horrendous treatment is often an indicator that a narcissist is already involved with another person.)

Through his journals Sandy read all about his affairs in both his previous marriages. She found it quite shocking to read about his alternative personality in his journals. Sandy found out the truth of who he was and she now understands that everything in his journal was his *true* self.

Although the pain of the betrayal in his affairs was unbearable (she found out about several more of them), Sandy counted herself fortunate. It was through these blatant journals that she was able to read who the *true* person was—in his own words and by his own hand. The wolf could no longer believably wear the sheepskin, as her eyes were opened.

In the end, the mask and manipulative words of a narcissist can be so deceiving and confusing that you question which person is real—Dr. Jekyll or Mr. Hyde? The journal told her very clearly—it was Mr. Hyde.

Money

After Janna's marriage to a narcissist went off the cliff, she knew she had to come up with a separation agreement that included a financial settlement. Janna was willing to compromise financially versus going to court as she already knew it would be a long and brutal battle with him. Janna's freedom from this abusive relationship and never seeing this cruel person again was so much more important to her than money. However, when her narcissist kept failing to pay her financial settlement, Janna began to dig. In her search, she found all kinds of information. The man spent $1.5M in a couple of months in order to hide his money. This included properties in a couple of different cities, large sums of money to his son, and a bank draft of an exorbitant amount to his mistress. Janna figured he was spending and stalling so that he could find ways of getting out of their prearranged agreement and pay her even less. When Janna confronted him about their agreed-upon financial settlement he raged at her, "That's MY MONEY!" Note: this was not about the $1.5M she knew he was hiding, but rather the money they had built together and had already agreed to divide.

Chances are, when it comes to finances, once again they won't tell you the truth and they will try to get everything they can from you. Their money is their money and your money is their money. They are entitled to your money and they deserve it. Regarding finances and honesty, a narcissist's creed is to "deny, lie, hide, and take."

To a narcissist, everyone's money is his. His; yours; the money of the company he works for; his parents'; the elderly lady's, the one he's befriended. It's all his. He will be charming to those he needs to be charming to in order to get the money.

Trait 20. Numerous Affairs Outside the Relationship

Experts seem to agree: cheating and narcissism go hand in hand.[8]

—Sophia Mitrokostas

Narcissists, sociopaths, and psychopaths all rank the highest personalities in terms of cheating. These three personality disorders have a complete disregard for the rights and feelings of others; they fail to feel any guilt or remorse when they have been abusive or cruel to another person; they are completely devoid of having empathy toward another human being.

Someone with a Narcissistic Personality Disorder will never be able to empathize with their partner and understand the hurt that he or she has caused. Even if the narcissist does break off their affair, the inability to empathize with their partner will never go away. Affairs are difficult enough to deal with, without having the cold, callous, and bone-chilling cruelty of a narcissist. How could there possibly be any healing or capacity to move forward in an environment such as this? In order for a marriage to recover from an affair, the instigator of the affair must be able to empathize with their partner's feelings of betrayal and to be willing to have some accountability for their harmful actions. A narcissist is capable of neither.

If anybody studying psychology wants a concrete example of what a narcissist looks like, I advise them to consider any man who cheats on his wife. These guys are the textbook me-firsters, the ones who think the rules don't apply to them, the ones who tell themselves as long as she doesn't know, there's no harm done.[9]

—Julie Klausner

Both narcissists and sociopaths have a much more lenient attitude toward infidelity than the average person. When the narcissist believes they are better-looking, more intelligent, more attractive, and more worthy than their spouse, somehow this leads them to believe that they are also entitled to cheat. The using and abusing of people never stops, even with the "other woman." This attitude causes the narcissist to think they are entitled to use their affair partner exclusively for their own sexual pleasure. Sometimes in extramarital affairs, the narcissist will attract another narcissist—since nobody in that relationship really cares about fidelity. Then it's just a matter of who uses who more, and who can discard the other person first. From an outsider's perspective, a narcissistic pair can be quite fascinating to watch as you witness some karma in action.

Another reason for numerous extramarital affairs is that many narcissists are also sex-addicts. Narcissists have a greater desire for casual sex—sex without the "emotional commitment"—since emotions are a foreign language to them anyway. It takes a very immature and selfish person to dismiss their partner's value, love, and trust, for the sake of doing whatever they want to do in the heat of lust. Rather than taking responsibility for their actions and the committed relationship they are in, they indulge in whatever they want to. Let's face it, anyone who cheats and has affairs is dishonest. Period. Most likely they already manipulate and use people in other life situations, at whatever the cost, in order to get what they want.

When someone is narcissistic, they don't see why they should sacrifice their own happiness for someone else's.

A narcissist is often described as someone who is convinced that they warrant special treatment and repeatedly takes advantage of others to satisfy their own desires. When it comes to relationships, the narcissist feels that the normal rules of fidelity shouldn't apply to them, and that what they want should supersede anything and everyone else in their life.

One of the biggest problems with narcissists in relationships is that they always believe that they can attract better people than the person they are with. They are in a constant state of discontentment and unhappiness. In their mind, you are easily replaceable. They also perceive their own attractiveness, sexual prowess, and intelligence to be above average. Being in a relationship with someone who operates in this way is a perfect setup for infidelity. Sydney-based clinical psychologist Jacqui Manning states, "People who have been conditioned to always think about what makes them happy and content—and believing their needs being met is the most important thing—are more likely to be serial cheaters."[10]

A narcissist can't be faithful. This is because—to a narcissist—"you" don't exist except as a mirror. When he looks at you, all he sees is his own reflection. Distort this reflection and he will go find another mirror. It's as simple, or as complicated, as that.

Their infidelity is driven by the need to fulfill their unending demand for narcissistic supply. It is good to remember that their infidelity is not driven by a dissatisfaction of you as their spouse or their main partner, but their unfaithfulness is a sadistic need for maintaining their narcissistic "supply." A narcissist is constantly looking for supply to fill themselves with happiness. They must get it from external sources since they are so devoid on the inside. Due to their deep levels of emptiness, their hollowness can never be filled by one person. This is why they will have multiple affairs.

When their primary supply starts communicating their own needs or desires, the narcissist will instantly seek out their secondary supply. When they move onto their next supply, you may feel like your relationship has suddenly gone off a cliff. They are discarding you while they feast on their new supply. They feel zero guilt for cheating on you and they see no obligation anymore to you or to your relationship. Even when they make marital vows, they are never really committed. (Although they will certainly expect *you* to uphold the values of the relationship.)

When he won't even give you honesty, you can stop expecting loyalty.

Remember that the rules apply only to you and not to them. You are expected to possess undying, unquestionable loyalty toward them while they play the field, shrug it off, and then rage at you for getting upset at their betrayal. They cheated and you are expected to forgive them instantly and move on without them doing the work of rebuilding trust. They expect loyalty and immediate trust while they never change and continue to cheat. After all, like everything in the narcissist's world of dodging responsibility, their cheating was "not their fault." They may go so far as to say that *you* "owe" them for their cheating, and it was all your responsibility. If you had only fulfilled their needs (which they never communicated), they wouldn't have cheated. If only you had served them better (you have already gone above and beyond and depleted yourself to please them), they wouldn't have cheated. By now you may realize it is impossible to fulfill another person, let alone a narcissist who is a bottomless abyss.

Other common ways for them to blame and degrade you, and escape accountability for their actions is to say that you are "not fun anymore," or you "lost your figure," or "they had no other choice." NEVER accept such garbage! In a healthy relationship, instead of cheating, a decent partner would communicate what is not working and would not expect someone to remain picture perfect one hundred percent of the time for the rest of their life.

Don't forget to watch out for this one—they may even resort to projecting their affairs onto you and accuse *you* of cheating when they were out with multiple people. Yep, this can come out of the blue. They do not have a reason or even a person to accuse you of cheating with, but somehow you are sleeping with the person you looked at, the person whom you talked with at a party, a co-worker, or whomever. Regardless of their projection, when it comes to a narcissist, you will always be painted as the "bad person" as they conveniently disregard any accountability for their cheating actions. In the process, they will likely accuse you of going crazy as well.

Trait 21. Abusive

When a person is abusive, they use another person (or many people) for their own exploitation and objectification. It is abusive when someone uses or takes advantage of you for their own personal gain without any regard for your feelings or needs. Shahida Arabi, in her book, *Becoming the Narcissist's Nightmare*, defines "narcissist abuse" as

> *chronic manipulation and devaluation of their victims, leaving the victims feeling worthless, anxious and even suicidal ... which includes an idealization-devaluation-discard abuse cycle where they "lovebomb" their partners, devalue them, then discard them until the trauma begins again.... This type of abuse can leave psychological and emotional scars that can last a lifetime.*[10]

Narcissists and sociopaths actually get sadistic pleasure from inflicting trauma on their victims through harming and abusing them. For them, relationships are all about power and control. People with Abusive Personality Disorder (APD)—and all true narcissists have APD—will never actually change (except by the power of God). If they are truly a narcissist, they will certainly not see the need to change because they are never wrong. Despite the horrific abuse they inflict, they are notoriously successful at putting on the charming act long enough to get what they want from you before they cruelly discard you in an instant. Self-acknowledged narcissist Sam Vaknin admits that narcissists know they are amoral. They just simply don't care.

The narcissist will always deny, minimize, or rationalize their abuse. They may make debasing or sometimes outright abusive comments and then attempt to cover their tracks with, "It's just a joke!" They have no shame, remorse, or desire to take responsibility for the damage they inflict upon others. Somehow they excuse, justify, and rationalize their behaviour with more abuse. No matter how kind and giving you are, no matter how beautiful, successful, and confident you are, when you are in a relationship with an abuser, they will inevitably abuse you. It is who they are. It is who they will always be until they admit they need to change from their destructive ways.

They burn the bridge and then ask why I don't visit.

Abusers blame everyone else for all their problems. They blame others for their foul moods and destructive behaviours because they cannot tolerate thinking that they have any part to play or that they have any faults. As abusers shift the blame, they also try to drive their victims insane, so the victim thinks, "I must be the crazy one."

Narcissists are masters of illusion. They play the victim while in truth they are wreaking havoc by torturing, mistreating, and abusing those they fooled into loving them.[11]

—Y. Clerebout

Narcissists can be abusive in any or all of the following ways.

Emotionally

Please note that with a narcissist, everything you have ever said, whether it is good or bad, CAN and WILL be twisted and used against you. In the beginning of your relationship, you created a deep, personal bond (at least on your part). You shared with that person your life experiences, your secrets, your past hurts and struggles. While this is all fine and safe with a normal person, when you do this with a narcissist it will ultimately come back to haunt you. Later on, when they are devaluing you and prepping you for the discard stage, they will use your personal information against you to degrade, belittle, threaten, and even harm you.

Narcissists have an incredible lack of empathy and humanity. The indifference they have when you are facing an illness, injury, emergency, or crisis is callous, inhumane, and chilling. One narcissist let his wife suffer through all her cancer treatments alone at home while he went on a five-star tour of Europe. She begged him to stay with her in this difficult time and he honestly couldn't be bothered, so he booked a luxury trip for himself because of all the stress she was causing him.

Emotional abuse also comes in the form of silencing you, when the narcissist belittles, minimizes, negates, and denies your feelings and perceptions while also not allowing you to express your point of view. You may hear things from the narcissist like, "That's stupid to think that." "It wasn't really that bad, you're exaggerating." "Your feelings are wrong," "That's not what you mean." "That never happened." The narcissist will communicate other disdaining and cruel comments to you because you are so much "less" than the narcissist. Stonewalling, silent treatments, and intentionally withholding kind words, emotions, or affections for the purpose of directly hurting you are all flavours of their abusive nature.

> *Emotional abuse is so damaging because it outlives its own lifespan. Not only does it damage a person's self-esteem, at the time it is done, it also sets up a life pattern that daily assaults the inner being.*[12]
>
> —Gregory Jantz, PhD

Narcissists will also use against you the accomplishments and strengths of which you are the most proud. Your strengths and independence threaten their image and their control over you. They will ignore, negate, show disdain, or mock you for whatever you accomplish. They will attempt to crush your dreams, your goals, your friendships; they will belittle your appearance, your values, your talents; they will negate your emotions, needs, and concerns.

A narcissist will suck all the fun out of what would be some of your best experiences. They may insult you or give you putdowns when you have been given an award. As sabotage experts, unless you are still in the love-bombing phase, they will sabotage any events that are important to you. You will find they are extremely adept at ruining birthdays and

Christmases. One woman who was married to a narcissist knew after a decade and a half of marriage, not to expect a gift from her husband at Christmas. However, she did ask him for a Christmas card. In the end she was given a gift tag with, "to B from F" written on it. He couldn't be bothered to get his wife a gift let alone a real card for Christmas. He intentionally didn't even write out her name because his aim was to be as cruel and as hurtful as possible.

Often times the abuser will seek to isolate you by taking you away from your family, friends, and the people who love you the most. They don't want you to hang out with other people, as they want to be the sole influencer in your life. It is too much risk for others to influence you and to point out the flaws and concerns they see regarding the narcissist. To further distance your relationships with others, the narcissist will discount your family and friends, assassinate their characters, and try to pit you against each other. They do this in order for you to be completely isolated and without support. The name of the game for them is *control*. Intentionally isolating a person from everyone they love and who loves them back is *very* emotionally abusive.

Abuse doesn't define you, it defines the actions of the abuser!

Cheating is definitely a form of emotional abuse particularly when it becomes a chronic cycle of infidelity. Especially when you combine it with gaslighting statements such as, "You're crazy, nothing happened, it's all in your head." Chronic long-term cheating or cyclical cheating can crush a person's self-esteem to the point of creating psychological effects such as panic attacks and PTSD. It is also very emotionally damaging when the narcissist blames you for their cheating, "You made me do it!" When a narcissist cheats, they violate your trust and destroy your relationship while remaining completely indifferent as to how or why you are devastated. You may have poured your heart and soul into the relationship but in the end, from their perspective, you were just an object to be used up by them to gain attention for a period of time.

I equate narcissistic abuse to "soul rape." The survivor did not consent to being deceived, betrayed, and abused.

Verbally

Verbal abuse can come in the form of anger, rage, insults, and threats. Whenever you challenge the "perfect" image that the narcissist has crafted for themselves, you attempt to hold them accountable for their actions. In doing this, you threaten to sabotage the illusion they have of themselves. If you in any way expose their true self to others, you will experience their narcissistic rage. In an instant, you will see this cool cucumber turn on you in a fury of wrath. You can expect a lot of ridicule, belittling, raging, threats, and other forms of abuse at this time. Narcissistic rage is when their charming mask comes off and they are now hell-bent on destroying you.

Verbal abuse also involves accusing, blaming, and shaming. It can include name calling, sarcasm, rage, and bullying. Verbal and emotional abuse can come in the form of criticizing every action, remark, or thought that the other person has. Other verbal abuse tactics narcissists use are spreading malicious gossip and creating smear campaigns or lies about you in order to attack your character or to turn others against you.

Many times the narcissist will make conditional agreements. This is when they keep changing the conditions or goalposts so that they don't have to fulfill whatever they have promised. These changing conditions can be based on their various fickle moods. For example, if you do something they don't like, if the weather changes, or whatever whim they have in the moment, they get to change the agreement. These types of persistent deception, in the form of not fulfilling their promises or intentionally lying to your face, are also forms of verbal and emotional abuse. Amidst their web of duplicity, the narcissist avoids their responsibility, negates the pain they cause others, and ends up doing whatever it takes to achieve their end results.

Other forms of verbal abuse include negative contrasting and triangulation. Negative contrasting is when the narcissist makes a comparison between you and other people, or between you and themselves with the intention of painting you in a bad light or belittling you. Here are a couple of passive-aggressive examples of negative contrasting. "It's amazing how the women at my office keep their bodies in amazing shape and are so sexy. I'm not quite sure why *other* women carry so much fat." "Sarah's husband is always taking her on trips. The other day he got her an expensive diamond jewelry set. I guess only *real* men can make that kind of money." Both of these types of statements are designed to demean you, to compare you in passive-aggressive ways to others, with the intent of making you jealous and/or insecure about yourself and your relationship.

Triangulation is when the narcissist deliberately brings another person or a group of people into the relationship dynamic to belittle you and make you vie for the narcissist's attention. When Tonya and her narcissist went for marriage counselling, the narcissist attempted to use triangulation with their female counsellor. He kept sending the counsellor emails listing all the "work" of personal growth and self-development he had been doing outside their sessions. Of course he never discussed any of this with Tonya. You would think that, with all the "effort" he was putting in for the sake of their marriage, he would want to keep Tonya in the loop. Fortunately, the counsellor was familiar with triangulation and was able to see through this ploy. She firmly stated that there would be no separate emails or phone calls to her but everything would be discussed openly between all three of them during their counselling sessions. Afterwards when they broke-up, Tonya kept seeing the counsellor. Her narcissist had never told her of any of the personal "work" he had done. It was all pure fiction to charm the counsellor to be on his side and to turn her against Tonya.

Unfortunately, his triangulation worked later on in another context, as he successfully turned an entire group of their friends against Tonya. Through his twisting of words, Tonya became the enemy to this group of people. Unfortunately they were once very close friends of hers. This group actually became so enraged with Tonya that they cut her off completely despite the reality that he had been abusive toward her and had cheated on her with many people. Narcissists use triangulation, negative contrasting, and other forms of verbal abuse to manipulate and become more powerful.

Financially

No matter how financially wealthy they are, abusers will think that all of their money only belongs to them and that all of your money should unquestionably belong to them as well. Financial abuse can include controlling your personal or joint finances, or by using any financial situation to control you. Most financial abusive scenarios play out when the financially dominant one calls all the shots to exploit the other person who must succumb to their wishes. They often have the power to bury you in court with unending legal fees because they can afford to. Unfortunately, this is more often the case with husbands who control their wives when their children are small. Perhaps the wife has not worked while bearing their children and is more financially vulnerable as she has been out of the work force for years. Such a woman can also feel powerless to leave because the husband controls the bank account and she would have no way of taking care of her children.

They can also control your finances through extortion, theft, manipulation, or gambling. Some narcissists will accumulate debt in your name or even sell your personal property. Never let a narcissist or financially abusive person manage your money. Always keep a separate bank account from the narcissist.

Physically and Sexually

Any type of violence or physical act done against you is abusive. To be explicit, this includes throwing things at you, pushing you, preventing you from going where you want to go, kicking, punching, pulling your hair, strangling, or pinning you up against something. These are all forms of physical abuse.

Regarding sexual abuse, without mutual consent, even in a marriage, when sex is forced upon the other person, it is rape and abuse. Period.

Spiritually

Narcissists do come in all forms and many of them are involved in faith or religious groups. Some narcissists will outright claim to be "God's anointed," while they live out a double life. Many will twist and distort the scriptures, using God's Word, or spiritual teachings and godly principles to suit their own agenda. However, you will always know them by the fruit they produce in their lives. Do they act with the grace and love of God? Or do they proclaim their own self-righteousness while judging and condemning the world? Narcissists can play the super-spiritual saint without any flaws, while you are the unworthy sinner to be condemned. All the while, they do the very things they condemn you for. It's even better for them when they have a bit of manipulated spirituality to back them up.

Narcissists have spent their whole lives as actors. However, after a prolonged time of seeing their true abusive self, you won't buy it anymore. It gets increasingly more difficult to believe in the "sheep" costume when the wolf has attacked you for so long.

PART II

How Did I Get Involved with a Narcissist?

Now is the time to dig deep and get to the roots of how and why this happened. This includes powerful psychological reasons, the narcissist's charm, unhealed wounds, and fixing our blind spots.

CHAPTER 5

HOW DO WE GET SUCKED IN AND WHY DO WE STAY?

In order to understand what you are going through, it is important to learn about the phases or cycles of narcissistic behaviour. True narcissists follow a textbook pattern in how they treat you. From the outside, it may be difficult to understand or easy to judge someone who stays in an abusive relationship. However, there are also strong psychological reasons as to why someone stays in an abusive relationship. Until a person has lived in this situation, they really have no frame of reference for the psychological conditioning that a victim experiences.

The victim often stays because they have learned to develop unconscious survival strategies such as numbing, abuse amnesia, trauma bonding, and Stockholm syndrome (to name a few). The abuser uses manipulative tactics such as intermittent conditioning, the Law of Diminishing Returns, and gaslighting to induce the victim to stay.

There are many reasons why you may find yourself in a relationship with an abusive narcissist. It is important to recognize and acknowledge what you are going through or what you have gone through in order to get to a place of freedom and healing.

You are certainly not alone.

Three Phases of Narcissistic Treatment

It is vital to know that there are three phases of treatment that the narcissist will cycle you through. The narcissist may go back and forth between these phases and sometimes they will go through the cycle many times.

Phase One—The Love-Bombing Phase

This is the phase where you are treated like gold. You feel such a strong connection with this person and the energy is high. You have "so much in common" and you believe that you have met your soulmate. In this phase you are put on a pedestal and treated like a goddess or a god. The narcissist will shower you with all kinds of attention, texts, phone calls, and gifts. It is the honeymoon stage of a relationship *on steroids* and it is the very best of the best.

The love-bombing phase is not the reality of how the person will treat you in the future. Or at least, not how they will consistently treat you in the future. When they feel you are slipping away, they will re-love bomb you. They do this in order to keep you hooked. Just know that this amazing treatment of you is temporary and will not last very long before you are in …

Phase Two—The Devaluation Phase

During this phase you will start to see some cracks in your wonderful knight, or beautiful damsel. You also discover that while you were once adored, now you are not considered in the slightest. In fact, if you are honest, you are downright disrespected by your partner and are completely devalued. Your accomplishments, feelings, thoughts, perceptions, and needs don't matter. You begin to see the narcissist display some cruelty and contempt as you are considered "less than" and "beneath" the narcissist. This is the phase when the blatant criticism of you enters, and you will find that your soulmate is actually filled with disdain and contempt for you.

In this phase you can expect emotional withdrawing, stonewalling, and the silent treatment. You will probably experience an incredibly sullen, moody, sulky person. Many times you may feel as if you are interacting with a toddler. This toddler starts to have fits when you won't do what they want you to do and they begin to experience that the world does not revolve around them. Then comes the dangerous territory. Whenever you question (which threatens) the false image they have of themselves, you will encounter their narcissistic rage. It is a hot anger that rages like a fire-breathing dragon attacking you.

It is vital to understand, and to be willing to accept, that the person you fell in love with at the beginning of your relationship (the charming love-bomber) NEVER REALLY EXISTED! It will get easier once you accept the fact that the person you fell in love with doesn't actually exist. This person wore a mask to deceive you and use you.

Phase Three—The Discard Phase

The discard phase is cruel, callous, and sudden. This is where the real person is revealed on a consistent basis and there is often not even a hint of the love-bombing mask that you once cherished. You may be blatantly ignored for long periods of time. In the discard phase, the narcissist has now moved on to their other "supply" (a.k.a., their next victim who is already in place or who will be in the anticipated future to give them the attention they desire). This cold, harsh treatment is due to the fact that the narcissist is now idealizing and love bombing that other person. Sometimes you will not actually discover their other "supply" as they are masters of living a double life, they are pathological liars. Their secret affairs may be hidden for months or years; however, what will be obvious is that their cruelty toward you has skyrocketed. Other narcissists are more overt. They will be parading their new prize on their arm to their friends and family faster than you can grasp what has even happened. Their intention of obtaining this sudden new supply is not only to gain attention for themselves but also it is to disrespect you and intentionally wound you.

You will find there is no attempt for closure—no attempt on their part to end the relationship with you. There are no efforts to make this easier on you or for you to feel better about the ending. In short, there are no kind, thoughtful, or humane feelings that you will receive from the narcissist. They have no guilt and no remorse for callously discarding you, lying to you, and cheating on you. Narcissists are incapable of feeling remorse or empathy. You are now no longer necessary in their life because by now you have seen the light of who they really are and you are no longer buying into their false image. It is likely that you will not be able to grasp how inhuman and how completely devoid of empathy the narcissist is, until this discard phase.

Mixing Phases

Now these three phases don't simply happen in a one, two, three order. The narcissist often goes back and forth between phases one and two many times before moving to three. However, when you are re-love bombed, it is never so great as the first time. Each time you are re-love bombed it gets weaker, and each time you are devalued it gets worse. Indeed, the devaluation treatment of you gets crueller every time. The back and forth between love bombing and devaluation can last for years or even decades until ultimately you will reach the discard phase.

Here's a bit of an overview of what this might look like. A narcissist starts with pure love bombing for six months, then eventually adds in a pinch of devaluation. If the target or victim confronts or breaks off the relationship, the narcissist will deny the devaluation treatment and begin anew with the love bombing. You think that maybe you have misjudged the person or you have misinterpreted the situation. After you are hooked a bit deeper by their amazing treatment of you, you will experience a bit more devaluation, followed by an onslaught of love bombing. This is meant to catch you off guard. You will begin to question your own judgement as the narcissist completely denies their bad treatment of you. The narcissist will accuse or persuade you that you are taking things the wrong way; they will convince you that they were "just joking." In your confusion, you have to admit that you are also seeing their good treatment of you. After all, nobody is perfect, right? The back and forth between these stages will continue until the narcissist is tired of you and they have found a new "supply," or sometimes a former "supply," for that matter. Either way, the third phase will eventually come and you will be promptly discarded without any feelings of regret or responsibility on their part. Actually without any feelings at all.

After the discard stage (and this can even happen years later even after the divorce or separation), if they have lost their new "supply," be prepared for the love bombing to begin again. And so their broken record plays on …

How We Get Sucked In and How We Can Get Free

If you are reading this, you may be reeling from the shock of what has just happened in your life, and you are trying to move through the debris and chaos left in the wake of being a narcissistic discard. You may be wondering how all of this could have happened, and how could it have gone so very, very wrong?

In my journey, I discovered, there are many reasons why we get sucked in by the narcissist and there are powerful psychological reasons as to why we stay. These reasons include the power of love bombing; our belief in their false self; intermittent conditioning; the hope dope; self-blame; abuse amnesia; cognitive dissonance; Stockholm syndrome, also known as trauma bonding; the frog in the pot theory; numbing; and the power of gaslighting.

Reason One—Love Bombing

Love bombing is VERY powerful, particularly when it comes to all the attention that a narcissist gives you. You were probably looking for your soulmate and then the narcissist walked into your world, showering you with all kinds of attention, constant phone calls, texts, gifts, and surprise outings. They made you the centre of their world and you did the same for them. You feel this new relationship is special, unlike anything you have ever experienced. You are convinced that this person is one hundred percent committed to you, your happiness, and your relationship. You believe that the narcissist is genuinely interested in you. Later you will discover that they were really only interested in making you dependent on their praise and attention so that they could get more praise and attention out of you and ultimately control you.

You are about to find out that even their interests and values are all smoke and mirrors. During this phase where you are idealized, the narcissist often will reflect back your hobbies, interests, feelings, and values. This profound synchronization makes you feel completely understood and cherished. However, it is a manufactured "soulmate" effect that seduces you into thinking that you've met the "one."

After a few years into the relationship, Kathy found out that all of the common interests that she and her new husband shared were not so common and nor was he actually interested in any of them. It turns out that he didn't like getting together with people. He didn't actually like her friends and family. They stopped travelling overseas and doing many fun, adventurous things together shortly after they got married. In the end, it turned out that even his Christian faith wasn't his true life and he willingly exchanged it for a Buddhist faith to mirror what his next victim wanted. That is what it is like to be love bombed and to have your interests, beliefs, and feelings mirrored by another person who, in the end, did not actually exist.

To get past love bombing, be willing to take your time and don't dive headfirst into relationships. See the person in many contexts with a variety of people to make sure they are consistent. Be sure not to idealize or romanticize a person to the point where you are not able to see any flaws.

Reason Two—We Believe Their False Self

What we have experienced in the love-bombing stage is the false self. It is not the actual person. The false self is the fake persona that the narcissist projects to the world. We buy into this amazing, fabricated person. After all, aren't people who they say they are? Don't their actions speak of who they are? That is why we question ourselves so much when we start to see their true self emerge. The wonderful false self whom we first met MUST be the real person; and the mean, disrespectful true self that we now see, must mean that WE are falsely interpreting their behaviour or the circumstances. (Especially since the narcissist bombards us by constantly telling us how our perceptions are off.)

Unfortunately, believing their false self will take an immense toll on you. Slowly your sense of reality and confidence will erode over time. This is what drives people crazy and leaves them with physical symptoms including nervous breakdowns, migraines, panic attacks, gut issues, and anxiety. Your gut and intuition know. Your deep-down perception of their true self is *not* wrong.

I compare the false self and the true self to a *character* in a film and the *person* who is the real actor. Think of a character from a movie that you were extremely attracted to. Perhaps it was the unwavering loyalty that he demonstrated in the film, his self-sacrifice and devotion, the romantic gestures that melted you on the spot, or it could be a certain masculine energy that you gravitate toward. (Change the gender to suit your situation.) You think of how wonderful this character was in the movie. Wow! How amazing it would be to embody the leading lady in this story so that you could be with someone like that!

In contrast, you then saw the real actor in an interview. He turned out to be an arrogant, condescending, womanizing, self-centred guy. Ah-hah! You realize that you fell for their movie character and that the actor is a completely different person. You would never in a million years be attracted to the real actor who is indeed a serious jerk and the polar opposite of who you saw in the film. Ding, ding, ding! The same is true with the narcissist. In the beginning you fell in love with their "character"—the fairy-tale "Prince Charming." Except this isn't who the real person is; he was just playing a role. When you see the mask come off the narcissist (the character) and the real person presents himself (the actor)—believe it.

> *Beware of people who seem to shape-shift suddenly before your eyes into different personas.*[1]
>
> —Shahida Arabi

Hmm, "shape-shift"; that's an interesting term, Shahida. How many personas and characters do they actually play? Heidi definitely saw this in her narcissist when he was with her sister's kids. Whenever he was with them, she saw a completely different person. Heidi had been with this man for a few years before she saw a different persona when he was around her nieces and nephew. The first time she saw it, she thought to herself, "Oh, that's cute. That's how he is with kids. What a goof." Then it got to be a bit much, to the point where she didn't even recognize who he was when he was around her nephew and nieces. It is interesting to note that the kids never knew when he was joking or serious and they felt very uncertain around him. Heidi had never seen any trace of this other person except when that personality manifested around those kids. Most likely it was a way to win them over.

This new persona was completely the opposite of who he was becoming. Around these kids he was always laughing, extremely extroverted, the life of the party, a performer, and a comedian. It was such a stark contrast to the introverted, moody, haughty, critical, mean-spirited person that Heidi had lately been experiencing at home. Seeing how this dichotomy became more extreme over the years, Heidi started to question things. It was like the more Heidi got to know the real sullen, mean person, the more extravagant and exaggerated this other personality became. Heidi also realized that the person she was now seeing on a daily basis was completely different from the charming man she dated years ago. First impressions are not always accurate!

Not only can narcissists put on various personalities; they are also very proficient at faking any emotion. They can turn on the crocodile tears, give "humble" repentant discourses, and say anything to win you over. They learn to imitate people, memorize speeches, and use ideas and lines from movies, books, and songs. They do this because there is no real emotion on the inside. They must learn to craft their responses and mimic the emotions of others. You may start to see how sometimes the emotion does not fit what is happening, or the intensity is not appropriate for the situation.

Rachel recalls a time that she fell off a short stepladder. She was not really hurt but her narcissist came in the room blubbering like a school boy and sobbing uncontrollably. The response was completely overblown for what the situation called for. She ended up consoling him and then he abruptly stopped sobbing as if nothing had happened. It happened in several instances—immediate crying and tears over seemingly nothing, with a quick shut off. She always found that to be strange and completely manufactured. And, of course, when it came to him being truly abusive in certain incidents, only the heartless person showed up.

While we do tend to believe their false self, there are many signs over time that something is off. Pay attention to gross inconsistencies in a person's behaviour, emotions, or persona.

Reason Three—Intermittent Conditioning

Intermittent conditioning is a type of unpredictable, reinforcement agenda that a person uses to gain manipulative control over another person. In this haphazard and confusing treatment, you are neither rewarded nor punished *consistently* for certain types of behaviour. American psychologist and philosopher B.F. Skinner coined the term "intermittent reinforcement" to describe a schedule in which a subject's desired behaviour is only rewarded occasionally, rather than every time.³

This random, erratic treatment keeps you on edge and can create an addiction to the relationship. You never know when you will be treated with cruelty and contempt, or when you will be treated royally and put on a pedestal. This type of inconsistent treatment is meant to keep you guessing and off-kilter. It is much like gambling. You never know when you will lose it all or strike it rich. It can be very addictive to see what might happen. Although with this type of track record, you have a high probability of losing, you know that when you do win, you have the potential to win big. It can almost seem *more* rewarding to *finally* be treated well after such horrific dealings.

> *The narcissist gets away with giving you less while getting more of your time, energy and effort.²*

Intermittent conditioning in a narcissistic relationship is the *re*-love-bombing stage where the narcissist feeds you some crumbs of niceness to hook you back into the relationship. This can cause you to question if the cruel treatment you have experienced is actually real. Remember, even the most abusive person can display charm at seemingly caring moments. They do this to control you. After treating you in ghastly ways, they will go back to their awesome treatment of you and please you enough so that you will stay in the relationship.

Unfortunately this trains a person to associate love with distress, anxiety, and unpredictability. Psychologists state that the potency of intermittent conditioning (of being treated amazingly only once in a while) is more powerful than having a consistently healthy relationship. Intermittent conditioning keeps us trying for that sporadic win of being treated like gold. This gambling effect on the brain creates more excitement because the rewards are so random, unpredictable, and rare; therefore, the thrill is magnified whenever there is a win.

Chemically what happens within us is that an *unpredictable* reward causes us to receive more dopamine in the brain when we finally do get that reward. Dopamine triggers release all of those feel-great chemicals such as oxytocin. This hormonal rush can be chemically addicting and keeps us going for more. To sum it up, dopamine flows more freely when the rewards are unpredictable versus predictable. Yes, you can become chemically addicted through the natural hormones that course through your body when a certain stimulus is presented.

Reason Four—Hope Dope

Hopefulness is a characteristic of healthy, optimistic people. It is great to have this expectation, as hope keeps us going during the difficult times in life. Every normal person wants a healthy, loving, supportive relationship. It is one of the greatest things most of us desire in life. However, this hope for love can sometimes cause us to fill in the gaps and imagine that love exists where it actually doesn't. Love can be the thirst in the desert that causes people to see mirages, because we so desperately want to. Thirst, combined with these illusionary mirages can drive us to keep taking action until we arrive at the place, only to find there was really nothing there.

We can be delusional about the love someone has for us or about who the other person really is. We can believe beyond all reason that something will change inside the other person. "One day they will 'get it.'" We can tell ourselves many hopeful tales. "Things will improve." "He must just be having a bad day." (However this can extend to a bad year or a tough life.) "Everyone goes through rough patches." "No relationship is perfect." "You can't expect the honeymoon stage to last forever." "We just need to find that spark again."

Where we get into trouble is when hope becomes our dope drug and it deadens our senses to the reality of what is actually happening. No matter how the narcissist acts, we sincerely "hope" that the narcissist will change. We even create excuses for them that they are just having an "off" day (or decade). We will be determined to do everything possible to get him or her to love us and to make this relationship or marriage work. One of the hope-dope lies we tell ourselves is "If I can just love him in the way that he needs, he will change, start treating me well, and love me back." It is as if we have a superpower over someone's life, and that *we* can make *them* change. This also, is a false illusion.

Psychologists, Dr. Henry Cloud and Dr. John Townsend, talk about defensive hope in their famous book, *Safe People*.

> *We use hope to defend ourselves against facing the truth about someone we love. We do not want to go through the sadness of realizing that they probably are not going to change. We don't want to accept the reality about who they are. So, we hope.... We usually have an old pattern of not facing grief and disappointments in many past relationships, dating back to childhood.*[3]

It is our responsibility to give up hope when it is false or defensive, or when it becomes an avoidance or a blockade to us facing our own grief and disappointments. If we are honest, many of us need to change our patterns of how we deal with our grief and disappointments. We must be willing to face the truth even when it is so desperately painful. We need to learn to face our own pain and grieve for what has happened or for what will never happen. Grief is difficult, and the only way out of it is to go through it.

The reality is it is EXTREMELY rare that a narcissist can, will, or even wants to change. One study had the statistic that only 3 percent of narcissists can truly change (and that is only out of the very few who admit they have a problem and are seeking help for it). From what I have experienced and read, it is VERY rare for a narcissist to first of all, acknowledge they are a narcissist, since they are perfect in their own eyes and never do any wrong. For your own sake, it is better to give up your false hope that they might see the light, feel the unknown emotions of remorse and empathy, acknowledge that they too have a dark side, and then genuinely change.

Honour yourself and keep your distance from such dangerous personalities. Don't get hooked on the hope dope. After all, have you actually seen any real fruit or evidence of genuine remorse, empathy, or change in their life?

Reason Five—You Blame Yourself

At some point, the narcissist will likely blame you for everything that went wrong in your relationship and even in their life. In a warped way, you may be inclined to agree with them. Of course it's you! Because the narcissist is such a different person to the rest of the world! His evilness only comes out when you are around; therefore, you MUST be to blame.

While it is healthy and good to acknowledge, own up to, and seek to change where you have gone wrong in a relationship, people are ultimately each responsible for the place where they are in their own life, and that even includes the narcissist. However, a narcissist will never accept the responsibility for where they are in life or for the pain they have caused others. They will push any blame and accountability on to whomever they can get to *accept* the blame. This is why it is crucial to set boundaries on what responsibilities you will accept. Perhaps you are also the type of person who over accepts responsibility in areas that you were never meant to take ownership of. You are not responsible for another person's actions, thoughts, words, moods, feelings, temper tantrums, or disrespectful and cruel behaviour so do *not* accept their false blame and guilt.

When the narcissist has their withdrawing and withholding patterns, they will also blame you for being the "needy" one as you respond to their hot and cold behaviours. At one point they were all too happy to give you all the love, attention, and affection you desired and then some. Now they have changed the game and when you come to expect the same treatment or dare to be vulnerable enough to express your needs, they regard you with contempt. In healthy relationships, connection, honesty, loyalty, and communication are all necessary elements for relationships to thrive. However, when you still want these things, you are now dismissed for being needy and, ironically, you are also blamed for not being enough for them.

Don't get sucked into confirming what they are declaring, by saying to yourself, "It must be me. Maybe if I were just more … (fill in your own word: loving, serving, submissive, beautiful, creative, wealthy, cultured, more intelligent, less intelligent, more outgoing, less outgoing), they wouldn't be so cruel." The truth is a narcissist will never have enough and you will continually be their target of blame. *No one can ever be enough for the narcissist.*

Reason Six—Abuse Amnesia

We have been told many times throughout our lives to "forgive and forget." Abuse amnesia does this all too well as a person not only forgives but also easily forgets the abuse. While forgiveness is very healthy and essential for moving on, in abusive situations you neither want to forget nor to continue to take more abuse. Abuse amnesia is an unconscious survival strategy. According to a domestic abuse recovery website, *Out of the Fog*,

> *Abuse Amnesia is a form of cognitive suppression where an abuse victim has trouble remembering episodes where their boundaries have been violated.*[4]
>
> —Sharie Stines

If there was any abuse in your home while you were growing up, abuse amnesia can intensify, because it is already familiar to you. This type of amnesia has been an imprinted way of coping, adapting, and surviving in your home environment. You are desensitized to the "red flags" that are obvious to others.

Counsellors often talk about the fact that 80 percent of your emotional blueprint is more or less set between the ages of eight and ten. However, this does not mean this is your destiny, or that you have to remain a victim to your past or present circumstances. It does mean that if you grew up in a home with any sort of abuse, you will need to be aware of it, and to acknowledge any abuse in both your past and present. You can *change* your emotional blueprint. You will have to do more intentional work than other people who did not grow up in such an environment. With deliberate and consistent work, you can be free from your past and the patterns that sabotage you, and you can chart a different course for your life.

It is stressful and traumatic to have abusive events in our lives. The way we often cope with trauma is to minimize the damage by focusing on the good times and by quickly seeking to move on from the past abuse. No one wants to stay in that place of trauma, so we seek to move on as quickly as possible. When we do this, we may also begin to deny, minimize, or rationalize our abuse in order to cope with the distress. Here's the test—you know you have abuse amnesia when you are in an abusive situation and both the victim and the abuser can carry on as if nothing ever happened. However, in order to heal, you *must* acknowledge what has happened. Often it takes a good counsellor, or sometimes your friends and family members, to help you see when you are being treated in abusive ways.

In the good times of love bombing, it is especially easy to forget the abuse. When we stay in a relationship with a narcissist, we may subconsciously justify that all the good parts of this relationship make staying worthwhile. This mindset of abuse amnesia helps protect us from the trauma we are experiencing when things are really bad. Emotional abuse begins in very subtle ways and builds over time. Trying to forget our abuse is a defensive way to survive by protecting ourselves. We learn to disassociate from our traumas and to suppress or minimize the suffering, especially after it has been chronic abuse.

When you end your relationship with a narcissist, to truly be free of abuse amnesia in the future, you will have to face the *reality* of *all* the traumas you have experienced in your life. This can be intensely painful.

However, when you truly and finally deal with and acknowledge all of your traumas in life, it can bring a deep and lasting healing. Ending your relationship permanently with a narcissist can be an avenue of recovery from the trauma experienced both in this relationship and from your past wounds.

Reason Seven—Cognitive Dissonance

Cognitive dissonance is when a person holds two conflicting beliefs at the same time. An example of this is when you experience the Dr. Jekyll and Mr. Hyde behaviours with the same person. How can someone be so kind and loving, AND be so incredibly cruel and bent on destroying you? It is very mentally disturbing.

Cognitive dissonance has been described as a hazy unreality of confusion. When a person is in this state, they are constantly trying to look for reasons to support one belief as being true and the other belief as being false. The person living in cognitive dissonance is facing a dilemma of dichotomy. After you have experienced the charming love-bomber in all their glory, it is wrenching to see the other persona of this horrific, callous abuser seething with contempt for you. You have now seen two conflicting personas. Which person is the real one?

It is impossible to accept that both personas are the real deal. We cannot rationally justify that our experiences with these conflicting personas can create a cohesive and true reality. One persona *must* be false because it is diametrically opposed to the other persona. We naturally want to believe that the charming, "loving" person who has treated us so well in the beginning and has put us on a pedestal is the real person. We choose to believe that the attractive persona is the real one. We negate the other personality and with it our own horrific experiences.

In *A Theory of Cognitive Dissonance* (1957), Leon Festinger proposed that human beings strive for internal psychological consistency in order to function mentally. Anyone who experiences internal inconsistency becomes psychologically uncomfortable and seeks whatever means possible to reduce the cognitive dissonance.[5] In other words, we cannot mentally function properly with psychological inconsistencies. When you experience such an internal contradiction, you are motivated to decrease this dissonance by making a choice that one is true and the other is false.

This type of mental abuse creates a sense of unreality and perplexity in which you begin to distrust your own perceptions of the situation. You try to find a way to reduce the overwhelm of both this unbalanced perception of the narcissist and the different personas you are experiencing. In doing so, your natural inclination is to either (1) adapt by justifying your horrific experience with Mr. Hyde or (2) become indifferent to what you are experiencing. In the first way of coping, you adapt to abuse. It becomes your "normal" and you even defend your abuser. The second way causes you to numb your feelings and use escapist strategies so that you avoid the pain. These two coping mechanisms are ways to seek to reduce your cognitive dissonance. Neither of them serve you.

Reason Eight—Stockholm Syndrome and Trauma Bonding

Stockholm syndrome is a condition in which hostages develop a psychological alliance with their captors as an unconscious survival strategy. Historically, the term came into being when two convicts on parole, Jan-Erik Olsson and Clark Olofsson, took four bank employees hostage during a failed bank robbery. This was the Kreditbanken in Stockholm, Sweden. The hostages were held captive for six days in a bank vault and were tortured with nooses and dynamite. What is inconceivable is that when they were released, none of the hostages would even testify against either captor in court. Instead, the former hostages actually began raising money for their captors' defense.[6] This psychological condition is completely illogical and irrational in light of the fact that these hostages endured torture and their lives were in danger from their captors. This reflex is a very powerful and unconscious survival response.

Stockholm syndrome is a form of trauma bonding. Trauma bonding is "a strong emotional attachment between an abused person and his or her abuser, formed as a result of the cycle of violence."[7] This violence is not limited to physical violence but can include emotional and psychological violence. In trauma bonding, the victim tries to develop an alliance with their abuser in order to lessen the trauma. Stockholm syndrome and trauma bonding are close cousins. Basically, interchange the words "hostage" with "victim"; and "captor" with "abuser" (or narcissist, in this case) and you have the same scenario.

Trauma bonding happens when we endure intense emotionally negative experiences from our abusers. This bonding happens over time with narcissists. The abuse often begins slowly with condescending remarks, degradation, disrespect, name calling, and manipulation until it crescendos into abuse, rage, pathological lying, and infidelity. In narcissistic abuse you will likely experience emotional, mental, and sometimes physical terror. However, much like the hostages in Stockholm, your survival mechanisms kick in and you must deny this terror if you are to outlast the relentless abuse. Anyone in terror turns to their nearest source of comfort to gain psychological rebalance. In other words, a person turns to the very one who is abusing them to receive comfort from them in their trauma.

A person in a state of trauma bonding, or Stockholm syndrome, feels progressively helpless and increasingly dependent on survival from their caregiver, regressing to a similar place of infancy. When we need to obey in order to survive, we become like an infant who clings to its mother. We can end up centring our life around obeying and pleasing the captor in order to survive.

What many psychologists have discovered is that, ironically, when a relationship offers both pain and pleasure it can create even stronger bonds than a relationship with pleasure alone. Therefore, unfortunately, the trauma bonds with a narcissistic abuser are much harder to break than the bonds in a normal and healthy relationship. However, it is possible. And now is the time to take back your power.

Reason Nine—Less Bang for Your Buck

It is inevitable that, when you are in a relationship with a narcissist, you will progressively be getting less bang for your relationship buck. While the amount of love that you provide, the extent of your giving, and your acts of service to your narcissist remain the same (or even increase), you will continue to get less and less back from the narcissist the longer your relationship progresses. You are likely depleting yourself of your emotions, resources, and your soul at an exponential rate in order to keep up to the ever-increasing demands from the narcissist. In fact, while the narcissist gets more of your time, energy, and efforts, they are getting away with giving you much less. They give you less love and fewer compliments, while somehow you end up paying all the bills and taking the sole responsibility for all the woes in your relationship. This is how they slowly settle into their abusive ways.

Narcissists will continually test the waters by ping-ponging back and forth between love bombing and devaluing you. It is subtle and gradual. They want to see how much they can get away with. I'm sure you have heard of how to boil a frog. If you throw a frog into boiling water, it will immediately jump out because of the shock. The immediate shock of the extreme heat sends it leaping. In the same way, if the narcissist were to treat you, in the beginning, the way they treat you in the end, you would run like hell. You would *never* accept the scarce crumbs that they are now giving you, nor the abuse that they are now inflicting upon you.

This is similar to the analogy of how to kill a frog. However, if you put a frog into a pot of lukewarm water and ever so slowly turn the temperature up, the frog will stay put and not notice that they are gently being boiled to death. This is how a narcissist works. The temperature is imperceptibly turned up over time and you hardly notice their transformation. Hopefully you will get out before you are boiled to the point of no return!

Reason Ten—Numbing

With psychological trauma, it is very common to cut yourself off from your own emotions. You may be unable to feel your emotions because you have suppressed so much trauma. You cannot fully connect with the nightmare you are presently experiencing. You feel shell-shocked. When you are unable to fight or to take flight, the response that is left is to freeze. You must freeze your feelings and dissociate emotionally as a way to survive. Numbing does serve you as a way to protect you from the overwhelming onslaught of abuse. However, numbing has some negative repercussions as well.

When you constantly have to numb your feelings, you can lose your voice and your true self. When you are with a narcissist who doesn't care to hear your voice or who outright negates it, you can begin to numb, dull, and lessen your voice and your emotions. Whether it happens through their abusive restrictions or you deliberately numb your own emotions (or a combination of the two), you ultimately lose your voice. You no longer speak your feelings, thoughts, needs, requests, opinions, and dreams. In order to salvage the relationship, the cost you pay in staying with them is that your true self will start to disappear. *No* price is worth this cost!

When you numb, you may feel a deep sadness, you may cease making plans with others, or you stop developing your own interests because nothing seems to matter. Subconsciously you will focus on saving your energy to fend off the next set of emotional attacks. When you become emotionally numb, you can also become deadened to any sense of joy or hope. However, this isn't the end of the story. There is hope and you can recover your voice!

CHAPTER 6

WHY WE ATTRACT NARCISSISTS

> *Don't be ashamed because you were a narcissist target. They target sweet, loving, caring souls.[1]*
>
> —Anne Brown

There are numerous reasons why we have attracted narcissists into our lives. Often, it has not only to do with our pain from past traumatic events, our blind spots, and weaknesses but also we attract them through our strengths and wonderful qualities. There is no doubt that the narcissist saw that you were unique and special, and they knew they could manipulate your empathetic heart. The goal of this chapter is to give you some awareness and to shed some light as to why this experience may have happened to you.

Whether you have some areas in your life that need healing, some blind spots (such as poor boundaries), weaknesses, or unconscious sabotaging habits or thought patterns, *now* is the time to deal with these things in your life so that this will *never happen again*. It is good to take an honest examination of our lives and to see the areas that we need to heal, and to acknowledge where we need to grow. As we say in coaching, awareness is the first step, so that we can have the choice to change.

The following could be explanations as to why you have attracted a narcissist.

1. You Are an Empath

After reading numerous articles, books, and interviews, I was surprised to find that the victims of narcissistic abuse varied quite a bit. What you might consider to be a stereotype of someone in an abusive situation was not necessarily the case. These targets did not seem to have *any* of the following things in common: confidence levels (whether high or low); degrees of attractiveness (or not); being introverted or extroverted; social status; financial status; or education levels. All of these characteristics varied across the board among the victims of narcissists; none of these traits, whether they were in high or low quantities, seemed to be a common denominator. These dynamics were not even consistent when the same narcissist chose different partners. Various studies showed the number one factor, which ALL the victims had in common, was that they all had a *high degree of empathy.*[2]

An empathic person, or an "empath," has the following traits:

- You are excellent listener. Complete strangers pour out their hearts to you and people easily open up to you.
- People from all walks of life are attracted to you. The same is true with animals.
- You are very much affected by other people's energies. You pick up on people's feelings and moods and can intuitively feel what other people feel.
- Empaths exude warmth and genuine compassion.
- You are enthusiastic, outgoing, joyful, and have a great sense of humour.

- You always strive for the truth and are constantly looking for answers and more knowledge.

- You are a free spirit and you love your freedom.

- You have a huge desire and almost an agenda to see others be in a place of healing, love, and growth.

- You seek out the underdog and have great compassion for anyone who is suffering or in pain.

- Self-sacrifice is a normal reaction for you. In fact, you tend to ignore your own needs in order to take care of what others need and want.

- While you may be able to talk openly and frankly, you may also find it difficult to express your inner emotions to others.

- You have a tendency toward people pleasing. The downside is that because you are so focused on pleasing others, it can cause you to lose yourself in the end.

- Disharmony is stressful for you. When you are in conflict, you seek to find a resolution as quickly as possible. Since you consider others' needs more important than your own, you will likely be the one to compromise in order to keep the peace.

If these traits characterize an empath, doesn't this make sense why narcissists prey on empathetic people? It is your compassion, your desire to heal, and your overly giving nature that draw narcissists to you. Empaths are natural givers whereas narcissists are the epitome of takers. You are a target because you will readily sacrifice yourself to see the narcissist be "set free" and "healed." The overly compassionate empath can easily be sold the lies that the narcissist has been the "victim" in all of their horrible life circumstances.

If you as an empath, do not understand how to protect yourself and you do not intentionally create boundaries with people, you can very easily and very quickly bond with a narcissist in an attempt to try to fix and repair any pain and apparent hurt that the narcissist has suffered in their life. The narcissist can lead you down a very dark and painful road as they prey upon your lovely, empathic spirit. This is why it is crucial that empaths learn to set and enforce healthy boundaries, stay in touch with their inner voice, and engage in regular self-care.

The good news of most narcissistic-empathic relationships is in the ending. After a difficult road and a painful breakup, most empaths will use this horrific experience for growth. After having a greater awareness from such an appalling experience, empaths are willing to learn from their mistakes. Following a narcissistic relationship, empaths usually come out of it stronger than ever.

Since you are an authentic person and are eager to live out your true purpose in life, you are likely to view this experience as a very painful awakening. Your growth perspective is that you have dodged a major bullet and that you can and have learned amazing things to help other people! This experience can be viewed as a place from where you can grow tremendously in otherwise impossible ways. You will use this experience as an opportunity to learn, to become better, to heal from your own past and hurts, and to come out stronger in the end. It is in fact this optimism that you have as an empath that will empower you to move forward.

2. You Are a Unique and Wonderful Person

Let's face it, if you weren't completely amazing, the narcissist would not go for you. They need someone who will give them attention and, more importantly, they need someone who will enhance their image. When they are with you, they both feel and look better. Maybe you are the eye candy, the trophy wife or the hunky husband who looks so good on their arm. You could be a savvy business person or someone who has a great deal of talent, prestige, or fame. Perhaps you have wealth, or youth, or a vibrant social circle from where they can access even more attention. Obviously your emotional intelligence (or emotional quotient or EQ) is off the charts and theirs is nonexistent.

Whichever distinctive attribute they have chosen (and it is probably a combination of many of your wonderful qualities), the bottom line is that *their* image is enhanced because of *you*. They admired you and boasted about you (at least in the beginning). Deep down they envy you, which eventually turns them against you. You will find that the very things they praised you for in the beginning will be the same things they will use to belittle you and destroy you in the end. The fact is, you were targeted for your amazing qualities. You are a unique and a wonderful person—*always* remember that!

3. We Are Unconsciously Trying to Fix Our Past Hurts

Our subconscious mind is *extremely* powerful. It permanently stores everything that has ever happened to us and it contains the awareness of all the things that our conscious mind cannot recognize. Your subconscious mind is constantly working to make your behaviour fit a pattern that is consistent with any of your emotionalized thoughts, hopes, desires, and beliefs. The subconscious does everything it can to prove and strengthen the beliefs that you already have, whether they are positive or negative. It also holds our deepest wounds and any toxic viewpoints and limiting beliefs that we learned in our childhood. While our subconscious can be powerfully good, it can also draw us to the wounded, unresolved, and painful places from our past. If we have had previous trauma, we can be more susceptible to both the bad treatment and the love bombing that the narcissist gives us. Deep down, we are still seeking validation, worth, and healing from our past wounds.

When we have had experiences in our childhood of not feeling heard, seen, loved and validated, we are conditioned to expect and accept less in our relationships. When we have developed a deep sense of unworthiness early on in our lives, we tend to gravitate to what is familiar to us. According to many counsellors, **80 percent of our emotional blueprint is set between the ages of eight and ten**. When I heard that during my own counselling sessions, it made sense. I had an uphill battle to fight. Some of the most difficult years of my life were between the ages of six and eleven.

Of course, I am of the beliefs that no one ever has to remain a prisoner of their past circumstances and that you can take back your power in your life. It *is* possible to change our unconscious emotional blueprint through a great deal of inner work and affirmations, and through intentionally reprogramming our inner beliefs. Most of us hold beliefs that are limiting, toxic, and unconscious. Unfortunately we can walk around for decades without being aware of what these beliefs actually are and of the full impact they have. It may take a good counsellor or life coach to create awareness of what these beliefs are so that we can recreate our thought patterns and transform our life.

Children who are neglected or abused experience a type of cognitive dissonance. As mentioned previously, cognitive dissonance is when you hold two conflicting beliefs at the same time. Since it is not possible to believe both opposites, you must get rid of one belief in order to honour the other. When a child has been abused or neglected by its parents, the child won't stop loving its parents, it stops loving itself.

Some part of every child believes that they are unique and special. However, when a child experiences abuse or neglect from one or both parents, this tells them a different story. A child can even experience a type of traumatic neglect based on no intentional fault of the parents. Life circumstances such as divorce, illness or the death of a parent, job loss or financial hardships, affairs, and addictions can all lead to a child experiencing neglect. However, the fact remains that a person cannot hold two conflicting beliefs for long without experiencing extreme stress and tension. A choice must be made. One belief must go.

Abusive or neglectful treatment demonstrates to the child that they are unworthy of love and affection. It is often easier to keep loving your parents and to see your parents as right in their treatment of you (which often means to see yourself as being unworthy of love) than it is to believe that your parents treated you wrongfully. When faced with a choice, a child will unconsciously choose to let go of the belief that they are special and worthy of love, and instead buy into the belief that this is how they *deserve* to be treated because they are unworthy of love.

Most of our behaviour is driven by our subconscious. Obviously, we would never consciously choose abusive treatment. In fact, when we "consciously" look at other people in the same situation, we are amazed that they would put up with such behaviour. How could they *possibly* be and stay in a relationship with an abusive person?

However, if you find yourself in this situation, in an inexplicable and unconscious way, you are trying to create a right way for another abusive person to rewrite your past and heal your previous trauma in life. If you have witnessed domestic violence as a child, or experienced a major trauma as a child in the form of bullying or emotional abuse, or experienced stress in your family situation such as a divorce, an affair, or addictions, you are predisposed to unconsciously choosing a narcissist. Psychologists call this "trauma re-enactment," when you attempt to resolve or fix what has happened in your past. We can unconsciously be drawn to unhealthy people to "fix" our past even as we try to "fix" the abuser. Until we have this awareness and we are healed, our unconscious mind will always seek to make things right in our lives. Even if it is by unhealthy means.

4. A Neurotic Level of Naivety

"A neurotic level of naivety" is something that the Spartan Life Coach, Richard Grannon, talks about. He is amazing! You can find many of his teachings about narcissism, divorcing a narcissist, emotional abuse, people pleasing, and other incredible topics on YouTube. In his video, "15 Traits of a People Pleaser," the Spartan Life Coach says that people pleasers have a "neurotic level of naivety."[3] This neurotic naivety is not seeing, believing, or acting on the reality that is actually presented to us. Instead of believing that the person you love can say such horrific things to you or can treat you in incredibly abusive ways, the neurotic naive one says things such as, "He's not *really* like that. He didn't mean it." "She was going through a rough patch. She'll get better." "I thought he would really change." "I can't believe she would do that again." In order to survive, we learn to deny or misinterpret the evidence that is right in front of our face.

Society has also made some very optimistic, yet unfortunate, *absolute* assumptions that we have adopted. An example of that would be that, "Everybody is basically good." Perhaps "basically" is true; however, there are numerous exceptions to this and it is not an ironclad guarantee that *all* people are basically good. By now you know and have experienced that there are some pretty horrific and *intentionally* evil people in this world. If you want a blatant example, think of the Nazis who dehumanized their victims to the point of treating them as less than animals before they annihilated them. It is also very difficult to argue that cold-blooded, calculating murderers and rapists are "basically good."

Another societal rule the Spartan Life Coach argues against is that "You shouldn't judge people." While it is good to be open-minded about others, you *do* need to be discerning for your own protection. It is actually very healthy to make judgements about people to help you decide those who are safe and unsafe, right and wrong, healthy and harmful. This "never judging" societal rule does not serve you. Judging people is not a crime and it can protect you from some truly treacherous personalities. If you need to reframe the word "judgement," then replace it with "discernment," "being smart," or "protecting yourself."

Another test of neurotic naivety that Richard Grannon gives is if you have ever heard yourself saying, "I *can't believe* how cruel he is being" or "I *can't believe* anyone would be that deceptive." If you find yourself in a constant state of disbelieving that people can do such things, you may have a crippling naivety that is working against you. When people are showing you their true (albeit *cruel*) colours, don't argue in favour of them or struggle against believing it. Trust the evidence that they are supplying you with through their actions, words, and characteristics.

Most likely somewhere along the way, in our past, we had a relationship with someone who was supposed to be good, but who did bad things. This can be why we struggle with not seeing and/or not wanting to see the reality of what is playing out in our lives. We could also have had other influential people in our lives who let another's bad behaviour slip by unnoticed or did not give out any consequences for such behaviour. For example, you had a father who cheats like crazy on your mother while your mother puts up with his behaviour and supportively stays with him. You've now learned from your mother to minimize both the behaviour and its horrific effects. You've now learned from your father that the lying, cheating, and emotional abuse is really "not that bad" and "this is completely normal and acceptable." Even when in reality, it is not. Or perhaps you have a mother who is a closet, raging, alcoholic and your father is constantly covering up for her. He has minimized her behaviour and has not set up appropriate consequences for his own good; nor has he given her any incentive to change. Her behaviour is allowed to continue and it becomes "normal."

In the examples above, due to the models you've had demonstrated before you while you were growing up, you learned at a young age to misinterpret the evidence you see before your eyes in order to survive. Through our experiences in the past, we may have adopted a mindset, a false belief, or an unwillingness to see the evil truths in life, which cause us to have this "neurotic naivety." However, this is not an excuse or a license to continue in neurotic naivety. And it certainly does not serve you! The awareness of being neurotically naive is meant to give you the insight and motivation to change, in order to now become both wise and empowered by accepting the true reality that is presented to you.

5. Ignoring Our Inner Voice

After the breakup from my narcissist, I really felt I had lost my voice. At first I thought I had lost my voice in the *relationship*, since every thought, emotion, or opinion was negated and deemed insignificant. At the end, I was told daily that my thoughts were "wrong" and my feelings were "stupid and wrong!" I was told, "You shouldn't think that." "You're being silly." "That's stupid." "That's not how you're feeling."

Toward the end of the relationship, I was not allowed to have an opinion or to share my thoughts or feelings around him. I finally felt a growing anger within me after being negated for so long. Rest assured, not all anger is bad. Sometimes anger can be a sign that something is desperately wrong, such as when our boundaries—including emotional, personal, financial, physical, and intellectual—have been violated. I was progressively feeling that my voice and my very person was being silenced. It had to stop.

In actuality, I lost my voice long before the breakup. And truth be known, *I* was the one who started it. Yep, I looked deep enough to find that it was me. *You can only be empowered when you take responsibility.* I had to go back to when, where, why, and how I lost my voice and how I allowed that to happen. I went back to my journals. When did I start to notice things change? Were there red flags I missed or ignored? What was going on that I stifled and silenced my voice? I looked back to some key moments in the relationship. Right before we got engaged, we broke up. Why did I break it off with him and why did I take him back?

It was during that breakup that I had really seen the mask fall off. I saw the true person who was behind his image. I had broken off the relationship because I had uncovered some devastating ways through which he had been deceiving me over the past year and a half. During the time of confronting him, I saw what I now know to be narcissistic rage. There was such anger, excessive coldness, and cruelty aimed at me because I had stumbled upon the truth of so many of his lies. There was no remorse for what he had done or for how he had been lying to me for the past eighteen months. I did not want to believe that he could be so callous and malicious or that he had done all these things. After all, it was so drastically different from what he was like the other 99 percent of the time. I couldn't believe that he was raging against me as if I was the one who had lied and betrayed *him*. In retrospect, I now know that this is the typical behaviour that comes out when a narcissist fights to maintain control of his image by holding onto his lies.

Both the excessive lying for such an extended period of time (eighteen months) and the callous treatment following the breakup should have been reasons enough to send me running. Actually, I did leave … for a time. During this time I had even written in my journal that he had done specific things that were "DEAL BREAKERS!" Why, then, did I not save myself years of pain, run like hell, and never look back?

There were definitely some unconscious drivers and I was convinced of his words and promises. Promises that he had "changed." Convincing words that he had such a "huge breakthrough from God." That he was not the same man as he had been five years earlier when he did the things he had been lying to cover up. I wanted to believe his words that he had indeed changed. I wanted things to be as wonderful as they were before. I wanted to believe his words rather than my own voice and my gut instincts. So … I did.

The experts know what they're talking about when they say that the biggest predictor of future behaviour is past behaviour. This is especially true when it comes to someone who has a history of lying. He had, in actual fact, no proven track record of living any other way. Although I was not to find out for several years, eventually the truth came out that he had a lifelong history of these kinds of behaviours— both the behaviours he was trying to cover up through his lies and his history of being a pathological liar.

At the time of our mini breakup, in all the confusion, I did write about all the things that would have to work in order for us to get back together. I clearly said that I could never date and especially marry anyone who was dishonest and who had been a cheater (the real reason why his second marriage broke up ... and apparently, as I was to find out years later, his first marriage too). I did not honour my own boundary or listen to my own needs. I also wrote that I needed to truly see some remorse from him for all his lying. After all, deep down I knew that if there were no remorse, he wouldn't truly change. I wrote that we would need to re-establish trust and there would need to be a track record of him actually telling the truth. I needed to know that his other addictions that he had covered up were gone. Also, we would need to successfully go to counselling together. My inner voice was telling me all the things I needed for myself in order to possibly move forward in this relationship. I also believe my inner-inner voice was truly saying, "Honour your boundaries and what you really want and need in a relationship! Don't settle! Don't stay with this man! RUN FROM HIM! AND DON'T LOOK BACK!"

Then, something insane happened. Instead of running and not looking back, I did the opposite; I took him back.

Perhaps there are others out there who can relate. I took him back without any of those things happening that I needed, such as a track record of truth telling, seeing some remorse for his past actions, knowing that his addictions were taken care of, and us both going to counselling together. Several years later, I discovered that the moment I took him back was when I started to ignore my inner voice and my gut.

I *chose* not to listen to my inner voice that day. I was the one who gave up my power. I didn't hear my own need to feel safe, to be honoured with the truth, to be listened to, to be loved and cherished. *I* negated my own needs and my own voice. No one else did that. My revelation was that it was not the narcissist who negated me (or at least he was not the only one who negated me, nor was he the first). I had started to deny my own voice long before. This onus was completely on me. It was now time to take responsibility and to reclaim ground that I needed to take ownership of.

I even discovered that after I took him back, I stopped writing in my journal for about three years. This is something I had never done. I hadn't even realized that I had stopped writing for such an extended period until years later when I was searching for the answers. Not journaling was a clear indicator that I was no longer listening to me. It made sense though. How could I listen to my own voice when I had bought into a deceptive one and gave his voice a higher place in my life than my own? I had to take responsibility and change that. I needed to take back my personal power that I had unknowingly given away.

It wasn't until I left the marriage and questioned how I could have ever ended up being with an abusive, narcissistic man, that I started to piece together how this could have happened. After all, I was *determined* to figure out what *my part* in this debacle was, because I never want to be in this place again!

We can never change another person; we can only change ourselves.

I looked back to the time of our breakup, which was two months before we got engaged. My lack of journaling showed that I unconsciously decided to shut up my own voice. In order for me to take him back, as is, and not follow through on the conditions and boundaries that I set out, I would have to stop listening to myself. *I lost my voice long ago because of me.*

Relationships do bring out our own weaknesses. Two of the most powerful things I have personally learned through this experience are that I needed to regain, speak, and honour my own inner voice and I needed to learn to set better boundaries with consequences. I needed to take responsibility for how I had allowed him to treat me. It is true that *people treat you how you teach them to treat you.*

How about you? Is there a part of you that has shut down or shut up? Have you unconsciously silenced your own inner voice? Have you been ignoring your own needs in order to make the relationship work, or just to survive in it? Only *you* can recover your inner voice.

6. Weak Boundaries

Boundaries are the borders that we create for our lives and ourselves. They include everything you *allow into* your life and everything that you *keep outside* your life. Where do your personal boundaries fall? Our boundaries include who you permit in your life; the ways you accept how people will treat you; the voices that you choose to influence you; and what will consume your time, thoughts, money, and energy.

When you have weak boundaries, you allow unsafe people to be in your life. Unsafe people include those who will use and exploit you. These are people who are more than happy to take advantage of you, and infringe on your space, time, emotions, property, and finances. Unsafe people are disrespectful to you; they can even be intentionally offensive toward you; and they frequently disregard your noes, feelings, thoughts, and values. Abusive people are unsafe people. Narcissists are unsafe people. However, when people have strong boundaries, narcissists do not stay in their lives for very long.

> *In relationships, you get what you tolerate.*[4]
>
> —John Townsend

When we have weak boundaries, we can find it difficult or impossible to say, "No" to people when they request something from us. Having weak boundaries can include saying yes to doing things you don't want to do or things you don't have time to do; allowing others' problems to consume your life; or taking responsibility for something that is not actually yours. Having weak boundaries include taking on responsibility for other people's problems, actions, choices, feelings, and happiness.

By having weak boundaries, a person can very easily cave to the narcissist's demands. Without strong boundaries you can allow verbal abuse and cruel treatment, and you can accept the blame they give you for something for which they should be accountable.

Having weak boundaries can cause you to feel it is up to you to right the wrongs in someone else's life. You may erroneously feel that it is up to you to make another person feel happy and be successful. You may take on responsibilities for areas in their life that they are not owning. It is up to each person to be accountable for the choices they make, the feelings they have, and how they live their life. Each person must be responsible for their own emotions and for the outcomes in their life.

When we don't have solid boundaries, we let bad things into our space and our lives. For example, when people have severely wronged us or have been deceptive toward us, rather than making them prove that they have indeed changed, we accept them back before we have clear evidence. Without the verification that they have changed, we often take harmful people back just because they say they are "sorry." We can end up giving people second, third, and eightieth chances because we are supposed to "forgive and forget." Forgiving someone is indeed a freeing and healing thing to do. However, "forgetting" or accepting a dangerous person back into your life when they have never proven to be anything different is *extremely* hazardous to your wellbeing.

Sometimes giving someone a second chance is like giving them an extra bullet for their gun because they missed you the first time.

When your boundaries are not solid, you may feel completely powerless or as if you have been backed into a corner. When our boundaries are chronically violated, we are either not communicating our boundaries, or we are not enforcing them by having a real consequence when someone violates those boundaries.

Strong boundaries keep harmful people out. Dr. Henry Cloud and Dr. John Townsend's book, *Boundaries* (which I *highly* recommend), talks about the "Law of Power," which states,[5]

You only have the power to change yourself. You can't change another person. You must see yourself as the problem, not the other person. To see another person as the problem to be fixed is to give that person power over you and your well-being. Because you cannot change another person, you are out of control. The real problem lies in how you are relating to the problem person. You are the one in pain, and only you have the power to fix it.

This law shows that in fact we CAN and DO have all the power that we need in any situation or relationship. We are ultimately responsible for whatever we allow into our lives. Empower yourself by not giving away your choices and responsibility to others. You always have control over what you will and will not allow in your life. Always remember that your boundaries ultimately have to do with *you*. Your reward will come with changing yourself and owning your boundaries.

7. Putting Everyone Ahead of Ourself

In his YouTube video, "15 Traits of People Pleaser Syndrome," Spartan Life Coach Richard Grannon names one of these traits as "Excessive Conscientiousness."[6] This is when you put everyone else's ideas and needs ahead of your own. It is when you consistently give more weight to what *others* want, think, need, or feel in comparison to what you want, think, need, or feel. When this happens, you are overcompensating and over-giving. You allow everyone to ask for and take what they want from you, yet you don't assert your right to be treated equally or fairly. Again, this is the difference between maintaining solid boundaries or having weak ones that others trample. When you constantly put others ahead of yourself, you end up being much more concerned about what the other person has to say and what their opinions are than you are about speaking your own opinions and feelings.

When you operate in this mode, it often ends up that you take responsibility for everyone else's happiness. You feel you are solely responsible for making the narcissist (or anyone else for that matter) happy and that it is your fault when they are not. You are now taking on what other people are supposed to be responsible for in their own lives. If you find yourself caught in this trap, you will always go the extra mile for everyone else at the expense of your own time, energy, resources, and self.

Watch out for the word "fair" especially when you are dealing with a person with a personality disorder such as a narcissist, a sociopath, or a psychopath. These people never play fair. The hazard in dealing with dangerous personalities is when you always feel that you should be "fair" in every situation, even when people are taking advantage of you and completely screwing you over. It is time to start asserting some boundaries by prioritizing your own needs. When you have excessive compassion and a desire to always be "fair," no matter the circumstances, you end up giving away too much of yourself. This is exactly the kind of person a narcissist will choose to exploit.

8. Denying Our Own Pain and Perceptions

Many people who find themselves in a relationship with a narcissist have been conditioned in their childhood to minimize their emotions or to deny the pain that they have experienced. Most likely minimizing and denying pain was also modeled by one or both of your parents. You may have been taught not to cry, to tough it out, because things weren't really that bad. Sometimes this tough attitude has served you well! It has caused you to develop resilience. You have grown a thicker skin, you don't stay down in the dumps for too long, and you can bounce back quickly from adversity. This is the bright side of the coin. However, you may also have learned not to pay attention to your pain, to ignore your hurts, and in extreme cases, to fervently deny when someone is mistreating or abusing you. This is the dark side of the coin—minimizing or denying your feelings. You will need to start getting back in touch with your feelings, your pain, and your perceptions in order to move into your healing.

At the unhealthy extreme of denial, people go out of their way to justify their abusers. They actually try, and unfortunately sometimes succeed, in convincing themselves that the abuser had a right to treat them the way they did. A person can buy into the story that the abuse was their fault. That somehow they made the abuser do it. They buy into the lie that "If I can just learn to do better, serve them more, comply with what they want, or make them happier, their abuse will never happen again." When you try to ignore and deny the abuse, you also learn to accept mistreatment as a normal part of your life. In turn, abuse will keep perpetuating in your life and in your relationships.

In order to move forward with your life, you need to quit ignoring, denying, and accepting abuse in any form. You must get in touch with your pain, and acknowledge your intuition when it says, "This is *not* right!" Stockholm syndrome and trauma bonding tell us that there is a natural tendency to minimize how appalling the abuse is. Now is the time to acknowledge your true value as the amazing person you are. Acknowledge that your perspectives are worthy and extremely important. You need to remember your value. Your true value and worth are in direct contrast with how you have been treated and the harm and injuries you have experienced in this relationship.

One of the only ways to heal is to allow yourself to recognize with a full dose of reality just how horrendous the narcissistic abuse has been. Your perceptions are real. Your initial gut reaction that something was off was correct. Your pain does matter. You do not need to ever accept such treatment again. To move forward, you must acknowledge that your perceptions are and were valid, and that the things the narcissist said and did to you were wrong. You have felt deep pain. You have a right to set boundaries, to protect yourself, and to be treated with dignity and respect at all times. A compassionate counsellor or psychologist who understands the Narcissistic Personality Disorder can help you work through these things.

9. Defensive Hope

Defensive hope is when we hold onto a hope that is not based on anything valid. People often hold onto such improbable hopes in order to avoid their pain. This is a survival and a coping mechanism. However, this hope has no real reason to exist. There is no evidence and no truth to support it. This is a hope that has no basis in reality. When we do not want to face the truth of who our narcissist really is ... we hope. We hope that they will be better. We hope they will feel remorse, that they will change, and that someday they will treat us better. We hope that we can save them, love them enough, and change them. There is a false expectation that if *we* can just be more loving and more sacrificial, that if we can simply be or do *more*, then the narcissist will stop being cruel, dishonest, and abusive. We falsely believe that we can change another person, and we hope in vain that they will change.

Holding onto a false hope that a person will change prevents us from seeing our own pain and the reality of the situation. When we focus solely on empty hope, we do not have to face how deep our own pain really is. Anyone who is in a relationship with a narcissist will suffer profound pain. Often a previous unconscious habit was established, which we do not see until we return to uncover former patterns of not facing our grief and disappointment. Most likely we have not truly faced the pain in some (or many) of our past relationships. This pattern is usually embedded in our past experiences. Your relationship with the narcissist is not the first time you have encountered extreme pain or mistreatment. It is never easy to face our sadness, grief, and pain. Nevertheless, in the end, this puts the responsibility of change on us. *We* must not negate our own pain. *We* must do something differently so as not to accept unhealthy relationships in the future. *We* must be the ones to put boundaries between ourselves and the people who treat us poorly. *We* must learn that we deserve better.

We must also learn to not expect or hope that people will change when we don't see any evidence of it. Words are meaningless when they do not accompany action. It all comes down to what a person actually does. Is there proof of their change and thus reason for you to actually hope? *When there is no reality to back up our hope, we must release our own expectations that the other person wants to or will change.* It is not realistic to expect that a narcissist will suddenly feel remorse or empathy toward you and start treating you with compassion, kindness, and respect when you have never seen any genuine evidence of it. It is unrealistic to expect a pathological liar to start telling the truth, to make confessions of their wrongs, or to assume that they even know what the truth is anymore.

By not facing the reality that some people are truly evil and that they really do intend to harm you, to take advantage of you, or to abuse you, you will stay stuck in this pattern of defensively hoping. Until you face and address your own unrealistic defensive hope, you will continue to attract more unsafe people like this into your future.

10. We Romanticize to Fill Our Unmet Needs

Believe it or not, we are also guilty of idealizing and putting the other person on a pedestal. In the beginning, we greatly admired and idealized the narcissist. We wanted them to be "The One." Some of this is of course normal in the beginning of a romantic relationship. That's why there is a "honeymoon" phase. When we don't fully know a person, the natural tendency in the beginning is to fill in the gaps of the unknown with what is positive and familiar to us. We make assumptions that they think and operate the same way we do. We might assume that they have the same desires and values, whereas, in actuality, we have yet to discover if we do or don't have these things in common.

We run into trouble when we stay in this romanticized phase by putting our partner on a pedestal and continuing to see only what we want to see. Of course when you add in the element of love bombing and the false self that the narcissist projects, you need that extra level of discernment and objectivity not to romanticize the person or the relationship. Perhaps you had such a strong desire for a relationship that you bought the grandiose idealized vision of the narcissist and were not able to see what was truly there. Romanticizing a person to the point of only seeing the good or their *potential* can be foolish. Idealizing can prevent us from seeing people for who they really are, with all of their good *and* all of their bad. Everyone has good and bad qualities. However, when we look through rose-coloured glasses, we only see the person's glowing qualities. We can further enhance these qualities with our own imagination and block out any of their less desirable qualities and/or their sometimes dangerous character flaws.

It is important to dig deeper into our own lives and to become aware of any of our own unmet needs. Our needs will truthfully be met one way or another. Either in healthy or unhealthy ways. What are some of your needs? To be cherished, to belong, to be important, to be complimented, or to feel secure? There are hundreds of personal needs. Each individual has their own unique set of needs and no needs are better or worse to have than others. Our needs simply *are*. When you are aware of them, and are working to fulfill them in healthy ways with safe people, you will not gravitate toward unsafe people to try to get your needs met. Take the time to become aware of what your needs are and make sure you are getting your deep needs met in healthy ways.

People who are perpetually caught up in the romantic have set themselves up to meet many unsafe people.[7]

—Dr. Henry Cloud and Dr. John Townsend

Romanticizing often happens when we are hungry enough and this person seems to soothe the ache within us. This is when we can idealize a person to be something they are not. In our eyes, the narcissist can be our knight in shining armour, our beautiful damsel, or our soulmate; all while we are blind to the truth that others can plainly see. Idealizing a narcissist to fulfill our unmet needs can be a scary decision because we can we miss the blatant red flags that are staring us right in the face. By idealizing them, we refuse to see their bad, their unsafe, and their abusive characteristics.

We minimize all these qualities in the narcissist at our own peril.

11. Codependency—Disconnection from Our Authentic Self

Yikes! This is a pretty strong label! I wrestled intensely with the thought that I might be a codependent person. After all, I consider myself to be a highly *in*dependent person who strongly values my freedom. I have lived all over the world, I have tackled new jobs in various locations, and have made many new starts without knowing a soul. I have prided myself on being independent and adventurous. However, I had to take a deeper, more honest look at myself when I read that every narcissist needs a codependent partner, otherwise they would never be able to maintain a relationship. After doing a lot of research, I conceded that it was quite a valid statement. You need to have the yin and yang. Someone who is a good mix of a giver, pleaser, fixer, and a codependent, often pairs off with person who combines being a taker, controller, addict, and narcissist.

When I read some of the characteristics of a codependent, I had to take an honest look at myself, especially with regard to my marriage. After looking closer into the definition of a codependent and hearing further examples, I saw myself in some of these illustrations and discovered that I had some real work ahead of me.

Maybe you can relate to some of these traits:

- having weak boundaries,

- not being in touch with personal needs or feelings,

- making unhealthy sacrifices,

- not asking for help,

- being overly responsible for others.

You get the picture. These were a few things that I personally had to work on. After all—the goal is to *never make this mistake again*. If I was to avoid a future of living in this hell, I had to take responsibility and ownership to learn from my mistakes and to change.

Here are a few definitions of codependency:

> *The traditional definition of codependency has focused on control, nurturing, and the maintenance of relationships with individuals who are chemically dependent, or engaging in undesirable behaviors, such as narcissism.*[8]
>
> —Linda Esposito

> *Codependency is a controversial concept for a dysfunctional helping relationship where one person supports or enables another person's addiction, poor mental health, immaturity, irresponsibility, or under-achievement.*[9]
>
> —R. Skip Johnson

I also discovered that, somewhere along the way, a codependent most likely had a model of codependency. Mental Health America describes a codependent person as someone who

> *forms and maintains relationships that are one-sided, emotionally destructive, and/or abusive. It is an emotional and behavioral condition that affects an individual's ability to have a healthy, mutually satisfying relationship. It is known as "relationship addiction." Co-dependent behavior is learned by watching and imitating other family members who display this type of behavior.*[10]
>
> —Mental Health America

It is safe to say that we all come from dysfunctional families, at least in some capacity. How a dysfunctional family can affect you by attracting a narcissist into your life is that you have *grown up in a family that does not acknowledge that problems exist.* Nothing that is dysfunctional or unhealthy is ever talked about or confronted. You learn very quickly to repress your emotions and to disregard your needs. The family doesn't talk about things and they intentionally block, ignore, avoid, or deny pain. This pain could involve emotional or physical abuse; the destructive effects of affairs on the entire family; the devastating effects of addictions to alcohol, drugs, work, food, or pornography. Everyone in the family learns to repress their emotions about these situations. Perhaps one or more people demonstrated to you what it was like to minimize or to deny abuse. Most likely you were expected to do the same. You in turn learned not to cry, and to deny, minimize, and repress your pain and hurt feelings. It is likely that your emotional development, and possibly even your identity were prohibited or at least stunted from flourishing and growing.

From our childhood, no matter how much we've tried to block out or repress painful events, the cycle of trauma that we now find ourselves in is often "familiar" to us. We are very likely to unconsciously repeat what we "know" from our past. It is highly probable that our family of origin gave us a defective emotional blueprint. This is not to pass judgement on our families. They were most likely doing the very best they could in their own life circumstances at the time, and had weaknesses within *their own* family of origin. Nevertheless, unless we go back and fix the origins of our wounds and those up until the present, this will not be the last abusive relationship we will find ourselves in. Many times we exhibit this unconscious behaviour of not acknowledging problems because we have repressed so much. A person must go through the intentional work of healing in order to have a different outcome in the future. *Our emotional health and healing is our responsibility.*

Although this is not an exhaustive list, below are 45 traits of a codependent person. How many do you identify with?

Family of Origin

1. You had a parent who was a codependent.

2. You experienced a parent denying their own needs, wants, emotions, and life at the expense of the other parent's addictive, abusive, or selfish lifestyle.

3. You learned to deny, repress, and minimize your pain and hurtful emotions.

4. You, in turn, have learned to allow hurtful, disrespectful treatment from other people in your life.

Unhealthy Sacrifices

5. You are constantly giving, sacrificing, and minimizing your own needs and are thereby consumed with the needs and desires of others.

6. You confuse extreme sacrifice and caretaking with loyalty and love.

7. You are stuck in a pattern of giving and sacrificing, without the possibility of ever receiving the same from your partner.

8. You give support and are committed to your partner at the cost of your own mental, emotional, physical, and financial health.

9. You will go out of your way to sacrifice your own needs to accommodate other people.

One-Sided Relationships

10. You often find yourself in one-sided relationships where you do the majority of the work.

11. Your partner's needs always seem to be met, while your needs and wants are ignored.

12. You feel the most comfortable when you are giving to others and you experience a great deal of discomfort when others are giving to you.

The Consummate Doer

13. You are convinced that you will never find a partner who will love you for who you *are*, as opposed to what you can *do* for them.

14. You struggle with self-love and self-acceptance and believe your worthiness has to be "earned." You are stuck in performance mentality.

15. You are over-functioning and often obsessive, saying or thinking, "I should be doing this or that."

16. You are terrified about not "doing what is expected of me"; "not pulling my weight"; "being a burden"; and "not holding up my end of the bargain."

17. You are über independent and do not ask for help.

Purpose

18. Your purpose in life revolves around making extreme sacrifices to satisfy your partner's needs.

19. You often feel empty, bored, and worthless if you don't have either someone else to take care of, a problem to solve, or a crisis to deal with.

Negative Feelings

20. In your relationships you feel unappreciated and used. Deep down, you feel sadness and sometimes anger.

21. You can become burnt out, exhausted, and begin to neglect other important relationships or vital interests in your life.

22. You let your partner have his or her way, and then feel overwhelmed with anger or resentment.

23. "Look at all I do for you!" is a common thought in your head or even a phrase that is spoken out loud.

24. You have a sense of powerlessness in your relationships.

25. When someone is giving to you, you can feel embarrassed, insecure, or guilty.

Enabler

26. You recognize unhealthy behaviours in your partner but stay with him or her in spite of it.

27. You enable another person so that they maintain their irresponsible, addictive, abusive, selfish, or underachieving behaviour.

28. You prevent the other person from being accountable for their actions and words, thereby preventing them from learning common and much-needed life lessons.

29. You're dating or are married to an alcoholic, a narcissist, or any other type of addict.

30. In the name of love, you do things for your partner that he or she can and should be doing for themself or the family.

31. Other people in your life acknowledge that you help this person too much.

Boundaries Need Work

32. Your boundaries are weak or nonexistent.

33. You have a hard time saying "No" to anyone.

34. You've allowed irresponsible, hurtful behaviour in your relationship, whether that is physically, emotionally, or financially.

35. You say "Yes" when you would really like to say "No."

36. You feel that others have crossed your boundaries and you feel powerless to stop them.

Your Feelings, Thoughts, and Needs

37. You have trouble when it comes to communicating your thoughts, feelings, and needs.

38. You are unaware of your feelings and needs because you are so focused on what other people's needs and feeling are.

39. You have trouble pinpointing your own feelings and thoughts, or you diminish and deny how you feel.

Over-Responsible

40. You feel responsible for your partner's actions, feelings, choices, behaviours, wants, needs, and even their destiny.

41. You're always talking about or worrying about your partner's issues. Sometimes you make their issues, your issues.

42. You are strongly affected by your partner's moods, both positive and negative ones.

43. You always want to know what your partner is doing, thinking, or feeling.

Attraction

44. You have a history of attracting damaged or unhealthy people into your life.

45. You cannot seem to avoid romantic relationships with individuals who are narcissistic—that is, individuals who are selfish, self-centred, controlling, and harmful.

With awareness, intention and work, it is possible to overcome codependency and to move to a place of wholeness, health, and strength.

PART III

Strategies

This section is devoted to how you can effectively respond to narcissists in your life, ways to prepare yourself to leave any relationship you have with a narcissist, and how to deal with that person long after you have left.

CHAPTER 7

NINE WAYS TO DEAL WITH A NARCISSIST

This chapter gives you nine strategies for how to deal with narcissists in your life. The first strategy is, as much as possible, to create distance from them. This happens by either moving to no contact or low contact with the narcissist—and this means for the rest of your life! You will also want to start writing down any past abusive incidents to acknowledge what is truly happening to you as these occurrences will be downplayed or denied by the narcissist. You will need to get past their smoke and mirrors and reconnect to the reality of who this person actually is (not who you hope they will be).

The next step is to get your ducks in a row and to arm and prepare yourself for the battle of your life. Be stealthy, gather information, and do whatever you can to prepare yourself to make a physical move, go to court, or do whatever you need to do for your own wellbeing and the wellbeing of your children. It is also essential at this point to reprogram your mind from the devaluation and brainwashing you have received. Keeping your boundaries firm is a "must-have" in life in order to deal not only with the narcissist at hand but also to repel any future narcissists that you may encounter.

The grey-rock strategy is brilliant if you do have to remain in contact with a narcissist (such as if you share custody of the children). During these years of shared custody, it is essential to do whatever you can to keep yourself safe and sane. You always need to be prepared to deal with their hoover manoeuvre! This is a manipulative tactic that a narcissist will try to use to suck you back into a relationship with them. This final strategy remains in play for the rest of your life, no matter how many months or years pass by after you end the relationship.

> *One of the most courageous decisions you'll ever make is to finally let go of what is hurting your heart and soul.*

1. Create Distance

Let's face it, you will never win with a narcissist. The longer you are in contact with them, the more damage it will do to your heart, soul, mind, strength, wellbeing, and sanity. You need to do everything you can to protect yourself. You are worth it. You do not deserve such cruel, inhumane treatment. In my very blunt opinion, the best way to deal with a narcissist is to

> *Create as much distance as possible.*
> *Create as much distance as soon as possible.*
> *Run as far and as fast as you can from them. Do not look back.*
> *Deeply know that you deserve better!*

(There will be more on this in strategy 8 "No Contact or Low Contact." If it is not presently possible to completely eradicate the narcissist from your life, do the best you can with low contact.)

The end goal is to remove yourself from any dangerous personality who is intentionally, continually, and relentlessly trying to bring you harm. Get away from them and keep them out of your life as much as possible. It may take you a more few steps to get you to this place. You may be in denial as to how harmful they really are and can be. You will probably also need to set things in motion strategically before you can make your exit. If children are involved, creating distance is difficult if not an impossible thing to do at this time of shared custody. However, whatever distance you *can* create, even if it only emotional distance at this time, DO IT. Narcissists who are at the far end of the scale are indeed harmful, dangerous personalities!

Do not take this lightly—your wellbeing, safety, and future depend on it!

2. Write a List of Abusive Incidents

Obviously keeping a "record of wrongs" is not constructive in healthy relationships because it is counterproductive to keep rehashing past conflicts and your partner's failings. However, in an abusive relationship, a different set of rules apply. You need this record to have clarity of the truth and to keep yourself sane as to what has *actually* happened. The narcissist will use denial, manipulation, and gaslighting to try to distort your reality and to negate or minimize the abuse.

Write a list of the incidents in which you have been abused and add others to the list as they occur. This might look something like

- Humiliated me in front of our friends.
- Stonewalled me and disregarded my feelings.
- Blamed me for her losing her job.
- Denied it when I confronted him with clear evidence about his affairs.

By writing down these incidents, you will be forced to see and admit what is happening to you. Despite the narcissist's dismissal of your perspective and the truth, you now have a record confirming and validating the reality of your circumstances. When you have heard their constant denial of reality, when you have experienced the switch from Dr. Jekyll to Mr. Hyde, the hot and cold behaviours, the truth gets muddy. Combine that with having the narcissist gaslighting you and attempting to convince you that you are going crazy and it becomes genuinely difficult to discern reality. Many partners of a narcissist actually DO feel like they are going crazy with all the mind-warping games that are being played against them. Writing down and acknowledging what has really happened to you will assist you in your healing process and it will help to keep you sane. You are speaking out the truth in your writings and are validating what has happened to you. This is very important, especially since the narcissist has tried to deny, negate, or minimize the abuse and your circumstances.

3. Reconnect to the Reality of Who the Narcissist Is

Although the truth can be harsh, *now* is the time to realize who the real person is behind the mask. The ugly monster who rears his angry head and seeks to devour you is actually the real person. That sweet, charming individual who treasured you and who "connected" with you in ten thousand ways, unfortunately, never existed. The brutal truth is that the narcissist only did those things because they needed you as their "supply" for that particular time in their life. They needed the adoration and the attention from you. They needed you to increase their image in society. They needed your empathy, your energy, your emotions, your finances, or whatever the case may be. Then suddenly, they had had enough of you! They found someone else, and discarded you. You were made history before you even knew what was going on. That person who has discounted and devalued you, and who became abusive and cruel to you in the end, *is* the real person. Believe it.

Realize that you will never be able to reason with a narcissist, or expect them to care and empathetically see your perspective. There can be little to no hope for change in a stonewaller who shuts down, who does not care about what you are going through, and who takes zero responsibility for where the relationship is. It is impossible to build a relationship with someone who is *never* wrong, who is only seeking to blame, and who chronically sees themselves as the victim in the circumstances for which they were the master architect.

In the same way that you would not expect a ruthless, bloodthirsty, cruel crocodile to suddenly transform into a cute, loyal, tail-wagging, loving puppy, you cannot expect a narcissist to all of a sudden have a humble attitude, admit they were wrong, change, and become genuinely kind and caring toward you. Narcissists don't change. Or let's just say, it is *extremely difficult* and *exceptionally rare* for them to produce any genuine and lasting change. This is especially true if they are at the far end of the narcissistic spectrum. Only a miniscule number of narcissists actually *admit* they have a problem. That is the first step. And of course the percentage of the ones who have gone through therapy and who actually *change* is even lower. Since most narcissists show no remorse for what they have done and "are never wrong," you can expect that the odds are stacked against you with regard to your narcissist changing.

Author Shahida Arabi says narcissists and sociopaths, being emotionally empty themselves, feed off the emotional pain of their victims. This is where they get their power. No matter how much love you give, the abuser will not change just because they are loved. There is nothing *you* can do to change an abuser. Narcissists feel superior and entitled. They desire control at all costs. Mix that with zero empathy and a complete lack of remorse, and you have a guaranteed recipe for relational failure. When you love them by doing "whatever it takes" to try to help them get to a place where they might want to change, this will backfire on you. Your serving and helping them only enables and empowers them to be more exploitative toward both you and others. The more you sacrifice, the more they will take and the less they will respect you (if they had any ability to respect you and others in the first place). Understand, this is the reality of who they are.

4. Get Your Ducks in a Row!

Now is the time to get prepared. Collect as much information as you can. If they are a full-blown narcissist, and you have discovered their true self, they will try to destroy you in the end. Count on that. Take pictures of any information you can find and might need. You may not know what you are dealing with at the time, and you may not always know what could be useful to you in the end. If you are living with a narcissist, be prepared: they will not want to give you a cent and they may even attempt to clean out your finances as well.

When things started to get bad for Jane, she began to dig. In the process she found several real estate contracts and deposits for properties that her husband was buying, which she knew nothing about. With all the properties he was suddenly purchasing, he was attempting to hide his money before his ultimate discard of Jane. She also found receipts for large cheques deposited to certain companies she had never heard of. At the time, Jane didn't know exactly what was happening in her marriage, but her intuition was saying, "Prepare!" Although they were going to counselling, her husband's treatment of her continued to be horrific and was actually getting worse each day.

Jane ultimately discovered, when their marriage ended several months later, that many of those mysterious cheques went to companies that his mistress owned. Toward the end, Jane's narcissist began to lock up all his files. Fortunately, months earlier, Jane had already photographed everything and started taking steps to protect herself. It came in very handy when he attempted to clean out her finances and wipe her off the title of their home. With the ace card of photographs up her sleeve, Jane showed him a few specific pieces of evidence and it was enough to make him settle out of court.

Your preparation can protect you and can give you enormous confidence to move forward—the narcissist might think twice about gaslighting a judge.

It is a good idea to journal and document everything! Now is the time to be factual and specific about each type of abusive incident, including the time and location of things that were said and done. Make copies of emails and texts, and start recording phone calls, especially when any type of threat is involved. This information can prove very useful in a court situation, or where you may need to create a restraining order or a peace bond against them.

These records can also be useful to bring to a counselling situation. A counsellor can provide an outside point of view that will likely confirm that you are *not* "crazy," despite the narcissist's attempts to convince you otherwise. A solid counsellor or therapist can help you see the covert manipulation and gaslighting the narcissist is using. Once you are out of the relationship and further down the road of healing, you can also reflect back on the reality of what you have lived through in order to grasp the remarkable progress you have made.

You need to glance in the rear-view mirror every once in a while, if for no other reason than to see how far you've come.

Aside from keeping good records, it's a good idea to get legal advice if you would like to proceed with a separation or a divorce. Find out what you are actually eligible for from a lawyer (not from the internet, movies, or well-meaning friends). What are the laws of your land with regard to marriage, common law, children, property, assets, and alimony? If you want to file for divorce and/or make a separation agreement and a settlement, what are the steps involved? It is a good idea to know everything you will need to specifically do if you choose not to hire a lawyer. If you do decide to use a lawyer, interview several of them before deciding on one. Figure out the costs of going to court, and what type of information you would need to win your case. In most cases, for a completely fair settlement, both parties will need to disclose all their assets. Most likely the narcissist will either not disclose their assets or will not do so honestly. You will want to map out a plan with your lawyer and brace yourself for the worst-case scenario, especially when there are children involved. Remember, winning in court is not always about justice or who is right. Winning in court is about who can argue the best.

Consider your long-term future. What you are legally entitled to? Don't just rely on what your friends say you deserve or on what they know other people have experienced. Family law is ever evolving so be sure you know the actual laws of your jurisdiction for the present time. What can you live with? What's your bottom line? What number are you willing to walk away with if you choose not to go to court? What are the potential costs and average lengths of time to settle in court? Again, know your worst-case scenario and recognize what you can personally handle with regard to stress, financial cost, and duration.

On the one hand, going to court can cost you a great deal of money, time, energy, and stress; the emotional toll can be extremely taxing. However, many times to get any type of fairness or justice, it is necessary to go to mediation or sometimes eventually to court. If you do decide to go to court, know what you are getting into and what your actual chances are. That being said, whether you go to court or not, what is finalized and agreed upon legally can affect your future in significant and, most often, permanent ways. Know your options and move in the direction that is right for you. Each person's situation is unique.

Make your exit strategy a silent one. Never let the narcissist know what you are planning until you have your ducks in a row. Line up a safe place to go to before you start making waves as things can get hellish in an instant. If you are the one staying on the property, have a plan in place for your security and safety. It's not a bad idea to talk with your local authorities about what the process is of getting a peace bond or a restraining order for your jurisdiction. Again, this depends on what your circumstances are. Do what you need to do to protect yourself. Any knowledge you can gain beforehand will keep you ahead in the game. Be prepared!

5. Reprogram Your Mind

It is important to realize that you have been brainwashed in this relationship. Narcissists often start by using a subtle form of control. When things are good, they subtly and inadvertently tell you of their disappointment in you. They might give you some recommendations or suggest ways that you should think or behave differently to help make the relationship even better. Their brainwashing begins imperceptibly over time with a few "helpful" suggestions and eventually grows to become monstrously controlling and abusive. Their agenda in this relationship is to make everything about themselves, no matter the cost to you. According to what they really think, your thoughts, feelings, emotions, and needs do not matter. A narcissist who has programmed you by using mind control does not care about your feelings or your pain. In the end, they will refuse to show you any form of human decency, respect, or kindness. In this relationship, your self-esteem and self-worth will take a brutal beating. It's time to hear some much-needed kindness and words of affirmation. Below are three exercises to build you up and reprogram you.

Exercise 1: Remember Who You Are in Relationships

One way of washing your mind from the abuse and getting a different voice in your head, is to reread old letters and emails from friends and family that have encouraged you in the past. Spend time with people who are positive, uplifting, and who will affirm you. Your self-esteem and confidence will most likely be shattered after this relationship. It is important to remember that it will take time to recover and heal. However, your inner confidence and self-worth can become even stronger than before this relationship.

Exercise 2: Reaffirm Your Abilities

Another way to reconstruct your self-esteem and self-worth is to acknowledge all the wonderful things you know about yourself. You can start with your accomplishments. Write out a hundred things that you have succeeded in and have done well at in your life. This can involve being a successful parent, graduating from university or other programs, creating harmonious groups, having lifelong friends, running a race, learning to play an instrument, or creating an amazing piece of art. Most likely the narcissist has downplayed, minimized, negated, and twisted your strengths and wonderful qualities into some contortion that is intended to beat you down and poison you. It's time to reverse that and to reprogram your mind. You need to rewrite the messages you've heard from them in the past and transform them into something positive.

Exercise 3: Reconnect with Your Best Self

Next, it's time to reconnect with yourself; recognize yourself for the amazing person that you *are*. Acknowledge and write down a hundred of your personal traits, the ones that make you unique. List the specific instances where you have brought light and life to others.

Some examples of your distinct wonderful traits might be these:

- your serving heart such as when you helped your friends paint their home,
- your hospitality and how you always bake goodies for others at Christmas,
- your sense of humour and how you can make others laugh,
- your commitment to excellence in whatever you tackle,
- your ability to empathize with others so that they feel comfortable opening up to you.

The first exercise is to fill yourself with uplifting and encouraging messages and relationships. The second one is designed for you to focus on your abilities—what you have done and what you can do. The third section is to emphasize who you are, and how others view you and interact with you. It is important to remember who you ARE! A wonderful, unique, kind, empathetic, talented, and amazing person! Remember what you deserve in a relationship and how you deserve to be treated.

> *You have a right to safe, healthy relationships that allow you to express you heart and feelings without ridicule, repercussions, stonewalling, and threats. It is your right to be free from psychological violence and physical harm. You do not have to have abusive people in your life. EVER. You are worthy of loving, kind, genuine relationships that build you up and enhance your life. You are worthy of receiving good things in all your relationships. KNOW that you deserve respect, support, honesty, loyalty, and that your voice deserves to be heard and honoured. You deserve to be cherished, loved, and cared for—so never settle for anything less!*

Read this text box as many times as necessary. Then write your own statements about the gem that you are and what you deserve! It is time to reprogram your mind!

6. Strengthen Your Boundaries

Those of us who currently have or who have had a close relationship with a narcissist, often struggle with boundaries. Either we have been conditioned to have our boundaries broken (such as with a narcissistic parent), or we have never learned to set effective boundaries in the first place (most households across the globe). By our having weak or unclear boundaries, not only has the narcissist been able to maintain a place in our lives, but they can often effortlessly gain more ground. Now is the time to take your life back and to keep your boundaries firm.

When someone has clear, solid, and definite boundaries, it is extremely difficult for a narcissist to be around that person. Either the narcissist will realize that they cannot bulldoze their way past this person, or they will go into rage mode and the person who has solid boundaries will promptly remove themselves from the narcissist.

First of all, it is important to know what our boundaries are. We must be in tune with honouring our own voice and knowing what we need in order to feel safe, protected, and whole. Since you are reading this book, you most likely have or have had a narcissist in your life. Perhaps over time, you have dulled your own inner voice to the point where it is not recognizable when someone completely violates your boundaries. We need to first sharpen our sensors.

A good test to know whether we are not upholding our boundaries is when we say "Yes" on the outside yet on the inside we really mean (or would like to say) "No." A sign of a weak boundary is when we say something is okay with us when it really isn't. Or when we remain silent when we should speak up. It is when we do things or *allow* things to happen around us while our inner self is screaming, "NO!" A person with weak boundaries also gives to others, or gives in to others because of fear, guilt, or obligation. These are all signals that we are not upholding our boundaries and we are not acting from our authentic self.

When have you said, "Yes," while compromising your own standards or wishes?

Part of maintaining healthy boundaries is only giving what we want to give of ourselves, our time, our money, and our resources. People with solid boundaries do not give out of compulsion, guilt, or fear of loss, and they do not bend to manipulation. When you are giving to others, do you feel joyful and have no regrets? Or are you giving in a way that eventually makes you feel used, resentful, or manipulated? If any of these negative feelings pop up, they are good indicators that you need to do some work on your boundaries.

Another good test about the strength of your boundaries is knowing that people with good boundaries will say, "No" if they are not one hundred percent sure about something. People who lack boundaries will say "Yes," amidst their uncertainty. In saying "No" as a first reaction, you are giving yourself some space to evaluate. You do not lock yourself into a promise that you do not want to keep (or are undecided on), and you are not compromising your gut instincts. We need to learn to listen to our inner voice when something feels uncertain or off.

When people such as narcissists continually bulldoze over your "no," you need to have a plan in place for a consequence. List the boundaries that you need the narcissist to abide by. Find ways that you can still maintain your boundaries even when the narcissist doesn't abide by them. An example might be, "I really don't like it when you invite people to stay over at our house at the last minute. Then I notice you get angry when I am not prepared and 'joke' with our guests about how you have to put up with me. I am happy to host people; however, I require a day of advanced notice. I also require that you treat me with courtesy and respect. If you are not able to do that the next time, I will not be able to stay for our guests and you will be in charge of feeding and entertaining them on your own."

By setting a clear boundary with a consequence in place ahead of time, you have given both yourself and the other person a choice about what will happen given option A or option B. Communicating your boundaries and following through on them is one way to deal with the narcissist and get your power back. It gives them a choice while also putting the ball in their court to accept your standard or not. You have been very clear about what will happen in either situation and they are free to choose what they want to do. Boundaries with consequences give both you and the other person the freedom to do what you need and want to do.

When the narcissist starts to manipulate or gaslight you, state your truth aloud to the narcissist, such as by saying, "That is not what happened." By persistently speaking up for yourself each time you are manipulated, you are stating your truth aloud for both of you to hear. And you are putting up a boundary from being gaslighted. You can go so far as to say, "I will not be able to have any conversations with you until you can be honest and acknowledge my viewpoints."

My how the tables will turn! It will come as quite a shock when you hold firm to your truth by putting up boundaries to protect yourself such as when you say, "I don't believe you" and "I am not willing to have any conversations with you unless you acknowledge my viewpoint."

Truth telling is another boundary that needs to be put in place. Do not let them get away with lying to you. Keep stating your truths to them aloud and that will help you keep your sanity. The truth will set you free and it is empowering. The more I kept stating my truth to the narcissist (especially when you use their own words back to them), the more it stunned him into silence. They may get to a point of raging, but deep down they also know that they are fraudulent in the light of truth. "I know who you really are," can be a very scary point of exposure to a narcissist.

In conclusion, one of the most significant things about boundaries is this: "A boundary without a consequence is not a boundary." Think of the mother who counts to three as a warning to her children and after "three" does nothing. She may think that the tone of her voice is enough, but kids can quickly see past empty words. They know if there is ultimately going to be a consequence for their behaviour or not. They quickly figure out that if nothing is actually enforced, they can get away with any and everything.

The same is true with a narcissist. Without any consequences there is no motivation to change. Why should they change if they can get away with treating you badly? Decide in advance what the consequences of crossing your boundaries will be, communicate it to them, and then enforce your consequences when they choose to break your boundaries.

7. Maintain Neutral Emotions

This is often referred to as the "Grey Rock Strategy." Basically, this infers that you are to be as unemotional and as dull as a grey rock.

Think of how deadpan and monotonous a grey rock is and emulate it with its dull personality and boring qualities. It does nothing, it feels nothing, it's just ... there. When you become boring and indifferent (versus vibrant, caring, or emotionally charged—whether that is with positive or negative emotions), the narcissist will get tired of you and will quickly look for another supply. When they know they cannot get you to either care or react, they will move on.

> *Ironically, if the narcissist sees that you don't love him anymore he will then be intent on making you hate him. Either way, he will feel powerful in his complete control over you. The one thing that narcissists can't stand is apathy—toward him.*

Even our bad emotions can bring about a thrilling feeling of power and control in a narcissist. They actually get off on your pain and negative emotions. They enjoy it when you cry, get angry, or are hurting. Rose was shocked when she discovered how much insidious joy a narcissist can get from another person's pain. It was the night Rose discovered her narcissist's affairs. Through her husband's writings, she read how one of his mistresses was the only woman he had ever loved. She read how much he despised Rose, and how it was God's will for him to have this affair. Rose was truly shocked and deeply devastated.

History sometimes repeats itself like a broken record.

This mistress was actually the same woman who broke up his second marriage. Rose read further about *all* his affairs in his two prior marriages. She had no idea that he was and had always been a serial cheater. His writings described how he detested anyone he was married to. Rose looked back in his journals to see if he had ever had a kind word to say about her, even when they were dating or engaged or at the beginning of their marriage when she thought things were absolutely wonderful. However, she found no kind or loving word. The cruelty he demonstrated in his writings was indeed indicative of the person she had been experiencing for the last year of their marriage. These texts confirmed the *real* person. Painful as it was, Rose felt fortunate to see his actual soul unmasked through his own writing, including all the perverse content about his numerous women, his selfishness, and his inhumane cruelty. *This* was the real person.

Later that night, Rose went into their bedroom with his journal in hand, and told him that she knew everything. Of course, her husband was incredibly emotional. Not emotional in the sense of remorse and shame for what she may have read and for what he had been doing in his multiple affairs—but emotional in the sense of *raging*. He was livid that she found his journal. After a heated discussion that lasted three hours and with rivers of tears flowing for realizing how deep his betrayal was, Rose was finished—body, soul, and spirit. In that moment, she genuinely felt devoid of any life or energy. That was truly the worst day of her life. Rose later said that was the most broken she would ever feel.

The next morning, her narcissist texted, "I don't know where we are at. Last night was the most meaningful conversation of our marriage."

Narcissists enjoy your pain. The more you show the narcissist your tears, the more grandiose they will feel.

After the most horrific day of her life, Rose felt broken beyond repair. She was stunned by the depth of his lies, betrayal, and cruelty. However, she was even more astounded at how much he fed off her pain. She was shocked that it was "meaningful" to him. It wasn't the seemingly happy times they once had together that were significant to him. It was her deepest pain, her hurt, her betrayal, and her agony. *That* was meaningful to him. What Rose learned that night and the next morning is that the narcissist—whether they are positively or negatively charged—feeds off whatever emotions a person has because the narcissist themself is so devoid of feelings. Since a narcissist has no emotions of their own (except for narcissistic rage), they prey off *any* emotional reactions you may have. The deeper your hurt, the more powerful they feel.

> *The only way to win with a toxic person is not to play.*[1]
>
> —Mark Twain

Toward the end of the relationship, when you are in the devaluation and discard stage, a narcissist will tend to devour your negative emotions because it gives them a sense of supremacy. What they enjoy is to seemingly control your emotional upheaval by stomping on all your buttons with malevolence and vengeance. After all, by now they already have their new supply for the good emotions that stroke their ego. They use your sad, fearful, and tearful emotions to flex their power over you.

However, your power is in using the neutral, dull emotions of the grey-rock strategy, and in doing so, you give them nothing. It is like turning off the channel so that they can no longer watch their favourite show. Think of a TV junkie who can only see a blank screen. When you refuse to be emotionally charged around a narcissist, they will eventually leave you alone because you are no longer providing them with entertainment and a buzz of power. Watch them unravel while you remain cool as a cucumber and dull as a grey rock.

8. No Contact or Low Contact

When it is possible for your situation, the first recommendation is to have no contact with the narcissist. It is much easier and more effective to rip the Band-Aid off your toxic relationship by severing connection. Being in a narcissistic relationship can become like an addiction, as you have actually become addicted to this person and/or your relationship with them. It's time to break off your addiction and become healthy. Getting out of a relationship with a narcissist by going cold turkey and straight into no-contact mode will end up providing you with greater sanity and clarity and a stronger sense of self more quickly.

Complete no-contact means that you have removed yourself from a joint living situation. And you do not respond to phone calls, emails, texts, Facebook messages, or have *any* form of contact. No contact means *NADA*.

When you go into No-Contact Mode, you are shifting the power back to yourself.

Going no contact can initiate your ultimate road to healing and recovery. Since you will have no contact with this toxic person, you will no longer have their audible, destructive voice around. This allows you to eventually get back in touch with your own emotions, intuition and perceptions. Don't worry about being "nice" and "friendly" as society so blindly tells us to do. Anyone who has been abusive to you, especially in an intimate relationship, does not deserve your friendship. When someone consistently treats you with disrespect and contempt, they do not deserve a place in your life. Ideally, the no-contact stage will last forever with a narcissist.

Stay away from people who can't take responsibility for their actions and who make you feel bad for being angry at them when they do you wrong.

On the flipside, maintaining contact with them will leave you to question your own sanity. It will make you a vulnerable prey to their Jekyll-and-Hyde mood swings and varying forms of treatment. Continuing to have contact with a narcissist can create more trauma bonds and allow them to have an even greater hold and control over your life.

Having no contact allows you to stop wasting your precious time and energy on someone who will suck the life and soul out of you. Getting out of the toxicity allows space for healthy, whole relationships;

for new interests; and for fresh possibilities in your life. You deserve it! Rediscover yourself!

> *Keep revisiting your past and you'll never make it to your future.*[2]
>
> —R.H. Sin

Of course, not everyone is able to go into "No-Contact Mode." The next best alternative is to go into "Low-Contact Mode" and have as little contact as possible! One of the only reasons to maintain any form of contact with a narcissist is when there are shared children involved. In situations like this it is best to have as little interaction as possible. Your mental, emotional, and psychological health and sanity depend on it. If this is your situation, create firm boundaries and use the grey-rock strategy (neutral emotions) when you are around the narcissist.

9. Watch Out for ... the Hoover Manoeuvre

"Hoovering" is a strategy the narcissist uses so they can get back into your life, in order to regain control of you. Psychologists have named this strategy after the Hoover vacuum because, like the Hoover vacuum, the narcissist will try to "suck" you back into the relationship. Time is irrelevant. It may be months or years after your relationship is over and you have completely severed contact with them. Then, all of a sudden, they want you back into their life ... well ... at least for a time so that they can get their fix from you.

Hoovering comes in many forms. They may apologize with huge crocodile tears for what they have done, charm you back by confessing their undying love to you, or promise to do "whatever it takes" to get you back. They may faux-mance you by offering to take you to nice places or buy extravagant things for you. Of course they assure you that they are completely different now and that you will have an amazing relationship with them.

When Gillian was dating, she broke up with her narcissist because she caught him lying to her many times. After these exposures of truth, she also experienced glimpses of cruelty when his mask slipped. At that time, she was naive as to who or what a narcissist really is, with all of his love-bombing and hoovering tactics. Gillian remembered being extremely confused by his sudden grandiose gestures after he had lied. After she was apart from him for an extensive time, he successfully "hoovered" Gillian back into the relationship. She bought into his transformation story: that "grandiose breakthroughs" had been made, and that he was finally "free" from the reasons why he lied.

Gillian ended up marrying this man, only to escape out of her abusive marriage just a few years later.

Unfortunately, the bottom line is that narcissists will charm, manipulate, lie, and say whatever you want to hear. Yes, for a time, they will do whatever it takes to get you back into their life. They know your empathetic heart, your unending optimism, your desire to help and heal, and they will exploit all of that for their own manipulative purposes to control and use you.

When Kailey was about to move out of the house, her soon-to-be ex-husband tried to hoover her. Over the course of several weeks, she received cards, specialty coffees, and offers to help her move. He was willing to do anything else that she might need. For Kailey's last night in the house, her soon-to-be ex-husband wanted to take her to the most expensive restaurant in the city. However, the weeks prior to these grandiose hoovering gestures, he had been a completely different person. It wasn't enough that she was basically giving him their home; this same man was threatening to take her possessions and to leave her penniless.

Kailey had a hard time reconciling who this nice-yet-evil person was. She remembered the extreme confusion and unsettling feelings when she reflected, "he was being WAY too Jekyll and Hyde for me!"

Shortly after Kailey moved out, her soon-to-be ex-husband was well entrenched into several other sources of "supply." Kailey and her husband had zero contact for over three months. Then suddenly, out of the blue, the hoovering began again. Kailey was bombarded with offers for coffee, to go out to dinner, ski trip getaways, and even to move to Europe with him for a fresh new start. This flurry of offers kept coming in, even though Kailey never once responded. In the end, she found out that he had lost his "supply" during the season when the barrage of offers kept coming. This is typical. A narcissist will hoover you when they lose their supply or when they want to make their current supply jealous. They do this because they need their attention-fix and they remember that you were once a good supply. They will try to do whatever it takes to get you back and fill their void.

One thing that I have learned about hoovering is this: DON'T get sucked in. If at all possible, DO NOT COMMUNICATE BACK! If you pay attention to the content of hoovering emails, phone calls, or texts, you will likely find that they are full of vain charm and devoid of any *authentic* apology or true change. In these charming communications, there is usually no form of remorse, love, or kindness. Despite the romantic gestures, hoovering often has the martyr-and-victim mentality attached, mixed with a pinch of blame in attempts to guilt you, and a whole lot of manipulation.

When Sabrina first experienced hoovering, she was tempted to reply to a particular email from her narcissist to clarify the truth and to defend herself. She was deeply upset by his comments and how he was completely twisting things around in an accusative way. However, she had already read about the power of hoovering and was not willing to take the chance of getting sucked back in. Instead, she did send a response. Not to him, but to a couple of her closest friends who understood what she was living through. It contained some bold and blatant truth-telling with a flavour of sass. Writing this message was a huge stress releaser and they all had some great laughs too!

Why Do They Hoover?

A narcissist hoovers because they are addicted to two things: attention and controlling others. Without attention, they die. Like the Wicked Witch of the West, without attention, they will scream, "I'm melting!" Internally, they are so empty and devoid of emotions, empathy, and feelings of love and significance that they have to get these things from external sources such as you and others whom they target as "supply." When hoovering is successful and they actually get you back, in their minds, it reinforces their control over you.

Hoovering is meant to confuse you into thinking that the narcissist misses you and that they are not such a bad person. In reality, their motive is to regain power and control over you. It does not matter to them that they are toying with your emotions and your heart. Beware when hoovering happens. The narcissist hasn't really changed so don't fall for the charming, manipulative mask!

When Do They Hoover?

A narcissist will try to hoover you and re-love bomb you when their supply is low. They need a backup supply and they need it fast! It is likely that things aren't going well with the new person (or the old person, or any mass combination of persons for that matter). DO NOT GET SUCKED BACK IN! Remember, you are only "supply" to them! Like a vampire, they will feast on you for a time until all the life is drained out of you and then they will move on to hoover someone else. You are only a quick fix for them, and you are only for a time. Also keep in mind, they may be hoovering several other people at once!

Unfortunately you can never be a narcissist's one true love. You will always be the lowest on their totem pole while they are securing their back-up narcissistic supply.

They are also more likely to hoover you within a shorter span of time if you are the one who discarded them first. However, there is no time limit. Narcissists can hoover you after you've had months and even years of no contact. Hoovering may not happen right away. You may have periods of being bombarded with texts, various forms of requests, and other ways of them trying to get back into your world.

Melissa briefly dated a guy for two months. As soon as she discovered he was a narcissist, she promptly broke it off. Within a few months after the breakup, she started getting texts from him every couple of weeks. This continued on for several years with zero communication on her part. Despite her lack of communication, and that years had passed since they had even seen each other, he was now offering to take her to Bali. Melissa never responded to any of his texts. His hoovering obsession lasted for three full years until she finally blocked him entirely.

How Do They Hoover?

There are various ways a narcissist will hoover you. It all revolves around getting back into your life and controlling you. Hoovering tactics can range from being flattering to frightening. Below are a few styles of hoovering.

Random Texts

After you've left and/or told them that you want no contact with them, narcissists will often send you texts as if *nothing* ever happened. Some texts may sound like this:

- "Hey, are you going to go to … (a certain event)?"
- "It's our anniversary and I'm thinking about you."
- "I can't seem to find … (a certain item). Did you take it? Can you please check your stuff and get back to me?"
- "Please call me. I need to talk to you right now." (And they never say about what.)

- "The roses in our front yard are really growing this year. You should come by."
- "Happy Valentine's Day!"
- "I've renovated the bathroom from our old home together. You should come over and see it."
- "You're the only person I've ever loved." (Ironically that wasn't the story when you were with them.)
- "It's God's will that we get back together."
- "We were meant to be together."
- "There's an event coming up that would really enhance your career connections. I have an extra ticket."
- "Hey, how's your evening going?"
- "What are your plans for the weekend? We should do something."

Fake Apologies

When someone hoovers, they may actually vocalize that they are sorry. However, there is usually something not quite right, incomplete, or inauthentic about what they have to say. They may apologize for other things that are completely unrelated to their cruelty, cheating, and abusive behaviour.

Colleen's narcissist became so apologetic over the fact that he did not do better to set them up financially. He went on to say all the ways he so generously provided for them (painting himself as the hero), but in the end he realized it just wasn't good enough for her (inserting blame and guilt). Colleen thought this was quite a random and strange apology especially since there was never a "them" financially. Colleen and her husband had separate bank accounts throughout their marriage. Her husband was actually a very wealthy (yet very stingy) man who never gave her a dime even when he had the chance. What could he possibly mean by setting "them" up financially?

What Colleen did notice though was that he did *not* apologize for his horrendous abuse, the threats, the lying, or the multiple affairs. Clearly there were no feelings of remorse about *those* things and he could not truly acknowledge any of the destruction and pain he caused. It seemed to her that the only purpose of this fake apology was to make himself look better and to inadvertently shift any blame onto Colleen.

Your gut will ultimately tell you if an apology is off. Learn to trust it. When you listen between the lines, there is usually some underlying blame and/or subtle manipulation, and it ends up being all about putting the narcissist in a good light. After they "apologize," it is very common that they will demand that you instantly take them back and blindly trust them again, pick up from the very best point of the relationship, ignore all the crap that happened, and move on right away without any real change taking place.

Sending You Gifts

Hoovering in the form of giving can include gifts of cards, flowers, books, jewelry, gift cards, tickets for an event, or even a new vehicle. Gifts can be strategically used as an attempt to re-love bomb you, to guilt or manipulate you, and win you back over to their dark side. This can be quite inappropriate. After you have clearly ended things, they pretend that the relationship isn't over. They act as if nothing's changed between you, and that nothing bad ever happened.

A Call For Help.

This type of hoovering includes all types of frantic cries for attention. The narcissist seems to be in dire straits or they are in desperate trouble of some sort. Such calls for help include these: they have no money; their business is going under; they are sick; they are dying; they are going to kill themselves. You, being the compassionate soul, just might fall for these pleas and try to go to their rescue. If you have been in an abusive relationship, do not take it upon yourself to try to help or fix a narcissist who is in distress (whether it is real or imagined).

These calls for help are often a matter of thrusting the responsibility onto you for their feelings, their actions, the consequences of their actions, or for taking care of themselves. It is better that they take their own responsibility, face the consequences of their own actions, or take the initiative to seek help from a professional. Do not get sucked into being responsible for the narcissist, especially when you are already out of the relationship. Remember, being hoovered is about trying to get you back into a relationship in which nothing has truly changed and where they are only out to use you.

Raging and Fits

They may go into fits and raging when all else fails to provoke a reaction from you. Remember, you are never responsible for another person's emotions or actions. You did not cause their anger and raging, and you cannot soothe or fix it. A narcissist may also intimidate or threaten you to gain back their control over you. If you ever feel in danger, you may need to apply for a restraining order, an order of peace, a peace-bond, or whatever is applicable with your local authorities regarding your situation.

Smear Campaigns

A narcissist may wreak havoc in your social life by spreading rumours about you personally. Smear campaigns are meant to show why we were never "worthy" of the narcissist in the first place. These campaigns are usually targeted to contact your family, children, and circles of friends. It is considered a form of hoovering because the narcissist expects you to contact them, so that you will attempt to make them stop ruining your reputation with their lies.

Telling lies about others is as harmful as hitting them with an ax, wounding them with a sword, or shooting them with a sharp arrow. [3]

—Proverbs 25:18

Ironically, the best thing you can do in this type of hoovering situation is to maintain no contact. They have usually carefully crafted their smear campaign in advance, during the time that you are still reeling from the shock of the devaluation stage. Before you even suspected that you were going to be discarded, they were already in the process of painting your relational picture to everyone else by way of them being the victim and the martyr in your relationship. You will never win with a narcissist by trying to defend yourself. They will use your defense as proof that you are "crazy" or "overly emotional" and "impossible" to deal with.

> *Arguing with a narcissist is like getting arrested. Everything you say can and will be used against you.*

In a smear campaign you are bound to lose friendships and other close relationships in the process. Look on the bright side. The shake-up is good because sometimes you would never know who your true friends are and who is worth having in your life until you are faced with something as drastic as this. Some friends may come back around, others never will. The truth eventually comes out about who the narcissist really is because the narcissistic cycle will repeat itself with someone else. No matter how horrific the lies are, you have the truth on your side. The best thing you can do under a smear campaign is don't get involved. Don't fall for this particular hoovering tactic to contact the narcissist. Keep your cool and allow the truth to reveal itself over time.

They Target Those Close to You

If they can't contact you, then they may hoover those closest to you. They may make claims to your family and friends that they have "no idea what happened" and that they have valiantly tried everything to salvage the relationship. Narcissists may attempt to win over your family members, your work colleagues, your friends, and especially your children. They want others to take their victimized side against you. They are trying to form bonds with those closest to you to rile you up emotionally, to control you, and to lure you back into contacting them.

How to Outsmart the Hoover Manoeuvre

The very best thing you can do when you are being hoovered is *do not get roped in*. Refuse to play their game. Maintain low, or better yet, no contact.

> *When your past calls, don't answer. It has nothing new to say.[4]*
>
> —Lionel Richie

Do NOT fall for their attempts at reconciliation; empty apologies; flattering words; or meaningless, charming expressions of love. Realize that they know how to manipulate you and prey on your emotional availability. They will not change, but *you* can. Do NOT respond to or contact the narcissist. Eventually, once they realize you will not play their games anymore and can't be controlled by them, they will move on to easier targets.

> *If the narcissist did not appreciate your presence, why not give them your absence?*

Be aware of your own emotional triggers. Recognize how they may have hoovered you in the past. Ask yourself, "Did they really change, or did I get sucked into a lie? How were they able to suck me back in?"

Have your support tribe to go to and to let them know when and how you've been hoovered. It is likely that they can objectively point out specific things you have not seen.

PART IV

Twenty-Five Ways to Heal from a Relationship with a Narcissist

You have experienced great trauma from being in a relationship with a narcissist. Your journey of healing will take a great deal of strength, courage, support, resources, affirmation, and validation. It is essential to address the wounds not only from this relationship but also the deeper wounds from the past. It is time to acknowledge those old wounds, the ones that are unknown, passed over, or wounds that have never completely healed. Now is your time!

At the point when you have a base understanding of narcissism and are actively dealing with your situation by going no contact, or have minimal contact by using the grey-rock strategy; you are in the place to begin to heal and to rebuild your life.

Part IV provides twenty-five ways to empower you and to bring about healing and renewal in your life. Let your journey begin!

CHAPTER 8

THE INNER WORK

Ways to Heal: One to Seven

The inner work of healing is a journey and it does not happen overnight. This chapter deals with seven ways of doing the inner work to heal your heart. You will have many different types of losses in this breakup and it is important to make the time to grieve all of them. In order to heal, it is also vital that you get back in touch with your various emotions. The time of numbing has come to an end. Now it is time to acknowledge the specific emotions you have had or are having on this journey. Seeking professional support such as counselling or therapy can also drastically move you through the healing process more quickly and can give you the tools and hope you need for a different future.

As an empathetic person, it is essential that you give yourself the same compassion that you would extend to other people who are going through a difficult time. If this is your first breakup experience with a narcissist, you will find that it is a unique experience compared with other breakups. We will get into the specifics of what you can expect to be different when you break up with a narcissist. One truth that is vital to realize is that although the relationship was real for you, from a narcissist's perspective, you were only their supply. It is helpful to change your expectations of receiving any empathy or compassion from them. Doing the inner work also involves making sure that you make the time to prioritize your needs and healing, not just at this time but for the rest of your life.

Let your journey of healing begin.

Healing Pathway 1. Grieve Your Losses

You will have to grieve your losses at some point in order to get to the other side of healing. Do not negate your pain or ignore it. The sooner you face your pain and go through it, the stronger, the easier, and the faster your healing will come. Remember, it often gets worse, before it gets better. By dealing with and uprooting the pain now, you won't have to deal with it in an exponential way in the future.

The sooner you allow yourself to be with the pain, the sooner it will pass. The only way out is through.

Here are some of the things you may need to grieve.

The Good Times

There is no doubt that you had some incredible times in your relationship with the narcissist. Let's face it, the love-bombing phase was amazing! To have someone give you so much attention combined with the unbelievable chemistry you had is perhaps incomparable to anything you have experienced before.

Perhaps you shared some amazing times that revolved around your interests (whether these interests were real to the narcissist or yet another façade). Now you no longer have a partner to go to the symphony with, to play tennis with, to go skiing with, to go on overseas adventures with, or to enjoy campfires with. Reflect and acknowledge the good times that you did have and what you will miss, even if those moments were a long time ago. Write them down. Whether or not the narcissist was using you during those times, *you* were sincere, and those moments were real to *you*. Acknowledge your losses.

Your Hopes and Dreams

You may have been waiting a long time for someone like this person and dreamed of building a life together with them. You could be dealing with the end of a friendship, the end of a relationship, or the end of a marriage. It is most likely that you were planning on having this person in your life for a long time and possibly for a lifetime. You had ideas for the future that involved celebrations, Christmases, dinners together, fun activities, living through the ups and downs, travels, and sharing your lives together in special ways. Now the relationship is over and although it's better for your own sanity and safety that you limit or sever any contact with this person, you still have losses and those losses are real. It is essential to grieve those hopes and dreams with that person before you can hope and dream once again.

Your Time and Energy

Chances are you have invested a lot of time into this person. Especially in the end, there is no doubt that you devoted a great deal of energy attempting to keep the narcissist happy and to salvage the relationship. Now that you are standing in the wreckage, you realize it was a losing battle. It is true that we cannot get back the time or energy that we expended in this relationship. However, perspective is all in how you view your past experiences. While you may need to grieve your losses of time and energy, nothing in life ever has to be wasted. We can learn from anything in life and become better people for it. You can grieve your loss of time and energy, while also taking the perspective that this experience had meaning, and that it can and will be useful to you. Perhaps new opportunities and relationships opened up because you went through this experience.

The Death of a Relationship

At the end of my relationship, I felt like I needed to have a funeral for my ex. It was the death of the wonderful Dr. Jekyll, and the evil Mr. Hyde had murdered him. I grieved for the death of the man I fell in love with, the death of the man I thought I married, and the death of the persona of someone who never actually existed. Grieve for the person you *thought* they were. You loved that person with all your heart and you believed they loved you too. It is time to bury that person and to make your peace. That "kind" soul that you once knew never existed and they will never come back.

Material and Financial Losses

Perhaps during the breakup, you have lost your home including all of its memories. You may have lost certain possessions, family heirlooms, property, joint memberships to clubs, time shares, or health and tax benefits. Our material and financial losses can add up and take a toll on us. Starting again financially with kids or in mid-life is never easy. You need to acknowledge what you have lost and take some time to allow yourself to feel your feelings and to grieve.

You may now have to live in a very different space—a tiny apartment or a basement suite that has no memories. Sometimes this can actually be a positive thing that can help you move forward. When you do move into that new space, make it your own. Add some things into your environment that are uniquely you and that make you feel happy, motivated, or at peace. Start creating new memories in your new space.

You may have a different lifestyle because of altered finances. There may be certain things you cannot do for a while due to money constraints. However, this can also be a beautiful time to explore new interests and avenues. Many times this is actually an opportunity for greater self-discovery and empowerment.

Your Identity

Being married or being part of a couple has likely been a huge part of your identity. Most likely it was an identity that you embraced and thrived in. Navigating singleness later in life and/or being a single parent are unchartered waters; you probably never imagined yourself traversing in them. You may have to grieve the loss of a beloved part of your identity and you will now have to carve out a new one.

You may feel that you have let others down as well as yourself. Others may condemn you for "quitting" or getting out of the relationship. You may have said, "I will never get divorced," and you are now flooded with guilt. There is no easy ending with a narcissist. Just because your relationship failed doesn't mean that *you* are a failure. Isn't it better that you did get out? Isn't it better that you "failed" rather than that you kept taking more and more abuse?

There is a difference between giving up and knowing when you've had enough.

It is nevertheless important to grieve your former identity in order to make way for and to create and embrace a new identity.

Having to Suffer an Abusive Relationship

The psychological games and emotional rape that you have been through are horrific. I believe it is important to grieve for yourself—for how you have been treated and misused, and for what you have suffered personally, emotionally, psychologically, financially, physically, and mentally. You were with a person who was cold, callous, who used you as supply, and then cruelly discarded you without any remorse. This is the time to have compassion for yourself and to grieve what you have gone through. You did not deserve this. You deserve so much better. You are a kind, loveable person who is worthy of all good things.

The Loss of Other Relationships

In this breakup, you are bound to lose friends. You may have had mutual friends to whom the narcissist had been recounting their victimized tale long before you even knew what was going on. Although you may not expect that your friends will have to choose between you and your narcissist, most of them likely will. You may be surprised to know that certain people will be completely out of your life and will possibly never speak to you again, because of what they have heard. Smear campaigns are powerful.

You will have friends and even some family members who will never fully see the real predator behind the charming mask of the narcissist. Remember that the narcissist was able to fool you too through their charisma and idealization. In the beginning you would never have imagined the monster behind the mask. It was only because you were in an intimate relationship and in close quarters with the narcissist (most likely over a long span of time) that you were able to see who they actually are. However, the majority of people only ever see the mask. Friends of the narcissist usually live in the continual idealization phase without experiencing the brutal devaluation phase and the ultimate, inhumane discard. After all, the narcissist only shows their true self to their "supply," and that is only after the supply has been sucked dry.

Recognize that the narcissist has created a "harem." These people are their fan club who also provide them with a narcissistic hit. These people have been won over because they have only experienced the narcissist in public and have only seen the false mask. They are willing to take up defensive arms for the narcissist and if the narcissist is extremely successful at smearing your character, they may take up their arms against you as well.

Stacey understood firsthand how this worked because she genuinely bought into her ex's smear campaigns about his first wife. That was until she actually met the woman two years later. Upon meeting this kind and gracious person (who was *completely* different from the raging psychopathic monster that Stacey was led to believe she was), Stacey began to question what she had been told. Years later, Stacey discovered the truth about who this woman was and, indeed, who her husband truly was.

Be prepared as most likely at some point the narcissist will smear campaign you to your friends and family. Some of your friends may only hear the side of the story from the charming faker. Others may be too upset to even speak with you because the narcissist did such a great job of deceiving them by painting themselves as the victim and you as the villain. Some people may actually believe the inverse truth—that you are the pathological abuser who gets to escape accountability yet again.

In such cases, it may be in your best interest to go "no contact" with some of these people. In the end, your friends and family either know you or they don't. It can be amazing to discover some of the people who will turn against you. You may have to let go of some incredible friendships. Although smear campaigns are powerful, trust that the truth will be known to the people who really want to see it. Fortunately, you will have some unconditionally supportive friends in your camp who will be with you through thick and thin. These are the people who will support you on the rollercoaster of your recovery. Some of your other friends will come around eventually. Yet there may still be others whom you will have lost for a lifetime. Grieve the loss of those friendships.

Healing Pathway 2. Acknowledge Your Emotions

Allow yourself to go through the difficult emotions that we often tend to evade or minimize. You must go *through* the process of pain to get to the other side of healing. Your healing will never come by trying to go around the pain or by avoiding it. Suppressing your emotions can delay as well as prolong your healing.

Your healing will progress when you become conscious of what emotion you are experiencing and then acknowledge it. Since it is likely that your thoughts, feelings, and emotions were discounted, disregarded, or negated while you were in a relationship with the narcissist, it is vital that you start to acknowledge what you are feeling now. If it is sadness, acknowledge it. If it is anger, call it out for what it is. If it is elation or relief, accept and embrace it. Allow your feelings to simply be. Learn to fully experience each of your emotions in healthy ways. It is also beneficial to ask yourself specifically why you are feeling the way you do.

On the flip side, while we want to experience and allow our emotions, we also want to make sure that we are progressing to a better place. You may want to set a time limit for exploring an emotion such as sadness or anger. Then when the time is up, do something that will give you energy or happiness. An example is this: I will allow myself to fully feel my sadness for one hour. I will explore the emotion, sob, journal, and allow all my feelings of sadness for that one hour. Then I will do something active to change my state, such as walk the dog, go for a run, or watch a funny movie.

You are bound to feel emotional during this time.

Sadness

It is good to validate and own your pain (since it was not validated in your relationship). An acknowledgement of your sadness must happen before it can be released. Admit to your friends how you are feeling. Be sure you give this emotion the time and place it needs. Sadness is a necessary step in the grieving and healing process. Crying after what you have been through is normal, healthy, cathartic, and healing.

Crying has its own specialness: it is a cleansing, purifying release.

Guilt

There is a genuine time for remorse if you have truly done something wrong. However, beware of the false guilt that comes from the narcissist, whether they give it in person or their toxic voice continues to play messages of blame, accusation, and condemnation in your head. It is likely you have been indicted of all kinds of things while the narcissist played the wide-eyed, innocent victim. What you can learn from this experience is to not accept false guilt or receive all the accusations that were thrown at you. Guilt is an emotion you will likely feel yet is not based on reality; you will want to release it. Although others may try, you are truly the only one who can allow yourself to feel guilty. You can still be humble to learn and grow in your areas of weaknesses, to own what you need to own, and to put yourself on a path of transformation. At the same time, acknowledge and release any false guilt and blame that you have received.

Shame

You may feel some shame or humiliation for being in an abusive relationship. It wasn't abusive in the beginning. The important thing is that while you didn't know how abusive it had become, you are seeing it now. You are getting out or have gotten out, and you will not allow such things to happen again in the future. Shame can be harsh, judgemental, and condemning. Some shaming thoughts might be these:

- "How could I not have seen this?"
- "How could I have been so stupid?"
- "How could I have allowed all of these things to happen?"
- "Why didn't I get out sooner?"
- "Maybe I really did deserve this?"
- "Is there something flawed in me?"

> *Shame is the intensely painful feeling or experience of believing we are flawed and therefore unworthy of acceptance and belonging.*[1]
>
> —Brené Brown

Shame is complete when it drives to the core of our being and becomes part of our identity. It can make us feel that *who* we are is seriously flawed. That's why the attacking judgement in our minds that it was "our fault" and "we deserved it" is shame based. Such thinking needs to be recognized and uprooted.

Shame isolates us and makes us feel that we have done something wrong. Shame is extremely common in abusive relationships. The truth is the abuse that took place was NOT your fault. Narcissists (and even friends, family, and society) often go into victim-shaming mode. The non-narcissists attempt to justify that there *must* have been a reason why the narcissist was so horrible to you. Do not buy into this for a minute! The narcissist acted the way they did toward you because that is who *they* are and that is how they treat the people who are closest to them.

Although you may be feeling this way, acknowledge that you do not have to allow this lie to become your identity. You do not have to accept the responsibility for someone else's actions, emotions, or choices. Each person has control over their own actions. By one person choosing to be abusive, it is never the victim's fault. There is nothing anyone could ever do to deserve to be abused. You do not deserve to be controlled, isolated, or disrespected. You deserve to be treated with respect at all times. Who *you* are has nothing to do with why the abuse took place. The abuse took place because the abuser is abusive.

In regard to the question, "How could I have allowed this to happen?," remember we all make judgement errors in life. You are permitted the same grace. The narcissist had a very believable mask. Look at all the people who are still sucked in by this person. It could have happened to anyone. It *has* happened to countless millions of people. You are absolutely not alone in this. Look at all the other intelligent, confident, courageous, gifted, beautiful people who have been taken in by narcissists.

Shame does not serve you, so ditch it. You know now. Shame does not deserve to be a part of who you are. If you focus on the *truth* of your identity (that you are a wonderful, worthy person) instead of what happened in this relationship, you will grow from this experience, you will heal deeply, and you will actually become a better person for having gone through this.

Anger

You are bound to feel angry at some point after being with a narcissist. In and of itself, anger is not necessarily a bad thing. Anger is our warning system to protect us when we have been wronged. It is a signal when our boundaries have been crossed and when someone is disrespecting or threatening us. When anger is stirred within us, often it is our survival mechanism kicking in to protect and preserve our worth as a human being. This strong emotion can signal when we are being disrespected. Others, especially abusive people, can disrespect us when we are protecting our basic needs and when we stand up for our deepest convictions.

It's actually quite disconcerting if you don't feel anger after being in an abusive relationship with a narcissist, because your self-preservation did not kick in. The warning that you need to remove yourself from this danger is not there. Not having any anger is like not having any sensation in your body when you put your hand in a fire. We need this sensation to tell us to get out before we get completely burned beyond repair.

Anger is not something you want to deny or completely suppress; if you do, it can bottle up and explode like a shaken bottle of Champagne. You don't want your anger to get out of control and send your cork through the roof one day. Find healthy ways of dealing with and expressing your anger. You may *feel* like slashing his tires, burning his clothes, and doing everything that Carrie Underwood says in her song, "Before He Cheats." These are not exactly healthy ways of dealing with anger. Although doing such things might give you some temporary relief, you ultimately wouldn't want to do something that you will truly regret later. This includes anything that could affect you in court further down the road plus anything that could jeopardize your future in any way. You may be angry *and* you do not have to be vindictive.

It is important to get your anger out and find healthy ways of expressing it. Anger must not be stored up within you for any extended period of time. Go sign up for a kickboxing or boxing class. Go for a run or hit the weights. Go yell in the woods. Purge and spring clean your home like crazy. Find ways of releasing your anger that are not harmful to another person, ways that are productive and serving toward yourself. Release this powerful emotion in a healthy way, then move toward making some changes in your life. Protect yourself and take back your power. Learn the difference between healthy anger—which causes you to get out of bad situations and to protect yourself—and destructive anger—which is damaging and vengeful.

> *Releasing anger starts with realizing you can't control people, either in what they say or how they act.*

Powerlessness

You may have had years of being bullied by the narcissist. You may currently have overwhelming feelings of powerlessness—of being trapped, cornered, coerced. You may think that nothing you do has helped the situation. It may feel as though the narcissist has had all the power. That they called all the shots. They might have controlled how you spent your time and your finances, who you interacted with, and how you dealt with many other areas of your life. The honest truth is that another person will never be able to control you, your mind, and your will. Unless you let them.

Now that you're done with the narcissist, it's time to take back your power. Get your power back by controlling yourself—your thoughts, your words, and your actions. What you *can* control are your responses, what you choose to focus on, how you make your boundaries strong, and how you will start taking action for a better life. You may need to first acknowledge in what ways and circumstances you feel powerless. Get clear on where you have false and limiting beliefs. Declare that *you* are now in control and that the narcissist no longer has a say in your life—in your actions or in your thoughts. Being empowered is *your choice every day.*

Relief

When you are out of the relationship and have low or no contact with the narcissist, you will start to feel a great sense of relief and freedom. You will feel like you can breathe again for the first time in years. You may even experience elation and healing in your body, such as a lack of headaches, better digestion, more calmness, and more energy at the same time! It's a wonderful and weightless feeling. You begin to see the light at the end of the tunnel and you have hope. These are all feelings to embrace and celebrate! You are on the road back to yourself and you have a bright future ahead!

Emotional Trip Wires

While you are on this emotional journey of acknowledging your feelings, there are a few emotions that you want to be wary of. There are four destructive emotions that you do not want to pick up. You want to ultimately move to a productive place of true healing and freedom. Be careful of these four trip wires that can sabotage you.

Unhealthy Anger

This is the type of anger that has a vindictive, vengeful quality to it. When anger becomes unhealthy, it is no longer about you protecting yourself, getting out of a dangerous situation, or standing up for justice. This type of anger wants payback—payback with some strong interest. Unhealthy anger can escalate to the level of a Hatfield-McCoy feud. Don't waste your time planning for payback and pain. When anger controls a person, it can be an unquenchable fire that is never satisfied. Use your time and energy to get healed, to move on and into your wonderful life.

Bitterness and/or Resentment

These twin emotions can control you and prevent you from moving forward. They stop the clock in your life and prevent you from seeing the good opportunities and relationships that are right in front of you. A person can waste valuable time (sometimes years) replaying in their minds, rehashing, and retelling past scenarios of hurt and abuse. Your wounds remain raw, infected, unable to heal, and often worse than the initial blow. Bitterness can consume you to the point where everything rubs you the wrong way. You'll always feel like you're on the defensive and you're not sure why. It can suck the life out of you and be a drain on your relationships when you stay stuck in these toxic moments.

There are a couple of differences between anger and bitterness. Anger can pass quickly and it is about a present hurt, whereas bitterness latches on and does not let go of what has happened. Bitterness is always about past hurts and involves a helpless feeling that change is not possible. Resentment, on the other hand, can be a persistent feeling of ill will that lingers on and on (and on and on). There comes a point when we must move forward and not allow the past or others to control us.

Blame

When you blame a person, you are giving them your power. You are in a sense waiting for *them* to change before *your life* can improve. Spoiler alert! You will likely be waiting forever!

Blame surrenders your control to the other person. When you are in this place, you often overlook the potential lessons that you can learn that will enrich your life. Blaming will keep you stuck in resistance and will prevent you from having deeper awareness, healing, and empowerment.

Instead of blame, use empowering phrases to reframe your situation for the good. It may sound something like this, "Everything has happened for a reason. There were parts of me that needed to heal. By taking responsibility for my life, I will learn and grow. I will empower myself by never allowing such a thing to happen again, so that I will never have to go through this pain again. I am healed, stronger, and wiser now." Humbly take responsibility for your life, and choose to move on and grow. Taking responsibility allows you the choice and option to create your life on your terms.

Depression

There are bound to be some extremely low moments throughout your healing journey. Gratitude and thankfulness are the best ways to stave off depression. We always have things to be grateful for. Truly! Choose to do things that make you happy and get you into a different emotional space. However, if you are suffering from serious depression, it is best to seek professional help. Severe depression symptoms include significant loss of appetite, drastic weight loss or gain, sleep problems, isolating yourself, having trouble getting out of bed or leaving the house, and frequent thoughts of death or suicide. If you are experiencing severe depression, get some professional help. Your life CAN turn around!

Healing Pathway 3. Professional Support: Counselling and/or Therapy

Counselling and/or therapy can be game-changers in your healing process. Vocalizing your experience to another person can help you to release trauma and reduce your cognitive dissonance (holding two conflicting beliefs). Working with the right person can also help to validate the reality of what you have experienced. These professionals can be the support that you need at this time. They can explain things from an objective point of view, they can help you to see some of your own blind spots, and they are often amazingly good at getting to the source of your hidden pain. In counselling, you may discover that you need to deal with some deep roots from the past or even with issues from your family of origin. What you knew as your "normal" growing up might actually have been neither normal nor healthy. Perhaps there are some past issues that need to be addressed and deeper wounds that need healing.

If you postpone the healing process, grief can return months—even years—later to haunt you.

It is very important to find a counsellor or therapist who understands and is trained to deal with narcissism. You will want to find someone who both validates your feelings and experiences and can lead you to a better place. You will also want to work with someone who has unconditional, positive regard for you. A great counsellor or therapist will make a huge difference in your healing journey. However, a bad one can set you back. Choose wisely.

Healing Pathway 4. Self-Compassion

It is essential to give yourself compassion rather than berating yourself by asking, "How could I have fallen for that?" "Why didn't I see it?" "Why did I allow this person to treat me like that?" Accusatory thoughts such as these can actually activate the pain regions in our brain. Be gentle, kind, and understanding with yourself. Rather than beating yourself up, blaming yourself for not knowing better, and for not seeing the abuse, choose compassionate tactics that are more productive toward your healing.

After reading hundreds of articles, books, listening to interviews, and watching YouTube videos, I realized how easy it is for any one of us to fall for the false mask. It is also common that it can be years before we see the real person behind the mask. *Anyone* could find themselves in your circumstances. Remember, you did not fall for the narcissist; you fell for their illusionary mask.

> *They have been sick longer than you have been reading about their disorder—they have the upper hand.*[2]
>
> —Rhonda Freeman

It's also very confusing and hard to believe who the real person is when their mask slips. Until you've experienced such harsh treatment, it's incredulous to think that someone you love and trust could be so callous and malicious toward you. You will likely be reeling and shell shocked to discover how extreme their conduct can be in the discard phase. Experts say that abuse actually rewires and reshapes our brains. However, we do not have to let this be our destiny.

We are responsible for our path of healing and must take positive action to move forward if we want to achieve healing. The abuser is completely responsible for their actions and will one day face accountability for them. Your experiences and your feelings are *VALID*. Abuse is *never* the survivor's fault. Remember, it's as if you fell in love with the character and had no idea who the actor really was. In the end, just like in the movies, we realize it wasn't the actual person we fell for, only the role that they played. Now is the time to give yourself some compassion, the same compassion, kindness, and consideration that you give to others.

Another reason to be gentle and extend self-compassion is that it will speed up your healing. Judging ourselves and using negative self-talk keeps us in a destructive cycle. At some point you will want to come to a place where you forgive yourself. Forgive yourself that you did not look out for your own best interests. Forgive yourself that you allowed someone to treat and abuse you this badly. Remember that you didn't know then what you know now. Narcissists fool people every day. You may have never known it was possible for a person to act in such ways. You know now. You have taken steps to remove and protect yourself. Now you know that your abuser will likely never change. You've learned so much and will not let yourself be in that place again.

Healing Pathway 5. Expect a Different Breakup Process

If you have ever dated and broken up with someone who is not a narcissist or psychopath, the experience will be very different than when you do break up with a narcissist. There will still be some of the same common elements of a heart-wrenching breakup but there will also be a few differences. With a narcissist, you will not have the benefit of fully enjoying your past memories as everything is tainted with their lies. You will have to deal with the harsher realities of their cruelty, plus you have to cope with the discovery that the person you fell in love with never actually existed.

The Absence of the "Casablanca Effect"

Whenever you break up with a narcissist, the relationship lacks the "Casablanca effect." This expression is named after the celebrated film, *Casablanca*. Toward the end of the film, in the closing moments when Ingrid Bergman and Humphrey Bogart must part ways, Humphrey Bogart says, "We'll always have Paris." Even though they both knew that it was the end of their relationship and they must go on living their separate lives, the pair could always remember and look fondly back at the lovely moments they shared together during their time in Paris. This is what happens in healthy relationships. After a period of time has passed following the breakup, you can look back and remember some great moments of true love. Those times can continue to genuinely live on in your heart as wonderful moments in your life. You have these wonderful memories because there was truth and authenticity on the part of both of you. However, when you look in the past of being with a narcissist, you question everything, until the reality hits—nothing was true on their part. You won't have those Paris moments to look fondly back upon because ...

Nothing Was What It Seemed

When you look back at the past, it is all muddled and nothing was what it seemed to be. There were no genuine feelings of love reciprocating from them; they were only using you. There was no authenticity within them. It was only a show of smoke and mirrors. What appeared to be a relationship or a marriage between two people was really only all about them. Nothing was genuine on their part. Every promise they made, every great moment you spent together is tainted with their lies and pathology.

Their Unusually Cruel Treatment of You

Another difference you will have is that you need to acknowledge the deception, manipulation, betrayal, and abuse that (hopefully) you have not experienced in your other relationships. When you are going through the harsh discard stage, you may feel that everything you've ever believed about the goodness of people has been contradicted in this relationship. Every thought about loyalty, truthfulness, compassion, and humanity is obliterated when you are in a close relationship with a narcissist. It is not normal to be treated in the way that you have experienced. Acknowledge that it *IS* normal for you to have a strong reaction to being abused and mistreated by someone you trusted and loved.

You're not recovering from love lost or even from the failure of a marriage, but from warfare.

You Were Conned

"How could I not have seen it?" I'm sure these words will ring through your ears, heart, and soul many times. You will feel like you've missed the red flags that no "intelligent" person would ever miss. When you think back, these flags were vividly evident in the discard stage; however, they were completely camouflaged with deception in the love-bombing phase. Being with a narcissist is a dizzying experience; it is disorienting to have your feelings negated. In the end, you are indoctrinated into thinking you are crazy.

Beware of putting yourself in the position of complete blame for having "not seen it." While it is effective to learn from this experience, it is very detrimental to your healing to criticize and beat yourself up over this. Consider all the people in this world who have been in a narcissistic relationship. You are not alone. Think about all the people in your life who still do not see behind the narcissist's mask and many of the people who never will. Replace your feelings of guilt and judgement with graciousness toward yourself, gratitude for being out of the relationship, and a humble attitude as a way to learn and grow from this experience.

Healing Pathway 6. Realize These Two Truths

There are two important truths, which, once realized, will speed up your healing process. The first truth is that a full-borne narcissist will never change. They are who they are. Change involves admitting there is a problem. It includes a person acknowledging responsibility for having committed some wrongs. A true narcissist will never own up to their behaviour and will not change since they have never done anything "wrong." You can neither help them come to account through logic and reason, nor can you help them to see the truth by killing them with kindness.

Narcissists are as likely to change and treat you with kindness and empathy as a crocodile is apt to transform into a compassionate creature when he is hungry and his delicious prey is right in front of him. Both narcissists and crocodiles are cold blooded, incapable of feeling any remorse for the pain that they inflict. They have zero empathy for us "lesser" creatures, their prey. Believing that a true narcissist can change is like expecting this cold-blooded, ruthless reptile to transform into a devoted, tail-wagging, loving, loyal puppy. Know the truth of who they are; protect yourself and accept who you are dealing with. A crocodile can only be a crocodile and a narcissist can only be a narcissist.

The narcissistic personality disorder is named by former FBI Special Agent, Joe Navarro, as one of the four most "Dangerous Personalities" in the world. He also concluded in his book, *Dangerous Personalities,* that there is a scale of narcissism. When a person hits a certain point on the scale and exudes a high degree of narcissism, they are very dangerous and to be avoided at all costs. Anyone who chooses to remain with them will suffer.

> *The narcissistic personality will grind you down, and in the end, you will suffer emotionally, physically, psychologically, or financially.*[3]
>
> —Joe Navarro

You cannot ever change a narcissist and your love will not be enough for them. They will abuse and suck the life out of whomever they are with, no matter how incredible that other person is. When they leave you for their new prey, be assured that in the end they will do the very same to the next person.

The narcissist will not be satisfied with who they are with. Even if you have become a doormat who pretends that the lies, affairs, abuse, and indiscretions don't exist, and even if you give them blatant permission to walk all over you as they please, they will never be happy. Even when they get everything they could possibly want, they will always show contempt and disdain toward you for being so foolish as to believe that their mask was their real self. You may have been a good supply for a time, but now they have used you up and they will seek a fresh soul to devour. Realize the depth of their sickness and understand that they are master manipulators.

> *Narcissism is an evil that masquerades as good. Like a Pied Piper this master illusionist can lead you to Hell all while making you feel flattered to be chosen to go there. Only when you wake up in Hell do you realize the real evil that existed in his fluted song. By then it's too late; not only have you fallen victim, but most likely you have paid for the flute, as well.[4]*
>
> —Tigress Luv

The second truth to grasp and one of the hardest things you will go through is the realization that you were never really loved by your narcissist. You were a resource to fill their horrific void. This is not because you are not worthy of love. It is not because you didn't love them enough or the relationship wasn't real for you. You were certainly not their supply because you are "crazy" and a horrible person.

The truth is the narcissist is not capable of loving and selflessly giving to another person. Relationships are never real for a narcissist. You were a fix for their addiction that they needed to feed. You served their supply need for a time and now they have a new drug (or possibly several drugs) of choice. Perhaps you will take comfort in knowing that they are also not capable of loving their new "supply" either.

You were just another source of narcissistic supply, so do not fool yourself into thinking that the magical connection that existed in the beginning was in any way real. It was an illusion, much like the identity of the narcissist was an illusion.[5]

—Shahida Arabi

You were the source of wonderful attention and praise. Perhaps you gave them significance by being the eye candy on their arm or you increased their wealth or status. In whatever way, you increased their own image simply by being with them. To be in a relationship with you is like driving a Lamborghini or having a Louis Vuitton purse on your arm. It makes them look and feel great; they in turn have more attention because you are valuable. Realize they consider you not as a real person but purely as an object, an extension of them and their image. When a person is objectified in such a way, no feelings need to be considered.

Unfortunately, for whatever reason, the emotions of your narcissist shut down a long time ago. They have a void where human emotions would normally be and that is why they seek emotions from you. They seek the love and empathy you give them in the beginning. At the end, they will feed off your anger and your tears just to feel *something* (albeit vicariously), because they are so devoid of feeling themselves. Although they may fake attachment in the beginning, they will never be able to make true connections in relationships because they are emotionally numb. The only emotions they may truly feel are envy and rage.

Acknowledging these two truths—that there is nothing you can do to change a narcissist and that you were only their supply—will help you to move on.

Healing Pathway 7. Recognize and Prioritize Your Needs and Healing

Those of us who have attracted narcissists into our lives can often be very disconnected from what we truly need. We are so concerned about meeting the needs of others that we do not take into consideration our own needs. Often times it is easier to make everything about the other person and to downplay or ignore our needs. Everyone has needs; it's part of being human. Your needs will get met in one way or another, either in healthy or in unhealthy ways. You can't ignore or avoid your needs without having consequences.

Psychologists say that a classic form of codependency is self-avoidance. It can be easy to "check out" when it comes to ourselves. When we avoid our own needs and pain, we end up making our lives about the other person and we often do this unconsciously. This makes it easy for narcissists to steer us into handing over our time, attention, loyalty, and resources to them at the expense of our own souls. In contrast, people who are aware of their own wellbeing, and who are fulfilling their needs in healthy ways will not sacrifice themselves for another.

It is essential to prioritize our healing at this time and to recognize in which areas we need restoration. We can be so caught up in healing things in the narcissist's life that we overlook the importance of making sure our own wounds heal and we are living in a place of wholeness. Much like the narcissist, we can lack self-awareness and not take responsibility for our inner wounds. This is an unhealthy form of self-avoidance and it is an area we need to own and take care of. When we heal our wounds and recognize our worth, we will never again tolerate abusive behaviours. Then we can forever be free from cycles of trauma.

CHAPTER 9

CONNECTIONS

Ways to Heal: Eight to Thirteen

Making powerful connections to the right things is a tremendous way to heal. Different types of connections can fulfill different streams of healing within you. Being with friends is a formidable path to restoration. Your friends know you, love you, and have journeyed with you. You have a shared history together. They can make you laugh and help you get back in touch with the best parts of you. It is also good to build new relationships with fellow survivors who have been at the receiving end of narcissism. These fellow survivors really understand your journey and they can deeply empathize with what you have gone through. They will appreciate your experience in ways that most of your friends probably never will. In turn, they can also share their experiences and wisdom. Another type of relationship to prioritize is connecting and reconnecting with yourself. It is time to reclaim your life and get back in touch with your real self.

Connecting to resources such as books, music, and movies can also bring healing. Insightful quotes can be tidbits of wisdom and can make you laugh too! Music helps your moods and emotions to flow out and be expressed. Movies tell stories that can make you feel that others have shared this journey (or even a part of this journey) with you. These films can serve as a warning or be a relief for what you saved yourself from. They can be humorous, insightful, moving, and inspiring. The movies listed in this chapter can help you see some of the same things you experienced—only this time you are viewing the circumstances as an outsider. All of these ideas for connection are designed to bring you into community and to move you to a place of wholeness.

Healing Pathway 8. Friends

Spending time with friends can be extremely healing. While not every friend may fully understand what you are going through, they can provide a listening ear, be there for support, and make you laugh again. Laughter is undeniably amazing medicine for the soul. Make time in your schedule to spend with friends and to go have FUN. Go out for dinner to your favourite restaurant, do an activity together, or take a day away with a friend for the sole purpose of connection and enjoyment.

Now is the time to rebuild your support system. Part of the narcissist's tactics were to isolate you in order to control you. Part of their brainwashing included separating you from those you love and care about, and from the people who love and care about you. There are likely many people who truly miss you. You will find that countless friends will love to reconnect with you and to assist in your healing process.

Healing Pathway 9. Fellow Survivors

After learning what a narcissist is, that I had been taken in by one, and was married to one, one of the biggest surprises that came to me was how many other people have experienced and lived through narcissistic relationships. The more I dug into this topic the more people started coming out of the woodwork with their stories. Numerous people had experiences with narcissists who were ex-boyfriends, ex-wives, ex-husbands, a sister-in-law, a brother, aunt, father, mother, grandfather, sibling, co-worker, and best friend. You are not alone in this! There are so many people with their own stories about narcissistic, psychological, and emotional abuse who truly do understand you and what you are going through.

It is important to have support from people who honestly understand and *get* what you have gone through. Unless they have experienced it, others will not understand the depths of the psychological games that have been played on you. Fellow survivors get it! They have lived through the warzone. It is likely that many of your friends won't completely comprehend what such an experience is like, so be prepared for that. You would have to personally experience someone with zero empathy or watch a plethora of Nazi movies to grasp how inhumane some people can truly be.

You can also expect that the mutual friends you had with the narcissist won't fully believe you because they have only seen the mask and the public persona of the narcissist (this same persona that you originally saw and fell in love with). Remember that narcissists only take their mask off for their intimate partners and family members. Fellow survivors also understand this.

It can be useful to join support groups or online forums that deal with those who are in relationship with a narcissist and/or who are getting out of these relationships. These people truly understand your experience. Many of the people on these forums are a few steps ahead of you in terms of their journey so you can glean some good advice from them. You can also see that these people are moving on to a better place and it can give you great hope for your life after the narcissist.

Healing Pathway 10. Get Back in Touch with the Real You

Narcissistic abuse can take a lot out of us. Many of us sacrificed numerous things we loved to do in order to pour our energy into both pleasing the narcissist and saving our relationship. After I left my narcissist, I went through a process of rediscovering who I was before the relationship. It was quite eye-opening! How had I neglected and let slip from my life the things that I loved so much? I had neglected or put things on the shelf that were a huge part of me for the sake of building a life with this person. First of all, I needed to take ownership of the fact that *I* had let things slip. It was time to reclaim my life, interests, and other relationships.

Who were you before the trauma occurred? What did you love to do? What activities have you stopped or have you put on the back burner during this relationship? It's time to rediscover and explore your hobbies, interests, and passions again. You may also look at the relationships you had prior to the narcissist. Since most narcissists like to isolate you so that you will be more dependent on them, chances are you have vital relationships that have drifted and become distant. Initiating and rekindling these important friendships can be extremely rewarding and life giving.

Think of your identity, your personality, and your essence. What did people say about you in the past? How did you identify yourself in the past? Do you still have these vital traits? Have some grown dull or are currently absent from your life? It's time to rediscover the real you and embrace who you truly are!

Healing Pathway 11. Inspirational and Funny Quotes

There are many quotes sprinkled throughout this book that I discovered on my journey of knowledge and healing. Some of these may be insightful by their resonating truth. Others may make you laugh and simply raise your spirits.

> *Better to have loved and lost than to live with that crazy person the rest of your life.*[1]

> *Trying to reason with a narcissist is like trying to nail jello to a tree.*[2]

> *I will heal. You will always be a sociopath.*[3]

> *Narcissists play dumb when they're CAUGHT. You should never feel COMPELLED to explain the basic principles of common courtesy to an adult.*[4]

If I could go back to the day we met, I'd turn around and walk the other way.[5]

Don't make excuses for nasty people. You can't put a flower in an asshole and call it a vase.[6]

After you, hell should be easy.[7]

Narcissist (n): a more polite term for a self-serving, manipulative, evil asshole with no soul.[8]

Never defend yourself against a narcissist. They already know you're right! They just want you to go crazy trying to prove it.

—Anonymous

To a Narcissist; I only existed when you wanted sex … WOW!

—Anonymous

A narcissist lives by a certain set of rules otherwise known as, "Double Standards." You will be expected to abide by these rules. However, these exact same rules won't apply to them.

—Anonymous

Narcissistic Personalities are created and sustained. No one is born a narcissist. It is a habitual choice to be selfish and to lack empathy for other people. Never forget that it is a choice.[9]

—Shannon Thomas

Did you know that narcissist spelled backwards is "Asshole"? Hey, if they can make shit up, so can we.[10]

A narcissist is someone who demands you give up EVERYTHING, in order to be their nothing.[11]

A narcissist paints a picture of themselves as being the victim or innocent in all aspects. They will be offended by the truth. But what is done in the dark will come to light. Time has a way of showing people's true colors.[12]

—Karla Grimes, quoted by Eddie Corbano

The paradox is that no love can prove so intense as the love of two narcissists for each other.[13]

—Norman Mailer

Don't underestimate how secretive, dangerous, and manipulative a narcissist can be.[14]

—Cynthia French

The smarter you become about narcissistic abuse, the crazier the narcissist will say you are.[15]

Someone who really loves you doesn't want to hurt you.

—Anonymous

Our marriage ended because of religious differences. My husband thought he was God and I disagreed.[16]

—Finding Your Feet

Healing Pathway 12. Music

Music can be both cathartic and healing. Kesha's song, "Praying," very accurately portrays a relationship with a narcissist and the journey toward empowerment. Christina Perri's "Jar Of Hearts" is also a particularly excellent song to depict hoovering after the narcissistic discard.

When I was going through the worst of it, I had songs for every occasion. There were

- the songs to let the anger out: Lincoln Park's "One Step Closer" and "A Place for My Head";

- the lamenting songs: Elton John's "Don't Let the Sun Go Down on Me";

- the revenge songs: Carrie Underwood's "Before He Cheats"; and of course,

- the empowering songs: Cake's or Gloria Gaynor's version of "I Will Survive"; Nancy Sinatra's "These Boots Were Made for Walking"; and Gotye's "Somebody That I Used to Know."

Music is a powerful avenue of healing.

Healing Pathway 13. Movies

Movies and entertainment can play an important role in your healing process. You can gain a lot of wisdom and insight through watching narcissistic tendencies from an outsider's perspective. As an audience member, you can observe both the narcissist and the victim. You can have a more objective viewpoint because you are not directly and emotionally involved in what is playing out.

Through movies, such as the ones listed below, you can see the commonalities, the traps, the patterns, and the games that exist within narcissistic relationships. You can also recognize (and probably relate to) some of the victim's vulnerabilities. There are countless narcissistic traits that you will become aware of as you watch some of these films. Below are a few that I recommend to give you a broad spectrum of different types of narcissists.

Gaslight

This is a definite MUST SEE![17] I highly recommend this movie because the original theatrical play is where the definition of "gaslighting" came from. After watching this film you will definitely understand how the narcissist can slowly and subtly manipulate you to the point where you think you are going crazy. Ingrid Bergman and Charles Boyer star in this psychological thriller. The movie was made in 1944, so you may have to order it on Amazon. And it's worth it! Seriously, a MUST-watch film!

The Other Woman

If you need a good laugh and would like to see the narcissist get back a bit of his own, then this is the movie for you![18] When the wife Kate (Leslie Mann), the mistress Carly (Cameron Diaz), and the girlfriend Amber (Kate Upton) find out about each other, they team up against the narcissist, Mark (Nikolaj Coster-Waldau); he has been playing all three of them at the same time. Ultimately in this film, Mark, the narcissist, must face the consequences of his cheating and embezzlement. The karma is very sweet!

Big Eyes

This film is based on the true story of Margaret Keane (played by Amy Adams).[19] It portrays the world-famous artist who is known for her paintings with the "big eyes." After escaping a horrific marriage and being instantly swept off her feet by the charming Walter Keane (Christoph Waltz), Margaret becomes bound to the ever-increasing demands of her narcissistic husband who is taking credit for all of Margaret's great artistic works. This film shows how magnetic charm can turn into abusive enslavement. It also demonstrates Margaret's journey of strength and courage to her final victory of freedom.

Dirty John

Dirty John is a Netflix original series, based on the true story of Debra Newell (played by Connie Britton) and sociopath John Meehan (Eric Bana).[20] There are many similarities between narcissists and sociopaths and there is a lot you can understand from watching this series. Perhaps the main point being just how deceptive and dangerous these types of personality disorders can really be. *Dirty John* is based on a true story. Debra's journey is incredible. You will have to watch this one to see how it turns out!

The Women

This film depicts a female narcissist who uses designer labels, sex, and her body to get whatever she wants.[21] The character of Crystal Allen (Eva Mendes) seduces the husband of Mary Haines (Meg Ryan). Although Crystal has a minor role in this film, it is interesting to see how the female narcissist operates. The lack of empathy, manipulation, self-centredness, arrogance, contempt for others, and the drive to keep up her appearance (especially sexually) portrays the traits of a woman narcissist.

The Other Boleyn Girl

Take your pick! The historical couple of both Anne Boleyn (Natalie Portman) and King Henry VIII (Eric Bana) are excellent examples of a narcissistic pair who come together.[22] Watch them vie for power!

CHAPTER 10

SELF-CARE

Ways to Heal: Fourteen to Nineteen

This next section of the healing journey is devoted to your intentional self-care. This includes your physical care; having an energy outlet and a healthy intake; and using journaling and gratitude to recharge and reset you. Your self-care is of the utmost importance at this time so find ways to do something to refresh your mind, body, and soul.

Healing Pathway 14. Physical Care

Many survivors of narcissistic abuse experience actual physical symptoms from the trauma that they have lived through. It makes sense since stress and trauma trigger physical reactions in the body. Physical symptoms of extreme stress can include migraine headaches, neck and shoulder pain, irritable bowel syndrome or other gut issues, chronic fatigue, adrenal fatigue, fibromyalgia, depression, panic attacks, and even pneumonia. At this time it is essential to take care of your physical wellbeing and to acknowledge that you have been through a great deal of stress.

When a person is put under stress, whether it is environmental, physical, financial, emotional (or all of the above), the body goes into fight-or-flight mode. This causes the adrenal glands to produce more stress and inflammation hormones in order to help you survive. In turn, this flooding of the body with inflammatory hormones wreaks havoc and can cascade into all sorts of physiological problems. Be aware of any physical symptoms you are facing. You may have been experiencing these symptoms for years or even decades without really noticing. Because of the fact that changes in the body can be subtle, you may have gotten used to living with these symptoms as your "normal."

When you are free from narcissistic abuse and when you no longer have the narcissist in your life, the physical differences you experience in your body can be both shocking and amazing. Many survivors have said that within a few weeks or months of being away from the narcissist they noticed a relief from anxiety, depression, migraines, high blood pressure, abnormally heavy periods, skin issues, allergies, irritable bowel syndrome, and other gut issues. Their bodies could finally relax because they were no longer being flooded with excessive amounts of adrenaline and the side effects thereof.

After leaving her narcissist, Val noticed within a few weeks that her chronic headaches and gut issues had vanished. She went to a naturopathic doctor five months later and did a hormone test. She learned her adrenal glands were completely shot. Val was diagnosed with adrenal fatigue and her body was experiencing polar opposites in the hormonal spectrum. The various types of stress and inflammation hormones were through the roof with their high numbers, which caused some of her other hormones to be so low that they were not even on the charts. After eight months of taking supplements, meditating daily, eliminating caffeine, and intentionally decreasing any additional stress, Val's chronic neck and shoulder pain left and her hormones started to regulate.

Stress needs a physical outlet and will always find a way to express itself through our bodies. It is important to address the ways that our bodies are reacting to our stress. Your physical healing is not an overnight process. It takes awareness, time, and being intentional to make your physical care a priority.

Healing Pathway 15. Energy Outlet and Healthy Intake

Get some exercise! Exercise will increase the endorphins in your body and it will give your emotional state an incredible boost! Going outside for some fresh air with a scenic view to get the blood pumping and increase your heart rate can definitely do wonders for your body as well as your mind. Whether it's walking, cycling, running, skiing, kayaking, or hiking, you will feel better by getting the blood pumping through your veins. You may even experience the feel-good endorphin rush!

Some forms of exercise are particularly great ways to let off some steam. You can pump some iron, go to a kickboxing class, throw some punches, learn a martial art, or hit some golf balls. Other gentle physical outlets such as stretching, yoga, dance, and Tai Chi are very effective for creating that inner calm. The latter types of exercises also physically lower your resting blood pressure and put you in a peaceful, feel-good state. Whatever forms you choose, exercise is a natural de-stressor. Your body will always feel great afterwards, and your overall moods will be elevated.

This is also the time when you need to get regular sleep. Sleep helps your body deal with stress and strengthens your parasympathetic nervous system, which aids in restoring and healing the body. If you are having trouble sleeping, try meditating right before you go to bed to calm your mind down. Essential oils such as lavender, Roman chamomile (rather than the German chamomile used for a tea infusion), and sandalwood are also excellent for enhancing your sleep. Put the oils on your feet, hands, your temples, the back of your neck, or on your pillow. Melatonin and magnesium are also effective natural supplements to deepen your sleep.

Although at times like these we would love to eat a pizza (or two), grab a few tubs of our favourite Ben & Jerry's ice cream, delve into a bottomless bag of corn chips (or whatever your comfort food might be), it is important to be mindful of your intake. Your nutrition and diet can greatly impact your body's ability to deal with stress. Anything that you can do to reduce your stress after being with a narcissist will help your healing and wellbeing. This includes having good nutrition. A healthy nutritional intake is vital to your recovery.

There are certain foods that actually help to de-stress the body. Stress-lowering foods are comprised of those that are high in antioxidants, vitamin C, and Omega 3s. Foods high in antioxidants and vitamin C include the colourful fruits and veggies such as blueberries, strawberries, raspberries, artichokes, oranges, peppers, beans, beets, spinach, and of course don't forget the dark chocolate! These antioxidant-rich foods boost our immunity, give us vitality, and lower our stress hormones. Foods high in Omega 3s, such as avocados, salmon, tuna, sushi, sardines, and halibut, are great for our brain health as well as for decreasing depression. At this time, feel free to go nuts! Pistachios, almonds, walnuts, and pecans are also full of the omega 3s that help to lower blood pressure and reduce stress.

The foods you will want to minimize or eliminate (especially in this stressful season) include white sugar (the biggest inflammatory food), white flour products, trans fats (mostly in fried and processed foods), and sweeteners such as aspartame. It's also a good idea to limit your caffeine and alcohol intake for now. Make an effort to have a healthy intake, an effective energy outlet, and a way to treat your body like the temple that it is.

Healing Pathway 16. Journal

Journal all past experiences and your ongoing feelings. Writing things down helps to acknowledge all that you went through—the narcissistic raging moments, the belittlement, the psychological violence, the gaslighting, denials, accusations, and the crazy making. Now that you are out of the relationship and you don't have the psychological torture of gaslighting, you can be more grounded in the reality of what happened to you. Although we don't want to stay in a place of trauma, it is important to acknowledge all that you have gone through. This can prevent abuse amnesia and rebounding back to the narcissist when the hoovering comes. It can also be cathartic to release the trauma that you have gone through.

Many times, those of us who have been in a relationship with a narcissist have been using numbing as a coping mechanism. One of the best things you can do for yourself to get out of the numbing phase is to acknowledge your emotions—both the good and the bad. Start writing down and even expressing out loud how you are feeling, by frequently checking in with yourself as you continue to write throughout your healing journey. Counselling, therapy, and confiding in trusted friends are other ways of working through the numbness.

People who end up with narcissists are often so focused on pleasing other people and meeting their needs that they lack the awareness of what their own feelings and needs are. Many of us have a habitual lifestyle of minimizing our own feelings. You may have grown up in a home where your feelings were never discussed or they were negated. You may have been told to "suck it up" when you were hurting or feeling sad. When you have never had the freedom or awareness that your feelings are significant and that your emotions are important signals to be listened to, you may be frozen and unaware of what you truly feel. This is where journaling can help build within you the important awareness for your wholeness and emotional health.

Also remember and record those moments when your gut was speaking to you that something was off. What were some of the signs that you chose to ignore for the sake of the relationship? This will help you get back in touch with your intuition and cause you to recognize the signs and feelings to watch out for when you run into another narcissist. Write down the things that your gut is telling you now. Part of recovering your voice is to pay attention to, listen, honour, and respect your voice and intuition. This will put you back on track to return to yourself.

Healing Pathway 17. Gratitude

Gratitude involves constantly finding things in your daily life to appreciate, no matter how small. You may be thankful that you enjoyed a great meal today, that you had a heartfelt visit with a friend, that you can cuddle with a loyal furry friend, or that you have beautiful views where you live. You can be thankful for a song you heard, that you are healthy, that you have wonderful friends, that you have the gift of sight, and that you have a roof over your head. *Feel* your gratitude by savouring and loving everything that you have. Open your eyes to all the amazing things that are in your life. Whatever the day holds, I promise, when you look at it with the eyes of gratitude, you will find so much to be thankful for.

Keep a gratitude journal. The beginning of your journey to freedom from a narcissist will most likely be a rocky one. However, each day you can find things to be thankful for because they put you into a grateful frame of mind. You can always choose to be grateful that you have survived this experience and can take valuable life lessons from it.

If you are having a really tough time finding something to be grateful for, go through old pictures and remember happy memories from different times in your life. You have had some truly wonderful moments in your life. Reflect on those memories and be grateful that you have experienced some pretty amazing things.

Being thankful really shifts our mindset and opens our eyes to the blessings we have.

Through gratitude, you will experience a shift and it will make a way for you to attract more good things into your life. Take time each day to be grateful. It is a game-changer!

Healing Pathway 18. Self-Care

Self-care is of primary importance at this time. It's time to focus on taking care of yourself. Self-care is any activity that we deliberately do in order to take care of our mental, emotional, and physical health.

People may be hesitant to engage in self-care because it is perceived as "selfish." This feeds into the frustrating misconception that anything we do that is not one hundred percent self*less* is instead self*ish*. However, when we engage in a high level of self-care, we are actually able to give *more* to others. Having a *lifestyle* of healthy self-care is vital to your wellbeing. You will notice that not only do your moods and relationships improve, you become happier, more at peace, and more gracious to others when you have a high level of self-care. The concept that "You are to put on your own oxygen mask first before helping others" is very real.

You cannot give from an empty cup. When you give from the overflow of your own cup, no one is ever drained.

Do something special for yourself on a regular basis. Doing little things for yourself shifts you from dwelling in your pain and past wounds and moves you to happiness and optimism. This gains momentum to create your beautiful new future. Self-care can be as simple as taking some time to curl up by the fire with a cup of tea and a good book. It can be going for a walk in nature. You can buy yourself a bottle of wine, get tickets to a see show with a friend, or treat yourself to a new perfume. Have your own home spa day complete with a mani-pedi and facial. Get a massage or buy some new clothes for your new life. Start making your own self-care the priority. You will feel amazing!

Self-care is giving yourself what you need.

How we see and treat ourselves is how others see and treat us. By engaging in self-care, not only will you feel better about yourself, you are also setting yourself up to be treated differently by others in the future.

Healing Pathway 19. Something New!

Engaging in a new activity or going to a new place can move us from dwelling in a haunting past to looking forward to a future with new possibilities! What are some activities that you've always wanted to do or learn? When we are in a place of new beginnings, the slate is wiped clean! It is an excellent time to do what you've always dreamed of doing. Perhaps it involves learning a new language, signing up for that marathon and completing the race, taking a class in painting or pottery, learning how to swim, going skydiving, or taking piano lessons. Embrace all that life has to offer!

Exploring a new place that you've never been to can also invite newness into your life. Take a day trip and discover a new area, whether it's a new location in your city or a different spot in nature. Seeing something different with fresh eyes renews the soul and jolts us into curiosity and exploration mode. Maybe there is an art gallery you'd like to investigate, an outdoor concert you can attend, or a different park you've never been to where you can go for a walk or simply read a book. Now is a wonderful time to be a tourist in your own city and explore some new sights in your local area. You can invite a group, a friend, or go solo.

Maybe it's time to book that big trip. I know numerous people, who, after getting out of a narcissistic relationship took the trip of a lifetime that they had always wanted to go on. Exploring a new culture or corner of the world can be just what you need to expand your mind and flood yourself with hope and optimism. Travelling, eating different foods, going on adventures, and trying new things can revitalize you like nothing else!

Now is the time to focus on and engage in many forms of self-care.

CHAPTER 11

EMPOWERMENT

Ways to Heal: Twenty to Twenty-Five

This final chapter on healing is about taking action to empower yourself. By the end of this chapter, you will have more tools in your belt to live in empowerment. The more knowledge you have about what you have experienced, the more you can move forward with confidence. Through having a deeper insight as to how narcissists operate, you understand their tricks. You can see through the false charm, manipulation, and gaslighting. You also have better insight and awareness of your own patterns and triggers. Because of this knowledge, you now have a choice to change. You have learned to reprogram your mind for healthy beliefs and you now know your true self-worth.

You won't need anything from them in order to move forward in your own life. Not even an apology. You have accepted that you will not get a genuine one and that's okay because you no longer need it. After reading this chapter, you will have an understanding of the difference between forgiveness and reconciliation. You will not be focused on controlling the justice of your situation as you know that justice has a way of working itself out and that a person always does reap what they sow. Ultimately, you know that you are the one to give yourself power and you are the one to choose to live in it from this moment on.

Let's continue in your healing and empowerment.

Healing Pathway 20. Arm Yourself with Knowledge

Knowledge empowers. The more awareness and understanding of Narcissistic Personality Disorder (NPD) that you have, the more empowered you will feel. Read books, blogs, articles, and listen to YouTube videos to help you understand what you are going through. It is very insightful to learn about NPD; how narcissists view people, relationships, and the world, and what their patterns are. It is also very refreshing to know that you were not singled out for their abuse. Narcissists ALWAYS end up treating the people who they are the closest to like trash. You were not the only one to be treated by them in this way, and they will continue to be abusive toward the next person they are close to. Arming yourself with knowledge also prepares you for their future text-book behaviours that they will engage in (such as hoovering).

Hindsight is everything. Many people discover who the narcissist really was and what their patterns were *after* they leave. It is eye-opening to see how people can truly be this cruel and devoid of empathy. Narcissists operate incredibly differently from normal people. They are not capable of remorse, empathy, or for truly loving and caring for another person.

As was discussed earlier, Kailey was grateful to read about hoovering before she experienced it. Kailey had been away from her narcissist for quite some time and had zero contact with him. However, true to clinical behaviour, four months after she left, Kailey was bombarded with all kinds of hoovering. Eventually it slowed down since there was no response from her. That's when he began to hoover Kailey's family. Kailey knew that this textbook behaviour would happen because she educated both herself and her family. When her family did not get sucked in and did not respond either, eventually the hoovering stopped. Being forearmed with knowledge will help you to not get sucked back into the manipulation and lies, and it will help you look at what NPD is all about from an objective outsider's point of view.

Healing Pathway 21. Reprogram Your Mind

In your relationship with a narcissist, you have constantly been bombarded with messages that your perceptions are false. You have been programmed to think that your feelings are invalid and everything is your fault. Obviously *you* are taking their abusive treatment in the wrong way since, after all, they were "just joking!" It's time to get rid of all the toxic projecting and gaslighting this person has tried to program into you.

Think of all the ways the narcissist has torn you down so that you can rewrite their scripts. What specific words did they say? What did you accept or falsely believe about yourself as a result of their words? Don't let your narcissist's words of tearing you down be the voice inside your head.

Now look at the truth of who you really are. Write down all the beautiful and unique things about yourself, and what other people love and appreciate about you. Go back and read cards and emails. Recall and write down specific positive words that others have spoken to and about you. Write out what others appreciate about you, what you love about yourself, and the relational gifts that you give to others. You will begin to rediscover the *truth* of who you are. Now write these words down and review them on a regular basis. It's time to revise the toxic, harmful scripts that have been playing in your mind and rewrite what is positive, true, and wonderful about you.

The journey of discovering your worth can be a bumpy road of change. When you stay the course, you will find you are equipped with tools of empowerment, and have arrived in the land of freedom.

Affirmations and meditations are other great ways to reprogram your self-conscious. Affirmations are positive statements that you speak over yourself. They are best used in the present tense and on a regular basis to uplift your spirits and put you on a positive track. A few examples of affirmations used in the present tense would be, "I am healing and getting stronger every day." "I am a beautiful, worthy human being who deserves kindness and respect." "I have healthy, wonderful relationships in my life."

The original significance of the word affirmation means "to make steady and strengthen." Affirmations help us to rewire our brains. They raise our feel-good hormones and shape our brains to think positive thoughts on a regular basis. Affirmations combined with guided meditations are wonderful to replace the destructive words that the narcissist has spoken over us and to transform and create new, life-giving thought patterns.

Meditation puts you back in the driver's seat of your wellbeing and empowers you. The previous emotional trauma from a narcissist can lend to a profound sense of helplessness. Having experienced severe trauma, the amygdala (the part of the brain that alerts us to a threat and sends us into fight-or-flight mode) becomes hyperactive. Even when something is not threatening to us, because we've been walking on eggshells for so long, the brain now looks for perceived threats everywhere. Trauma can actually sever the communication between the emotional and organizing parts of our brain, and it can shrink the hippocampus (which affects our memory and learning).

However, daily meditation diminishes our automatic reactions to the fight-or-flight response, which tends to go haywire after trauma. Regular meditation also helps to change our thought patterns and strengthens new neural pathways by increasing the grey matter density in our brain that relates to our emotion regulation. Meditation allows greater awareness and mindfulness of your thoughts, emotions, and needs, which you have likely shut down in order to survive.

Healing Pathway 22. Learn to Accept the Apology You Will Never Get

You will never get an apology from the narcissist, not a real one. A genuine apology would mean admitting they have done something wrong and that they are not perfect. In the eyes of a narcissist, they themselves have never done anything wrong. They continually view themselves as the perpetual victim in life where everything that happens is someone else's fault.

The rare time that you might get some sort of faux-pology, it is likely to be a half-hearted, self-righteous form of a justification that skirts around the issue and is often (when you listen carefully), disguised as a deeper accusation toward you or a covert compliment of themselves. Narcissists won't apologize for the emotional, verbal, physical, sexual, and financial abuse that they inflict upon you. They won't acknowledge or feel any remorse for their pathological lying, the psychological warfare, or their serial cheating. Do not expect or bother to wait for an apology from them.

> *Accept that you're never going to get an apology, because they're incapable of feeling like they've ever done anything wrong.*

Once you accept that you will never get an apology (or at least a real one), it is so much easier to move on. If you need to, write a letter to yourself with the words that acknowledge the wrongs they have done and the type of regret and remorse you would like to hear in a heartfelt, sincere apology. Writing this letter can help you to recognize the pain of what you have been through and all that you have experienced. No matter the orator, it helps to hear the words expressed: "I'm sorry." Create the apology you need to hear. Just recognize and accept that it won't come directly from them.

Healing Pathway 23. Forgiveness and Reconciliation Are Two Different Things

Many times people unknowingly interchange the words forgiveness and reconciliation; however, they are two very distinct acts. Reconciliation requires forgiveness; however, forgiveness does not require you to be reconciled with the other person. It is also important to note that neither reconciliation nor forgiveness are about one person being a doormat and the other person being a bulldozer.

Let's start with what forgiveness is and isn't. Forgiveness is not about excusing, ignoring, or downplaying what happened. Forgiveness is different from condoning something or failing to see that a certain action is wrong. Forgiveness does not mean that you accept abusive behaviours, nor does it mean that you will return to an abusive relationship. To forgive is to release a debt owed to you from past wrongs (whether the debt is real or perceived). Forgiveness involves releasing resentment and/or vengeance against another person.

On the other hand, reconciliation means the relationship is being restored. In reconciliation you are actively dialoguing with the other person about what happened and *both* people are actively seeking to restore the relationship. Reconciliation involves the sharing of and listening to feelings from *both* people. There is often remorse from one or both people, a strong desire to re-establish trust, and a commitment from both parties to rebuild the relationship. *Both* parties must actively be involved for reconciliation to happen. However, there are some people with whom it is not possible, safe, or healthy to reconcile and you should not seek to restore such a relationship.

Herein lies the difference between these two terms. Forgiveness is a solo act and does not involve participation from the other person in order to be completed. You do not have to have an active relationship with the other person going forward when you forgive them. Whereas you can release the other person through forgiveness without having a present or future relationship with them, reconciliation requires involvement from both parties and means that there is and will be a relationship going forward.

When you forgive another person you are no longer demanding repayment for the wrongs that someone else has done to you. You have made a deliberate choice to release any resentment or desire for vengeance toward the person who has harmed you. In essence, you are choosing your *own* freedom by letting go of negative emotions, bitterness, and resentment. The narcissist may not deserve or even want your forgiveness (since they have done "nothing wrong").

However, you don't forgive them for their sake—you forgive them for your own.

A grudge acts like termites to your soul. From the outside you may look fine, but you are slowly being eaten away.[1]

—Lee Jordan and Beth Jordan

Not forgiving can have physical affects in our bodies. Carrying the hurt or anger of an offense leads the body to activate stress hormones such as adrenaline and cortisol. These are hard on our hearts, raise our blood pressure, cause inflammation, and affect our mental health and outlook in life. When we don't forgive, we think we are punishing the other person, but the real person we are harming is ourselves.

Harboring unforgiveness is like drinking poison and hoping your enemy will die.[2]

—Joyce Meyer

Forgiveness on the other hand has many positive physiological effects on the body. It decreases our stress, anxiety, our inflammatory hormones, gives us a stronger immune system, and increases our self-esteem.

It is equally as important to acknowledge your own missteps and to extend that forgiveness to yourself. You must forgive yourself for "not seeing it." Or for sensing that something was off and yet still moving ahead in the relationship despite what your gut was telling you. You might need to forgive yourself for putting you or your family in harm's way from the narcissist. You may need to forgive yourself for staying too long, or for returning back to the narcissist too many times. It's time to let go of punishing, resenting, or seeking payback from yourself. Holding a grudge against anybody (even yourself) imprisons you. Forgiveness, whether it is for the other person or yourself, ultimately sets you free.

To forgive is to set a prisoner free and discover the prisoner was you.[3]

—Lewis B. Smedes

Forgiveness helps us to store things differently in our memories. When we don't forgive there is always a sense of injustice, an edge, or a grudge that is stored in our remembrances. However, when we forgive, the memories don't carry that bitter sting and we aren't held captive to them in the present moment. I'm sure we've all been around the person who continually relives their pain and bitterness to the point that it seems fresh, raw, and stinging as if it had happened yesterday, when in fact it was decades ago.

When you experience the opposite of someone who lives in forgiveness, they still remember it, they just aren't living it. It is a part of their history and clearly not part of their present. Their experience is not an open, raw, and festering wound. Rather, it is a scar from the past that has become a mark of wisdom, which has truly made them better in the present.

Perhaps you have heard the classic story of two prisoners of war who are reunited after many years. The first man asks, "Have you forgiven your captors yet?" The second man answers, "No. And I never will." "Well," replies the first man, "then they still have you in prison."

Forgiveness is an internal process where you work through the hurt, gain an understanding of what happened, rebuild a sense of safety, and let go of the grudge.[4]

—Ryan Howes

It is true that you have had a unique and horrific experience. It is likely that no one will ever know exactly what you went through. Forgiveness is a personal matter. And forgiveness is ultimately your choice.

Healing Pathway 24. Karma Waits

Realize that their destruction is inevitable in some form. No one is immune to escape the universal law of sowing and reaping. In time, for better or for worse, we will all reap what we sow.

In the beginning it may seem like everything is going amazingly well for the narcissist. After all, they do not even have the sadness, pain, or remorse in the breakup process because they have callously discarded you. It may seem that they have managed to escape the consequences for their abusive behaviour since they most likely also took the lion's share of your finances and property. They may have their arm around some new eye-candy as they boldly proclaim to the world that they have finally met their soulmate. They may appear to have this fabulous new life and have gotten away pain-free without having accrued any costs.

While this might seem to be the case at first glance, researchers have always been intrigued by the fact that narcissists are ultimately playing a losing game as they are prone to self-defeating behaviours. Although the narcissist can initially make a good impression on people, their relationships almost always fail miserably over time. They only have other people's admiration, a fickle sense of superiority, and feelings of power for short bursts of time. When people catch onto their mask and no longer admire them, they must start again. They never really get what they want as their behaviour self-sabotages them.

To the core of their being they are deeply discontented and unhappy people. Combine that with the fact that they have to live with their own company for their entire life. Can you honestly think of a worse punishment than that? You were with them for a time and it became unbearable. They must be with themselves 24-7 for their entire lifetime. That's quite the sentence! Not only do they have to live with themselves, but their deepest fears will come to haunt them at one time or another.

It has been said that narcissists have many great fears in life: fear of exposure for who they truly are; fear of being alone; fear of any indifference toward them; and fear of their victim's success after they are away from the narcissist. Their greatest fears revolve around both their image and maintaining control.

Fear of Exposure

Narcissists will fight like hell to keep their perfect image of their false mask in place. The risk of other people discovering who they truly are is more than they can bear. After all, even they cannot look at their own true self. It is too repulsive. Having their true self exposed is their worst nightmare. This is why they will lie, deny, and manipulate the people around them to believe their false mask. The danger for them is when you know the truth. You know what really happened and you know WHO they *really* are. Since you could be a threat because you could expose them, you must be destroyed. This is why they project their evil deeds onto you and others.

Fiera was told by her narcissist that his first wife cheated on him multiple times, was mentally insane, and even physically abusive to him. A few years later, when Fiera actually met the woman, she had a hard time believing a word of it. The narcissist's first wife seemed to be a very generous, kind-hearted, gentle, and extremely loyal person. Years later after Fiera's own divorce she finally talked to the first wife and heard her side ... it was ironic how it completely mirrored Fiera's experience! The first wife knew his true self and so the narcissist had to say or do whatever was possible to turn the tables on her so as not be found out. Since his first wife could expose him, he had to paint her in a such horrific light as to refute her credibility and falsely discredit her character.

Fear of Being Alone

Deep down, narcissists do not like who they really are. They cannot face themselves. Have you ever heard of a narcissist being alone for a long period of time to work on themselves or even to take a break between relationships? It doesn't happen. Many times they overlap their intimate relationships or partners. They MUST find a person to give them attention and to fill their void. This is why they will go to great lengths to win you over in the love-bombing stage, particularly if they haven't had their "hit" of attention in a while. They wear the mask so they don't have to be alone. Narcissists have no real emotional connections and if they are alone, they will have to face themselves and potentially see their true self. It is during the miniscule times between supply (if any), that they are living one of their greatest fears.

Fear of Indifference

When a person uses the grey-rock strategy or goes into no contact with the narcissist, it is one of the narcissist's worst fears coming true because you are now *indifferent* toward them. When the once bubbly, empathetic person is no longer there to give the narcissist attention, affirmation, and accolades, a piece of them dies. They expect your adoration. Your love validated their false mask and stroked their larger-than-life ego. Now that's gone.

Then they expected you to be reactive toward their abuse and manipulation. Your anger showed them that they are in control and that you can indeed be activated and provoked by the words that they speak. However, when you do nothing ... it completely overturns their world. Your indifference means they don't have power over you. Not only do you no longer give them the supply they need, but you are absolutely not affected by them. Since they cannot generate their emotions from you or on their own, they will need to find another supply and find it fast!

Fear of Your Success

Another one of a narcissist's deepest fears comes to life when their partner leaves them and becomes more thriving, successful, and vibrant than ever before. Success is your best revenge and it will serve your own life as well.

> *A narcissist's true nightmare is a survivor who is able to transcend the abuse and use it to empower himself or herself. That is the type of revenge that lasts a lifetime.*

Enjoying life, having healthy self-respect and self-care, along with having amazing relationships and being successful is truly the best revenge. Ideally, your motive for being an incredible success is not for the sake of revenge (because you are not even thinking about the narcissist who is not worthy to occupy space in your precious thoughts). You are doing this for yourself. You absolutely deserve to thrive, to be your best, and to fall in love with someone who deserves you and who will treat you with kindness, honour, and respect.

The best part is that when you have forgiven, released, and moved on with your own life, you won't even give a second thought to what the narcissist is doing with theirs. Neither the bitter path nor the codependent path is for you. Your past with them is in the past and you are now using this experience to become a wiser, richer soul.

Healing Pathway 25. Empower Yourself

Take the responsibility to heal and empower yourself. You are the only person who can own your life. Make sure that you do not allow yourself to fall into victim mode. To continue to see yourself as the victim would be on a par with the narcissistic *modus operandi*. A couple of the ways that the *Merriam-Webster* dictionary defines a victim are

- one that is subjected to oppression, hardship, or mistreatment
- one that is tricked or duped[5]

While you may have been a victim for a time, this does not have to remain your story. It is essential that you do not stay in this place. In order to escape the powerless victim mentality, you must start taking responsibility for everything in your life and decide how you will grow into becoming an even better person. When you take the responsibility to heal and grow, you will create your own happiness. By taking responsibility, you don't have to wait for someone else to fix your life for you. Your healing can begin now with a decision to take complete ownership of it. Do everything that you need to do to get healed. Be humble enough to learn in what ways you need to improve to become the person you ultimately want to be.

Rather than viewing what happened *to* you, look at how everything has worked *for* you.

It takes a radical mind shift to believe that our worst circumstances are working for us and toward something good in our lives. When we can focus on what we have gained from this experience rather than on what we have lost, we become less reactive and more proactive. A big part of empowering ourself is taking this mental shift in belief.

Believe that tremendous good will come out of this situation and that this experience is transforming you into an even better person. Despite what you may have experienced, choose to believe right now that you are worthy of an amazing life and wonderful relationships.

Find creative and fun little ways to empower and build yourself up. Give yourself reminders of who you are and the bright future you are going to have. Priscilla changed the name of her narcissist on her phone and emails to, "YOU DESERVE BETTER!" While she could have changed the handle to all kinds of colourful, descriptive words that were floating around in her head at the time, she instead chose something positive for herself. Every time she got a text, a phone call, or an email from him, she saw this empowering reminder. It was a constant message that she was not limited by that abusive relationship, that she did deserve a kind and loving relationship, and that she was now creating a different, uplifting future for herself. Priscilla never did respond to anything "YOU DESERVE BETTER!" had to say to her. She would simply smile and remember her empowering truth.

You are an amazing person who always deserves the best. Never settle or accept anything less. Never.

PART V

Expel and Repel the Narcissist

This section is devoted to detecting the early warning signs that you might be in relationship with a narcissist, as well as making some shifts so that you become a person who repels rather than attracts narcissists.

CHAPTER 12

SIXTEEN EARLY WARNING SIGNS

Okay, I would like to put a BIG DISCLAIMER on this chapter to say that some of these early warning signs do not necessarily mean you are in the presence of a narcissist—although when you see multiple signs, consider it a good possibility. Some of these traits can be regarded as yellow flags (proceed with extreme caution) or red flags (run like hell!) for any relationship. Regardless if you discover the person to be a full-blown narcissist or not, these traits forebode difficulty; they are unhealthy signs in a relationship. Take your time with a person who has these characteristics. Look a little deeper with your eyes wide open to see who they really are.

1. A Fast and Furious Relationship Start

The fast and furious can happen in a romantic relationship or even in a friendship. It goes something like this: You have *everything* in common. You feel like you have never been understood so well by anyone in your life. They text you and call you on a regular and/ or consistent basis, to the point where sometimes it feels like an obsession. You have this amazing connection that you've never had before. You've met your soulmate.

For example, after only a few months of casually dating, Gwen was told by her boyfriend that he had never shared such a deep connection with anyone before, including his previous two marriages. This statement could mean many things and it is worth investigating. It could range from the man being an overly enthusiastic romantic, to a codependent, to a love-bombing narcissist.

Although this is the stuff that movies are made of, most often, when it seems too good to be true, it probably is. Remember, all that glitters is not gold. Hopefully for your sake something like this would be a genuine connection and this can sometimes happen. However, keep your eyes open. You could be getting the socks charmed off you in the love bombing stage. This is when the narcissist is mirroring you and getting to know everything about you, including your ultimate weaknesses. Later, when the time is right, through this deep knowledge of you, the discard will be that much easier for them. Remember, when you are "love bombed," it *seems* that you have met your soulmate and that you are on top of the world. You have "never" had attention like this before. Most relationships that start like a house on fire end with great devastation and destruction. At least now, you have the wisdom and experience to know how the fast and furious can go.

New love is always exciting and it is natural to tend to lose our heads in the beginning.

You can completely get caught up, spending so much time with the other person and cocooning in your new relationship. However, pay attention. Something in your gut may tell you the relationship is going a bit too fast. You may start to feel a little out of touch with your world of friends and interests. Pay attention to this! TEST IT!

- Find out if you actually do have *everything* in common. Look for some genuine evidence that they are doing what they say their interests are. Do their past experiences and actions match their present talk?

- Be intentional to slow things down, give it time, and pay attention to the subtle shifts in the relationship. Chances are their fast and furious pace will be difficult to keep up in the long run.

- Keep in mind that a good time to introduce your new significant other to your friends is early on in the relationship. Introduce this person to your friends, the ones who you know will have your back and speak the truth to you. It is more likely they will give you their objective opinion and tell you what they see with both the good and the bad in the beginning of the relationship and before you are established. People are much less inclined to say what they really think when it seems that you have made a solid commitment. When you include people early on in your relationship, it helps to slow things down compared to when you are more isolated to just the two of you. You are also able to experience this person and who they are in different contexts.

2. Something Feels Off

Although this may seem like a vague, rather than a concrete clue, experts say the fact that something feels off is one of the top indicators of a narcissistic relationship. Your gut knows. When things aren't lining up or when there is any type of insincerity about them, trust your gut and look deeper. Never ignore that nagging feeling; it can save you from much heartache and pain. Narcissists appear to have it all together so it is difficult to see behind their mask and hear between their lies. If discernment isn't your top strength, make sure you have an intuitive person in your life to be a second set of eyes for you. Some people have the gift of knowing the essence of a person within one meeting and they are bang on in their assessment on every occasion. If you have people like this in your life, ask for their open and honest evaluation.

Afterward, when Jutta was out of her relationship, she found out that several people had a bad feeling about her husband after getting to know him. Others had a distinct, sharp, negative feeling after one single interaction with him. Unfortunately no one said anything until after she left the marriage. It was then that Jutta realized she had been ignoring that intermittent "off" feeling for a long time.

Love is blind. Pay attention to your gut. Ask for and consider what the discerning people in your life have to say.

3. A Lack of Gratitude

All the narcissists who have been present in my life seem to have a lack of gratitude in common. Now it can also be that some people have bad manners or they are unaware and careless of courteous behaviour or they are just plain selfish. I think each of us has failed to express a well-deserved "thank you" at one time or another. We may have felt grateful, had wonderful thoughts about the other person whom we are receiving from, and have simply forgotten to express it.

When you see a lack of gratitude on the part of the other person, look a little deeper and see if this a consistent way of life for them.

After a while you may begin to notice that it's not just a lack of gratitude, but an entitlement attitude. This is when you really need to pay attention. How do they receive from the people who have been in their life for a long time? Do they consistently lack gratitude or do they have any entitlement attitudes with long-term friends or family members? Is a lack of gratitude along with an entitlement mentality creeping in whenever they receive anything from you or are served by you in some way? If you notice their character is moving toward entitlement, you could be dealing with an immature and selfish person, or you could be dealing with a narcissist.

4. A Lack of Curiosity About You

This is an intriguing one. When Olivia was dating her narcissistic husband, she commented several times that it was interesting that he never once asked her about her past relationships. Olivia wasn't referring to personal or sexual details about past relationships. She simply thought that it was odd that he didn't have a natural curiosity about the person he was dating and some of her relational history. In normal relationships, people ask questions because they want to get to know the other person, they care about them, and they are doing some due diligence for their own good. This is especially important if you are considering spending the rest of your life with this person. Olivia even noticed that after they had been married, he still never asked her questions about the various chapters in her life before they met. Olivia realized there wasn't a curiosity or an inquisitiveness to go deeper and really get to know her because he simply didn't care. She also felt the contrast after dating a couple of different men post-divorce. These men asked a great many questions. Yes. Curiosity is definitely a huge part of any healthy relationship. If you are dealing with a narcissist or perhaps someone with extremely poor relational skills, a lack of curiosity is not a good sign.

In another instance, Ava had a narcissistic friend who would ask her questions. When Ava would start answering, her friend would interrupt and tell her what she thought Ava's experience was. There was no true listening involved and no desire for insight into the other person. Ultimately, there was no hungering for further knowledge from a desire to understand the other person, even though that is something that happens in healthy relationships.

Nevertheless, just because someone has a lack of curiosity or poor listening skills does not necessarily mean that this person has crossed the line into being a narcissist. And yet, with a lack of curiosity you may begin to see that your relationship is not balanced and that it has become one-sided. Now is the time to set some new boundaries and standards and intentionally choose relationships that are mutually fulfilling.

5. A Lack of Affirmation and Acknowledgment

In healthy relationships, your partner and your friends affirm you, encourage you, support you, and celebrate with you. Solid relationships are often a motivating, driving force for success and your thriving relationships will champion you on to greater heights. Pay attention to how the people who are the closest to you acknowledge and affirm both you and the other people in their life.

When Isla was in a friendship with a narcissist (they had both been single gals for years and both wanted to find their forever love), she began to notice that whenever amazing things happened in her life, there would be no congratulations or affirming words from her best friend. It seemed the whole world (or at least the other people in Isla's personal life and in the world of Facebook) would be congratulating and applauding her for some accomplishment or for passing a huge milestone. Yet whenever the topic would come up around her best friend, her friend would swiftly change the subject back to herself.

When the time came for Isla's wedding, her "best friend" gave Isla nothing. Although Isla treated her best friend to everything for the wedding—hotel room, her dress, professional hair and make-up, jewelry, and a day of zip-lining at the staggette—her BFF couldn't be bothered to get a shower gift, a wedding gift, or even a card for the biggest day of Isla's life. All the while, her friend flaunted about how she flew first class to come to the wedding and how she was making a lovely holiday for herself for a couple of weeks following the wedding. That should have been a huge red flag, except Isla didn't know about narcissism at the time.

Although you may have people in your life who perhaps are not in tune with how you would like to be supported, when things reach this extreme, realize that this is very unhealthy. You could be dealing with a narcissist.

While there may be people in your life who will not be your best cheerleaders, pay attention if those who are closest to you are adverse to giving you any type of acknowledgement or affirmation. Let them know how you feel and what you need. If they are still not supportive of you or if they actually demotivate and discourage you, move on! You deserve better and you may be dodging a landmine.

6. Disrespect and Overstepping Your Boundaries

When you have disrespect in a relationship, it is impossible to have a solid bond. Period. Disrespect prevents intimacy and closeness. It is a huge barrier to relational success.

Respect involves valuing another person's thoughts, opinions, feelings, and experiences. When respect is present, you are free to be yourself, to feel safe, and to be connected in a relationship. In contrast, when you are disrespected in a relationship, the other person disregards what you want and need, and is only concerned about their own desires and concerns.

> *There is a message in the way a person treats you ... Just listen.*[1]
>
> —R. H. Sin

Here's a test of respect. After giving someone a definite no or setting a firm boundary, see how they react. Can you agree to disagree? It is possible to have polar opposite needs, concerns, and values while still showing respect and regard for another person. What truly happens when you draw a line in the sand? Does the other person honour what you have to say? Or do they plow through your requests and boundaries and do what they want anyway?

> *Disagreement is one thing; disrespect is quite another.*[2]
>
> —Richard V. Reeves

Psychologists Dr. Henry Cloud and Dr. John Townsend write in their book, *Boundaries On Dating*, "Respectful people don't lose respect over time, they increase it ... This is a character trait. It is stable and not dependent on situations. So people who seem to stop respecting you over time, in all likelihood, *have never had true respect for others' needs and feelings.*"[3]

This clearly states that disrespecting other people is a *character* issue. It is not dependent on the recipient's behaviour. Disrespect has to do with the person being disrespectful and has little to do with the person being disrespected. There is nothing you can do to make a person respectful of you. This is their choice. Your choice is who you allow into your life.

> *A grown adult should NEVER have to be told to be respectful. Showing disrespect is not only immature, but it is a common trait of narcissism. Never tolerate those who are disrespectful.*[4]
>
> —Amreet

At its core, disrespect is deeply self-centred, which is a classic trait of a narcissist. When you tell a narcissist that you feel disrespected, they will deny, project, rationalize, or blame. They will neither apologize (faux-pologies don't count), nor will they change.

> *Pay attention to when people react with anger or hostility to your boundaries. You have found the edge where their respect for you ends.*

Although disrespect may not initially indicate that the person is a narcissist, the moment you start to set boundaries and you see rage, projecting, or blame, consider it a great possibility that you *are* dealing with a narcissist. Narcissists never accept boundaries or other people's noes. They will become enraged because they can no longer control and manipulate you. They may fear that you are onto them, that you will see the cracks in their façade and who the real person is underneath.

7. Materialistic: As a Matter of Superiority

Some people may take great pride or place a high value on their material things and it doesn't necessarily mean that they are a narcissist. Other people who are in certain professions may feel the need to maintain a certain lifestyle for business reasons. Still others may simply love and value certain luxuries items and a high quality of living. There is a type of healthy materialism (or stewardship) through which we take good care of ourselves and our possessions, and we can be generous to others through our wealth. However, when these material items become essential for the maintenance of an identity (or a false identity), you will want to look deeper.

Narcissists can become obsessed with money and materialism for the reason that it makes them feel superior and gives them the power, status, success, and fame they desire. Narcissists feel they raise their own worth in the eyes of others by acquiring certain things, which they use to maintain an image of superiority. Narcissists typically gravitate toward the high image possessions such as expensive cars, homes, watches, and clothes. Materialism to a narcissist is more about a means of making themselves superior to others.

Male narcissists tend to focus on the importance of a powerful position and status symbols such as certain exclusive memberships, their portfolio, their latest car, watch, or boat. Female narcissists on the other hand will focus on the physical image of their bodies, eternal youth, clothing, labels, jewelry, and accessories. Women narcissists tend to be in excellent shape and wear extremely revealing clothes in order to gain attention.

When someone is materialistic, you are not necessarily dealing with a narcissist. However, you may want to take the time to investigate their motivations and see if they are using materialism as a means of maintaining an image to gain superiority and control over others.

8. Past Behaviours

When someone has a questionable past, pay attention. Pay attention, pay attention, PAY VERY CLOSE ATTENTION! While it is good to believe the best in people, it is not wise to give unquestioning faith to someone who has had certain behaviours that you know you cannot live with.

When people feel genuine remorse for mistakes they've made in their past and when they have a desire to change, that's a start. Unfortunately many people do not make it out of the initial stage of desire toward actually moving forward to the action of changing. More often than not, their past behaviour will once again become their future behaviour. Make sure they have a long, proven track record of genuine change and that they are not the same person they were when they had their destructive past behaviours. *See* the fruit of their change, rather than just hear about the good intentions of doing it in the future.

The biggest predictor of future behaviour is past behaviour.

If they have been divorced or had some severed friendships, what have they learned? If they have not learned anything and/or everything was the other person's fault, take that as an indicator that they will be playing the "blame" game with you sometime in the near future. You will also want to know whether there has been a proven genuine character change where there has been destructive behaviour in the past.

Also note that it is difficult to know the truth when you are dealing with an experienced pathological liar. When possible, try to hear their former partner's experience. When the stories are diametrically opposed to each other, investigate further by asking outside parties about their experience with both people. The more you look for it, the more the truth will eventually surface. Hopefully you will know the truth before you have a hellish experience.

9. Other Relationships

It is a good rule of thumb to pay attention to a person's closest relationships. Do they have solid, healthy relationships in their life, or do they have a series of falling outs with people, both personally and professionally? What are their relationships like with their other family members? While there may be occasions to distance oneself from abusive and toxic family members, it's good to know what the real situation is. Narcissists will have a series of falling outs and broken relationships, and usually with amazing people. In general, are their relationships healthy or broken? What is behind that? Regardless, you want to be with someone who is capable of forming healthy relationships.

It has been said that you become the average of the five people you surround yourself with the most. When you think about this person you are getting close to, remember that axiom. Are the central people in their life trustworthy and full of integrity? Or are they deceptive and disrespectful? Get to know who the main people in their lives are. Are these people the average of who *you* want to be with and ultimately become?

10. Personal Responsibility

A big question to confirm with anyone who is close to you is this: Does this person take responsibility for their life? A lack of ownership of one's own choices, behaviours, and emotions can range from an annoying yellow flag to a blaring red narcissistic sign. Sometimes people can lean toward irresponsibility and they just need to grow up a bit. However, listen closely if they play the victim role in every circumstance of their life. What are they actually taking ownership of?

Are you dealing with someone who is lazy or has never learned to take responsibility for their life? Or are you dealing with a narcissist who vacillates between blaming others and being the victim? A narcissist loves these four roles: the blamer, the victim, the rescuer, and the martyr. Do you hear them blaming others for every wrong that has happened in their life and yet they take no ownership for their part? From their past experiences and relationships, do you ever hear that they have learned anything? Do they accept some level of responsibility or is the other party completely and solely at fault?

Blaming and being a victim can come in the form of ridiculous statements such as, "I was threatened into every one of my marriages," and, "I had nothing to do with any of my divorces." A narcissist will blame because they must avoid any type of shame or guilt. When you hear a lot of blaming, beware.

With a narcissist, you may hear them fill the rescuer role about how much they do for everyone else. They tell their own daring tales of the many sacrifices they have made for others and how it cost them everything. If you are dealing with a narcissist, you may discover a fake morality and a false humility. Most people don't brag about their sacrifices or make statements such as, "I'm always the only one who ..." With a narcissist you will often see an extreme amount of self-pity and one who plays the martyr.

A key to having healthy, thriving relationships is to build them with people who take complete responsibility for their lives. The way to a successful thriving life for yourself is to be a person who takes complete responsibility and ownership of your life.

11. Remorseless and Cold

It is true that some people lack social graces and be completely unaware that they have hurt you. People have different sensitivity levels. Some people are feelers whereas others are thinkers. Not everyone will be able to relate to every other person's experiences or emotions. However, it is when you see a complete lack of empathy that you could be dealing with someone who has a personality disorder.

If you are in a close relationship with someone and have been hurt by them, tell them how you feel and see how they react. *The answers are often in their response.* If there is either some empathy and an attempt to understand your point of view, you are likely not dealing with a narcissist. A true narcissist doesn't have the capacity for empathy. They cannot understand, feel, and respond to another's emotions because that part of them has been shut off. If they have hurt you and they know it and they still remain indifferent or are dismissive of your feelings, this is a red flag. If you continue to notice that they do not have the ability to empathize—run!

12. Not Wanting to Associate with Certain People

There are many reasons why people choose to limit their social circles. Some of these reasons are valid and wise; however, there are certain motives that you will want to pay attention to. One obvious bona fide reason for a small social circle is that a person is simply an introvert. Some people prefer an intimate few and can be extremely private or choosey with whom they allow to enter their life. At times one may be in a different season of life and may need to set certain limits with specific types of people. Perhaps those who keep small circles just don't gel with certain people or have a desire to. Fair enough. These are not reasons to sound the alarm bells.

The cautionary side of not wanting to associate with certain people is to be cognizant of the motive (such as if being seen with certain people might taint their image). A motive such as this can be an early sign of narcissistic disdain: that certain people are not sufficiently worthy or good enough to be around. This is not a matter of escaping "bad company," such as avoiding a type of person for your own safety. This is about not wanting to associate with genuinely good people because they may happen to be in a different financial bracket or they may not be as genetically gifted in brains or beauty. Does the person in your life not want to associate with others because they are poor, they are not attractive enough, they don't have a high-enough status, or they grew up in a different part of the country?

For these reasons alone, narcissists can disdain and not want to associate with genuinely good people because it might affect their image. They may feel their very image will be tarnished and they themselves will be diminished due to their association with these people. Truly, when it comes to narcissists, they only want to associate with those who will enhance their image or will praise and admire them. Narcissists tend to prioritize the image and status of another person with whom they associate.

Notice if your significant other or friend wants you to start cutting out or limiting your time with the important people in your life. With a narcissist, this divesting of your relationships happens gradually as they slowly start to isolate you. When dealing with a narcissist, you will find that they start to undermine and disdain your relationships with the people who are the most important to you. Out of "concern" for you, they may declare it is better for your own wellbeing not to hang around such people. They may claim that you are "different" after hanging around them, or that your "energy seems to be drained" from that relationship. What starts out as "care and concern" for you will transform into a contempt and disdain for others. A true narcissist does not want you to have outside support or other people's opinions. A narcissist's control comes by isolating you.

Note that everything with a narcissist starts out subtly. Be discerning if your significant other or your friend (narcissists can be in any form of relationship) does not want to associate with certain people, especially those who are important in your life. Why is that? Is there a valid reason for that or is this a warning to you about this particular person?

13. Lying

We've all been guilty of lying. However, people who have mostly good intentions and who are not pathological liars have some remorse when they lie. Harmless people take ownership when they lie to others. They see both their lies and their lying as problems, and they seek to make things right. Perpetual lying is a character problem. When a person habitually lies to you, they are not a safe person to be in a close relationship with. Regardless as to whether you discover this type of person to be a narcissist or not, you will never win or have a quality relationship with someone if their lies are more important to them than anything or anyone else.

> *If someone lies to you, they are unlovingly disrespecting you and your relationship.*

While not all liars are narcissists, I have never heard of an honest narcissist. A narcissist uses lying as a strategy to manipulate and control their relationships and circumstances in order to put themselves in a good light. When they are caught, they will defend their lies like a dragon defending her treasure. This happens even when you present them with obvious evidence to the contrary. Their strong reaction when they are found out can be a good clue to distinguish between a people pleaser who lies and a dangerous personality who lies.

Narcissists and psychopaths live a whole other life that most people in their circles know nothing about. Narcissists use and deceive others to get whatever they want from them. They have a charming way of doing it too—so, watch out! Remember you deserve to have honest and respectful people in your life.

> *When you keep someone in your life who is a chronic liar, and you keep giving them new chances to be trusted, you have a lot in common with this person: you are both lying and being unloving to yourself!*

14. Strange Accusations out of Nowhere

Occasionally people can make strange allegations from seemingly nowhere, because they have misunderstood or been misinformed about a situation. Still others can blindly accuse you out of their own filters of paranoia and suspicion. However, there is a difference when you are dealing with a narcissist.

Narcissists use crazy accusations as tactics for covering up their own shame or guilt in order to divert that specific attention off themselves. Often their charges against you are the specific acts that they themselves are guilty of. When you are faced with such horrific accusations, the natural knee-jerk reaction is to spend your energy defending both yourself and your honour against these crazy allegations. These outlandish charges are all sorts of things that you would never do. Some examples are that you are having an affair; hiding money; stealing money; being a gold-digger, a pathological liar, mentally unstable (usually you are "downright crazy" with a variety of mental illnesses), stingy, cold, callous, a horrible parent, raging, and selfish. A narcissist will project all of the unhealed areas of their own life that they have not dealt with, onto you, because they can't and won't take any responsibility for these areas.

Jocelynn remembered when she was reeling from a shattered marriage and the devastation of finding out about her husband's affairs. She was shaken with how and why their relationship could have taken such a drastic turn. At that time, Jocelynn was a week away from moving out of the house and she knew that her husband had had a secret mistress for several months already. Out of nowhere, Jocelynn was accused of cheating and not only cheating, but of having "multiple" boyfriends. Jocelynn found out later that her husband had not one, but three mistresses (multiple *girlfriends*) at that time.

In retrospect, Jocelynn found these accusations interesting. She then recalled all of his allegations against his first wife. His former wife had an "affair" (when in fact he had had dozens). She was the "master manipulator" (while he constantly exploited others). His first wife was a "horrible parent" (while he was cold, absent, abusive and had troubled relationships with all his children). She was "mentally unstable" and "crazy" (a classic narcissistic accusation). In hindsight, Jocelynn discovered that everything he accused his first wife of, is exactly what he did and who he really was.

All this to say, if someone ever throws strange accusations at you, examine them. Has this person simply been misinformed? Maybe they have some paranoia issues or hastily jump to conclusions. Or deep down, is this really a projection of who they actually are, and indeed they are using a strategy to try to keep you reeling and on the defensive?

15. They DEMAND Trust Rather than Earning It

It is normal for people to need time and a track record for trust to be established. Trust breakers are usually willing to give the other the time and space that is needed to do that. When people start demanding trust after a short amount of time, or they demand it directly after a huge breach in trust (such as an affair), pay attention. Narcissists think that they are entitled to trust and that they are above having to prove their credibility and character to anyone.

Natasha and her narcissist had done some business deals together. Natasha was a savvy project manager who put together and oversaw many business deals. Before they started dating, her ex had done three different deals in the same type of business. In contrast, he made zero profit and completely lost all his capital as well. Fast forward, through the two deals they did together, and Natasha netted him as much as he had earned in his regular job. He did not have to do any work, he merely needed to invest money. He trusted her without any demands.

When things started to go south between them, Natasha had an opportunity for another deal. He agreed to go into the deal, except he wanted 100 percent of the control of the deal and wanted the total profits while she did all the work. However, based on *his* track record in such business dealings, she did not trust his abilities. Her narcissist demanded control and flew into a rage when she did not surrender the deal with her contacts and strategies. He claimed she was completely unreasonable, she was not being a good wife, and she always had to have control and her way in everything. Despite all the money she made with him, he went on to say that she was completely incompetent in business and investing. He demanded that she trust him with her money, even though he had done nothing to earn her trust in this area.

Many narcissists will also just want you to "get over it" after they've broken trust by lying and having affairs. In reality, they have no track record of honesty, remorse, or change, yet they DEMAND that you instantly trust them. In fact, they will claim that it is *you* who are such a horrible, ungracious, petty person, for not giving into their mandate for complete, unconditional, and blind trust. This is definitely a red flag (and a run-like-hell signal) when a person is more concerned about you not trusting them instantly after a betrayal than they are about their own past shady behaviour.

16. Slipping of the Mask

None of us is capable of being flawless in our relationships. We each need to extend some grace when people have bad days. Most people don't respond in the best ways during times of extreme stress. Sometimes we don't understand people, we have different goals and views, and other times we simply miss the mark and blow it. We've all had those moments when we did not respond as we would have liked to or we reacted poorly out of stress or exhaustion.

When you are dealing with a safe person, they will have remorse for those moments of treating you badly. Often you can talk these things out and leave with a better understanding and respect. With safe people, although everyone has their moments, for the majority of the time you will see them live out kind and respectful behaviour toward you.

This is very different from the slipping of a narcissistic mask. When a narcissist's mask slips, they are not just having a bad day, they are revealing who they truly are. The slipping of the mask may involve bullying, rage, attacks against you, and passive-aggressive self-pity.

There are many reasons why a narcissist's mask will slip. Criticism is one. One of a narcissist's greatest fears is being seen as less than their perfect image. When other people find out who they really are, the narcissist is at risk of having their true actions exposed. They can be relentless and without mercy to the point where you will wish that they'd just put the nice mask back on! Eventually they *will* put their mask back on and pretend that nothing happened. You are of course "going crazy" by bringing up any of their mask-slipping brutal behaviours.

The mask also comes off when you fail to do everything they want. This includes failing to let them have their way all the time, failing to pay all the bills, not serving them dinner at a moment's notice, if you gain weight, or whatever whim they might have in the moment. You can guarantee the mask will come off when you stand up to them by enforcing a boundary and telling them a clear, "No!" When the mask slips, there is a reptilian coldness and you will see no empathy. Pay attention to that. Of course this will only be temporary (unless they have reached the discard stage with you).

The slipping of the mask is neither a bad day, a time of stress, nor a lapse in behaviour. It is a flash of brutality in an abyss of empathy, before the mask is put on again and you must forget that such a thing ever happened. You will find the truth in their denial or in the defense of their mask.

CHAPTER 13

HOW TO NARCISSIST-PROOF YOUR LIFE

If you are reading this book, it is likely you are in a position you never thought you would ever be in. Perhaps you are in any number of these situations: separation, divorce, an abusive relationship; or fighting for your home, your children, or your finances. These are circumstances we never intend for our lives and we often think it happens only to "other people." That is, until we find ourselves in this very situation.

I never envisioned leaving my marriage. I waited a long time to get married and I was in this relationship for life! After suffering the emotional violence and extreme abuse that only a narcissist can give, I fled my marriage. Many questions raced through my mind. What did *I* allow into my life? How could I have married a narcissist? What did I need to change within myself? I wanted to learn everything I could from this experience. I wanted to make sure this would *never* happen again. I wanted something different for my future. Yes, there were many things that I had to change.

After reading countless books, scanning through blogs, and watching hundreds of YouTube videos, I finally understood who and what a narcissist really is. I realized this wasn't my first encounter with a narcissist. After my rude awakening, I began to recognize other narcissists in different chapters of my life. People I worked with, family friends whom I've known all my life, a couple of my best gal pals, religious leaders, men I've dated, and even a boy I went out with in junior high. In my journey, I discovered that narcissism is *way* more common than one might think. My friends and even random strangers started coming out of the woodwork with their own experiences of being in a relationship with a narcissist.

This chapter is about some of the areas I discovered that I needed to personally learn and grow in. We can never change another person. We *can*, however, take responsibility for the part we played in the relationship and learn from our blind spots (which are always initially unknown to us). Then we can be different, move on, and have a fabulous life, a fabulous life that is free from narcissists, and one that is rich in true relationships.

Once you lock into these principles, a narcissist cannot exist in your life for very long and you can actually become a narcissist repellant.

> *It's so nice when toxic people stop talking to you. It's like the trash took itself out.*

Let's look at eleven ways to expel and repel narcissists!

1. Part I of Boundaries: Keep the Bad Things Out

Don't allow people into your life who disrespect your boundaries. Period.

If this is new territory for you, keep in mind there will be an adjustment period for both you and the people in your life as you navigate the new waters of setting boundaries. It may take some time and training for others to accept your new ways (especially if you've never set boundaries before and suddenly start setting them now). You will also need some practice on communicating your limits. Many people gain success by first starting to declare their boundaries with the safest people in their life. They get experience and feedback before progressing to the more challenging individuals.

After some practice, if you notice that people consistently cross your boundaries and continue to disrespect you, accept that they are not safe people to have in your life and move on from them. You never have to put up with disrespect. There are plenty of amazing people out there who will treat you with respect and honour your boundaries.

You are allowed to set boundaries. You are allowed to wave goodbye to anyone who doesn't respect them. Without apology.

To reinforce what has been previously said, an actual boundary must have a consequence. We may *communicate* our wishes and boundaries; however, if there is no real enforcement, there is no true boundary. These "consequences" are not about threatening or controlling another person, they are more about stating what *you* will do based on the given circumstances. A lack of boundaries can make a person feel frustrated, angry, disempowered, and out of control, whereas having solid boundaries will create more peace, confidence, and empowerment in your life. Not to mention it will provide a pathway to better relationships.

While we can never control another person's actions, we can control our responses and what we will allow into our lives. It is important to learn to communicate clearly what *you* will do if certain actions take place, and then follow through on what *you* will do if that happens. A simple example would be this: "It is very important for me to be at this event on time. I would love it if we can go together. I will be leaving at 7 p.m. If that works for you we can go together and if not, I'm sure you will be able to find your way there."

In this statement you are clear in determining what you will do regardless of what the other person chooses to do. With good boundaries, both people have freedom. You have empowered yourself and you will not get upset if the other person arrives at 7:45 p.m., because you will not have missed your event. Your boundaries let the other person know what you will really stand for. You are protecting and honouring yourself, regardless of what the other person does. Boundaries with consequences clearly let the other person know what *you* will do if they choose x.

> *Your personal boundaries protect the inner core of your identity and your right to choose.*

In the book, *Boundaries,* Dr. Henry Cloud and Dr. John Townsend have this to say:

> *A boundary always deals with yourself, not the other person. You are not demanding that your spouse do something, even respect your boundaries. You are setting boundaries to say what you will do or will not do. Only these kinds of boundaries are enforceable, for you do have control over yourself.[1]*

Learning to set and enforce boundaries takes time and practice. How do you know in which areas of your life you need stronger boundaries? While it is different for everyone, you may have some clear signs. These signals can include when

- you have that awful feeling in the pit of your stomach;
- you feel disrespected;
- you have a have rush of anger (this often signals that danger is present and you must protect yourself);
- you have a sense of shock in how others respond to you;
- you feel powerless in a relationship.

These are often signs that someone has crossed one or more of your boundaries, regardless of whether you have communicated your boundaries or not.

When you feel any of these indicators, action is required on your part. People will never know how you feel or where you draw your line in the sand unless you communicate it to them and ask them to stop. If they ignore what you have to say, let them know what *you* will do if they continue to disrespect your boundaries. There is no power behind merely asking a person to stop, especially when it comes to a narcissist. You must take action.

Without having any type of consequence to back up your boundaries, you will experience frustration and they will perceive you as a nag. Let them know that they have a choice and so do you. A few examples are these: if they choose to yell, you will walk out of the room; if they are late, you are going without them; if they choose to cheat, you are out of the relationship. There is actually a great freedom in setting boundaries and it is fundamental to turning your life around.

I know, I know, I stood up for myself. I'm such a bitch.

Once you start enforcing your boundaries, you will be more empowered and you will stop attracting people who seek to manipulate and control you in a relationship. Healthy boundaries keep you safe and having them is a clear sign of how others may treat you. Boundaries are about respect and what is allowed and not allowed in your relationships. Narcissists and abusers will detect your strong sense of self. They will leave you alone and will look for someone who has weak boundaries. Solid boundaries are kryptonite for narcissists.

The only people who get upset about you setting boundaries are the ones who are benefiting from you having none.

2. Part II of Boundaries: Let the Good Things In

Another part of boundaries is to allow and keep the good things in your life. Dr. Henry Cloud and Dr. John Townsend compare boundaries to a walled castle or a fortress. Boundaries act like a defense to keep the bad things out. However, castles do have doors and drawbridges to allow the good things in as well. If you have a narcissist in your life, it is likely that you struggle with what Dr. Henry Cloud calls, "reverse boundaries." Reverse boundaries are when a person has no boundaries to keep the bad out. They also erect boundaries where they shouldn't have them so the good things are not allowed to come in. When this happens you can end up putting walls and boundaries against healthy people who seek to be nourishing you and meeting your needs.[2] Obviously, the goal is to restore the order in life by keeping the bad things out and allowing the good things in.

Many people with reverse boundary problems tend to be classic avoiders, who don't allow the good things to come into their life. As an avoider, you would rather painfully struggle alone than ask for help. In fact, you likely withdraw from others when you are in need and choose to face your battles and struggles alone so that you won't be a burden to people. Somewhere along the way, you grew to believe that having needs is wrong, destructive, or weak. You likely find it difficult to accept support from others even when they offer it to you freely and joyfully. Because an avoider thinks their own needs are wrong, they often reject any legitimate needs that they have. Unfortunately, this can eventually train others to dismiss your needs as well.

Healing avoider tendencies happens by first recognizing and acknowledging your needs. *Everyone* has needs and it is not wrong to have them. Feeling worthy of love is essential to attracting and maintaining it. Accept support from others when you are going through difficult times rather than withdrawing. Learn to ask for help and let the good things and the good people into your life.

3. Recalibrate Your Radar on Safe and Selfish People

After being in a relationship with a narcissist for any length of time, most likely your gauge is off for recognizing who is actually a safe person. Unfortunately you have been living with an unsafe, predatorial person and that has become "normal." Your tolerance has increased for many things that, earlier, you never would have dreamed of permitting. Your "normal" of what a good and healthy relationship involves is now skewed. Your "normal" has become dangerous. You may wake up one day thinking, "How could I have possibly allowed that narcissist to say and do these things to me? How could I ever have been with a person like that? When did I get so off track?"

At some point in life you likely learned to become a compliant person who melds with other people's wishes, demands, and needs. Compliant people don't rock the boat. They become chameleons and blend into their environment. However, abusive behaviour is NOT to be tolerated and you never want to allow that in your life. Any hint of abusive behaviour ought to scream alarm bells for you to get out and remove yourself from danger! Now is the time to recalculate your internal radar on who is safe and who is not.

How have you seen some of these unsafe characteristics play out in your past relationships? Which qualities have you allowed into your relationships? This is also a great time to be honest and to do a self-examination to see if you have any unsafe qualities or if you have any addictions to unhealthy relationships. Below are a few contrasts between unsafe and safe people. The first four bold print statements are quotations from Dr. Henry Cloud's and Dr. John Townsend's book, *Safe People: How to Find Relationships That Are Good for You and Avoid Those That Aren't*. I highly recommend reading this book in its entirety!

Demanding Trust

"Unsafe people demand trust instead of earning it."[3]

People who are not safe insist on instant trust even after they have brutally violated it. Rather than acknowledging their severe breach of trust and what they have put you through, rather than humbly changing their ways and finding the means of earning your trust back, they immediately mark you as a bad person for not trusting them. They don't want to put in the real work of having a good track record over time and have to do the things it would really take to earn back your trust. When you are in a relationship where trust has been broken and you find yourself being coerced, manipulated, or guilted into moving forward before the trust has been restored, know that this is not a safe relationship.

Safe people on the other hand most likely won't obliterate your trust in the first place. Although we are all human and we do fall short, safe people will not get to the place where they betray or abuse you. If, however, some trust has been broken, safe people will give you the space that you need to allow that trust to grow again.

Empty Apologies

"Unsafe people only apologize instead of changing their behaviour."[4]

Yep—do a fruit check to see what is manifesting in their life. Is there any genuine *change* or are these just empty words? Saying "Sorry" and adding crocodile tears mean absolutely nothing unless a person backs their words with a change of actions. Don't settle for academy award winning performances that are devoid of any actual substance. Many unsafe people will give you convincing words and empty promises. However, the proof is in their actions. Unsafe people can maintain the same behavioural patterns for decades while continuing to give their persuasive Oscar-worthy performances of apologies ... and still *never* change.

Safe people back up their words with their actions. With safe people, you will see genuine change take place.

No Ownership

"Unsafe people blame others instead of taking responsibility."[5]

Safe and healthy people own up to when they make mistakes. They take responsibility for their actions. Unsafe people deflect responsibility and blame others for everything that happens in their life, including their own words and actions. "He made me angry." "She caused me to say …" "It wasn't my fault!" "I can't help it. They forced me to …" Unsafe people take no responsibility for their actions, emotions, and choices. They try to escape accountability by blaming others.

In everything, we are ultimately responsible for our own lives, emotions, words, and actions. A safe person owns their life.

Dishonesty

"Unsafe people lie instead of telling the truth."[6]

It is vital to be truthful in relationships. I think the statement below sums up the futility of having a relationship with a person who is dishonest:

> *There is no way a relationship can prosper and grow if one person is a liar.*[7]
>
> —Henry Cloud and John Townsend

They Cannot Stand It When You Say "No"

An unsafe person will turn against you when you aren't compliant with everything they want. Unsafe people in this context only surround themselves with people they can control and who will submit to whatever they want. This is a good litmus test in relationships. In safe and healthy relationships, you each have the freedom to say no. Control, coercion, guilt, or manipulation are not part of a safe relationship. Safe people do not try to make you do something that you do not want to do. Before getting too deep into any relationship, try out a "no" and see what the other person does with that. This is an excellent gauge as to where you will stand with them. This is also a good assessment as to how they will respond when you have an even bigger "no" to tell them later on.

Safe people will respect you when you say "no." They also will not be controlling of your choices, as any healthy relationship requires some deference.

They Lack Empathy Instead of Having Compassion

Liz was an avid runner. As it goes some days, you can have an off day with racing. No matter how rigorous and strategic is the training you put in, no matter how perfectly you fuel your body the night before, no matter whether you hydrate properly during the race itself, long distance races can take unexpected turns and drastic tolls on the body. Liz was experiencing one of those times. Races were usually easy and fun for Liz; however, this particular half marathon was a struggle. By the time she got to the finish line, it was not a pretty sight. It was downright ugly!

Liz's friend was also there and saw Liz's unusual staggering condition at the finish line. Her friend was quick to bring water, to get Liz to lie down and to put her feet up. However, there was no compassion or assistance from her husband. Rather than care for her, the man even crossed his arms and completely avoided looking at her. He disdained that Liz was weak in the moment. Apparently her condition made *him* look bad.

This man was a cold fish, devoid of empathy for her condition. Her friend was in absolute shock at his treatment of Liz. Later she sat Liz down and let her know some of her serious concerns. Unfortunately, that race day was just the tip of the iceberg. Her husband's private persona was much worse and he was growing extremely abusive. Thankfully, Liz got out of her unsafe marriage. Now she only allows safe people into her life.

Unsafe people lack empathy. They despise vulnerability and, in the end, they will never have your back. In contrast, safe people show care, concern, and empathy. They are there for you when you are having a hard time in life. They will support you and you will know beyond a shadow of a doubt that they will have your back.

They Are Incredibly Defensive Rather than Being Open

Sue was having a most difficult time communicating with her partner in one of her dating relationships. Her relationship was only good when it was sunshine and roses. Whenever she wanted to bring up *anything* that might involve a bit of conflict and require some problem solving, her boyfriend's extreme anger came out. She couldn't say anything without offending him. Sue tried dozens of ways to communicate with him. She never understood this extreme defensiveness. She even asked him the way he would want her to say something. When she used his exact words to communicate with him, he yelled that her tone was wrong. She tried out different tones out on him.

Finally she said, "So if I'm understanding this correctly, it seems like if I have a problem with something, you would rather that I don't say anything at all. It feels to me like you don't want to talk about things. You would rather I just pretend that there are no problems and that I am only happy *all* of the time." His emphatic response was, "YES! Fake it 'til you make it! I don't want any drama! I don't want to hear about problems or anything negative!"

Since Sue was only bringing up minor issues—she dared not bring up some of the real issues that were surfacing—she took a pass on that relationship and found a safe person who she could actually talk to. Someone who was not extremely defensive and who did not avoid confrontation and real discussions. You need to have the ability to confront and express your concerns safely in a relationship. If that is not present you will likely find yourself in another abusive and/or emotionally unavailable relationship.

They Are Emotionally Unavailable Rather than Emotionally Intimate

Being emotionally unavailable is an interesting dichotomy. With emotional unavailability, the same person who can indeed make you feel amazing on the surface level can simultaneously wound you on a deeper emotional level. Although the beginning is fun and you are on a high (probably because of the pedestal you are put on), you ultimately end up feeling alone in your relationship. This type of person takes the form of the charmer who makes grandiose and romantic gestures yet is who is emotionally unavailable when it matters. Their charm and love bombing never last. Often behind the façade is an emotional void that permeates the relationship and ultimately stings your heart. The wounds from emotional unavailability include not supporting you in your pursuits, values, and dreams; constant criticism; shutting down and walling up; being shoved far down the totem pole of your partner's priorities; and a lack of acceptance for the person that you are. With this type of unavailability in a relationship, you are likely to feel rejected or unimportant.

Emotionally unavailable people are very competent at flattery, charm, and short-term intimacy; however, that's it. Think of a fire cracker: they are loud and bright and then … the show is over and you're left with darkness and smoke. Be sure that all the romance, flattery, physical affection, compliments, and dinners out are not covering up for the lack of emotional intimacy or the emotional wounds they are giving you either covertly or overtly.

Vulnerability is the key to emotional intimacy. People who have addictions are emotionally unavailable because they attempt to avoid pain and vulnerability by numbing through their addiction. Their addictions will be more important than you are, which makes the person unable to emotionally connect with you or make a commitment to you.

In contrast, emotionally available people are able to sit with difficult, upsetting, or challenging emotions. An emotionally available person doesn't dismiss, negate, or minimize emotions. They are able to lean into the difficult and painful emotions. They are courageous and will risk vulnerability to allow themselves to be fully known—the good, the bad, and the ugly.

Their Relationships Are Addictive Rather than Healthy

In unhealthy relationships, addiction tendencies often show up by way of denying the differences or problems in a relationship. Denial is a symptom of any type of addiction. When differences and serious problems are ignored, minimized, or rationalized, we are not truly seeing or loving the whole person. In healthy relationships, both people are able with love, to confront, to communicate, and to provide solutions to problems rather than avoiding them or sweeping them under the rug. Sacrificing your values or standards to be with someone is a sign of a relationship addiction. In every healthy relationship, both people are true to themselves first. While there may be circumstantial compromises in relationships, there is not a compromise in the essence of a person's being, of who they *are,* and what they value.

Staying in a painful relationship out of fear of abandonment or loneliness is a sign of addiction. This is not love. It is important to know what our true motives are in relationships. Clinging to a fantasy love, trusting too much, idealizing the other person, ignoring your differences, expecting perfection, or trying to change another person are all signs of relational addiction. Underlying relationship addictions are fears of loneliness and emptiness.

In contrast, in healthy relationships you begin as a whole person. You are full and complete, you honour your voice and your values, and you don't feel lonely even when you are alone. Out of this place of wholeness, you are able to fully accept and love the other person for who they are. You have a deep base of friendship and you are comfortable to be fully yourself. You feel completely supported and loved and the feeling is mutual. There are no strings attached. You feel a deep peace in the relationship versus having feelings of underlying anxiety and performance. There is also a desire to become more and more committed to each other out of pure respect and love.

Hopefully these points help you to identify more clearly how to gauge whether a relationship or a person is safe. And in turn, how to become a more whole and safe person yourself.

4. It's All About Respect!

Having respect in your relationships centres around having respect for both yourself and others. When you have solid boundaries, you only allow respectful people to come into your life. You, in turn, are fully respectful toward others. You honour what others have to say, even when they disagree with you or refuse to give you what you are asking for. Respect is also about honouring your own voice and what *you* have to say. When you deeply respect yourself, you will teach others to do the same.

Ask yourself how you measure up on the following 21 traits for honouring yourself. Are there are areas you can work on in your life regarding your own self-respect?

When you respect yourself,

1. you treat your body, mind, and emotions with care and honour. This includes intentionally nourishing your body, holding onto healthy emotions, and getting rid of toxic thoughts.

2. you are completely true to your inner voice and your unique calling. You listen to your intuition and honour your purpose.

3. you never allow anyone to take advantage of you or to speak down to you.

4. you create and enforce your boundaries with others. This means with everyone in your life.

5. although your opinions and values may differ with others, you only have respectful people in your life.

A great test for mutual respect in a relationship is when people have drastically different opinions and views. Despite these differences, both people are free to be themselves, and both feel deeply respected around the other person whose viewpoint is opposite to their own.

6. you release people from your life who are boundary-busters. (Those who disrespect or plow through your boundaries.)

7. you feel completely congruent in every area of your life. Everything is in alignment. When things are aligned, you don't feel embarrassed or sad for having compromised a part of your true self.

8. you recognize that your time, energy, and resources are valuable and you only use them where and when you want to.

9. you only give your time, energy, and resources with complete joy; rather than giving out of guilt, fear, or obligation.

10. you know when to follow through, and you do so by leaving an unhealthy situation or a toxic relationship.

11. you accept yourself fully with compassion. You admit your flaws and then work to improve them.

12. with an appropriate amount of humility, you can confidently speak about your strengths.

13. you speak about yourself in respectful ways. You do not demean yourself in front of others (or even in private, for that matter).

14. other people's opinions and criticisms don't shake who you are.

15. you no longer have a need to impress others, to gain their approval, or to make other people like you.

16. you are living out your values and priorities to their full extent. You don't give in, or sacrifice parts of yourself in order to please others.

17. you take personal responsibility for your actions. Always.

18. you treat others with respect and you expect them to treat you respectfully.

19. you never apologize for who you are.

20. you genuinely love and value yourself.

21. you never give up on yourself and you continue to press forward in life.

These are all traits of a person who is resilient and who deeply respects themself.

If you want to be respected by others, the great thing is to respect yourself. Only by that, only by self-respect will you compel others to respect you.[8]

—Fyodor Dostoyevsky

How respectful are the people in your life? Another gauge in relationships is when you are able to openly express your heart and feelings, especially when something is bothering you or hurtful to you. Do others respond in a respectful way? (A big assumption here is that when you are discussing things and bringing up situations you are unhappy about, you yourself are not angry, bitter, attacking, or hurtful.) When you come from a calm, genuine place of clearing up a misunderstanding with a desire to restore the relationship, or confront something that is bothering you, how does the other person respond? The answer to where your relationship stands is often in their response. Do they pass over your feelings, negate, minimize, or dismiss them? Are they overly defensive and angry, and start accusing you of things? Or are they respectful of you and want to work toward a solution? Do they listen to your point of view? Do they care?

It is very freeing and extremely empowering to no longer have disrespectful, unsafe people in your life! By having your own self-respect in place, you will also repel people who are consistently disrespectful. You can become the person who asks for respect in all of your relationships and you can be that person who only attracts healthy, loving people into your life.

5. Listen to Others' Actions

It is vital that you put more weight into what a person does and how they live out their life versus putting stock into the words that they speak. When you are dealing with a narcissist, their words can be very convincing, yet at the same time very confusing as their actions don't line up with what they say. They can charm the socks off you in a group of people; however, you will experience them acting out their disrespect, shutting down, and voicing their cruelty and abuse only when they are alone with you. They will paint themselves as either the hero or the victim in the picture. Again, pay attention, as their actions will not line up with their words.

They may speak about all the sacrifices they have done for you and for your relationship, but a true narcissist's actions indicate the opposite. They may talk about being the ultimate provider, while conversely the reality of their actions is that they have never given you a cent and they are taking you for everything you have. A narcissist will likely tell the world he is father of the year and he's done everything for his kids. In reality, he finds excuses not to take the kids on his allocated days and when he does have them, he complains and is miserable.

Narcissists will often apologize or give you empty promises of a "changed heart," a "new revelation," or a "breakthrough." However, listen to their *actions*. Have they actually changed? Is there any true remorse? Or do they faux-pologize to you?

> *When a person or a situation has truly changed and is worthy of our investment, we will be able to see tangible reasons to believe them.*

Saying "sorry" is not enough. Insist on seeing the actual fruit of their actions to prove that they are genuinely different. There must be a verifiable change in a person's actions. In Dr. Henry Cloud's book, *Never Go Back,* he says,

> *There must be fruit, results, or a real change in life or the situation that gives reason to believe that something will be different this time.*[9]

Narcissists will deceive you with their words. Their love bombing is incredibly convincing. In the end, their ultimate *actions* give way to who they truly are. It is not worth sticking around to see if, "maybe this time," they will change.

Have you ever watched a movie while turning the sound off? You can tell a lot about the characters just from their actions. With a narcissist, try turning the volume down on what they are saying and only pay attention to their actions. Who are they *for real?* You need to beware of the deception in what a narcissist will say, as they are pathological liars and master manipulators. Keep a sharp eye out for the truth and avoid them as you would avoid the plague. Do not even pity them. Pity can lead you down the garden trail of further abuse. Do not fall for their words. If they are living in integrity, their words and actions will line up and you will not live in confusion. Listen to a person's actions.

6. Equality in Relationships

You know what it is like to be in a relationship where you have given everything that you have of your time, your resources, and your love. If you are reading this book you have likely also experienced what it is like when nothing is appreciated and more is constantly demanded of you. Stop allowing this into your life. You never want to get to the point where the life is sucked out of you and you walk away, exhausted from the relationships that you've invested in only to be disdained, abused, and despised. Now is the time to ONLY allow healthy and equal relationships to exist in your life.

> *A healthy relationship is a feast of affection and giving for both people. It is not one person receiving crumbs and trying to convince themselves it is enough.*

Ideally, you want to invest your time in relationships where the giving and receiving is balanced. You may not have equal giving and receiving in the exact same areas as the other person, but generally there is an overall equivalence of give and take. It's good to evaluate as to which ways you give and which ways you receive in your relationships. How do you specifically contribute in your relationships? In what ways do you receive from the other person? As relationships are often a balancing act, ask yourself whether there are ways to improve and grow in either area.

How do others receive from and give to you? Be wary of people who are solely takers. When relationships suck you dry or you start to feel exhausted from being around a certain person, pay attention to that. Is it just on occasion when your spouse, friend, family member, or significant other is going through a hard time and may need more from you? Realize that this can be particularly challenging if you are both going through a difficult season at the same time, and you may both need more simultaneously. Understand the season that you are both in.

Or are you chronically giving out much more than you ever get back and end up feeling a little more depleted each time you are with this person? Are you always the one on the listening end or do you feel deeply heard and understood by them too? Does the other person care about what is going on in your life and ask questions about you? In a healthy relationship, the other person will be curious and will care about you too.

Looking back, Geneva found it odd that in the two years she had dated her husband before they got married, he really never asked her any questions about her past relationships or her life experiences. Geneva recalled, "I mean, *no questions*. I mentioned it to him a couple of times that he never asked anything about my past relationships. He simply shrugged his shoulders. Even after being married, he never asked about any of my current friendships, my job, or anything related to my activities or interests. Actually he never asked about anything that was significant or important in my life. It's like he didn't care about getting to know me as a person. After I left, I evaluated my other relationships in terms of equality. I realized that one of my closest friends and I had a very unequal relationship. What was my part in all of this? I had not opened up and communicated my need to either of them that *I* wanted to be heard as well. I'm learning to look for and expect more from the people that I am seriously going to invest my time in."

Do you need to set a boundary for others on what they can take from you? Or do you need to set a boundary on yourself for what you will give and will allow? When we give more than we have to give of ourselves, this can be unsolicited by the other person. They may not be asking for or even wanting us to give so much. In either case, it can cause feelings of resentment on our part. Be sure that you only give what you want to give with no strings of people-pleasing, obligation, or guilt attached. If you are starting to feel any exhaustion or resentment, do a boundary check with yourself as to what you are giving and allowing to happen in your life.

In relationships, we get what we tolerate. If you feel as though you have some inequalities in your relationships, be authentic and speak up about how you feel. When you genuinely open up to people about your needs and concerns and you still feel the relationship is draining, it may be time to take a step back. In order to get a different result in your relationships, you have to raise your standards and seek out equality rather than one-sidedness.

This is another way to repel a narcissist as they do not want equality in their relationships. They seek out those who give too much and are poor receivers. Become a balanced person in your relationships. Unfulfilling one-sided relationships only hold you back from the wonderful life that awaits you. There are plenty of amazing people out there who are both healthy givers and receivers; you can form healthy relationships with these people. Go out there and find them, and be one yourself!

7. Learn to Receive

In order to have a wonderful equality in our relationships, those of us who have been with a narcissist need to learn to receive without guilt, dread, or feeling as though we are being a burden to others. The majority of people who are in relationships with narcissists have learned to negate their own needs, to make ridiculous sacrifices, and to squelch their own voice for the sake of serving others. Oftentimes we are great givers and terrible receivers. In the best relationships, however, both people are able to give and receive. When we don't learn how to receive, we simply won't be able to accept all the wonderful things being offered to us. Those people who are wanting to give to us won't be able to and we may be unintentionally shutting the good people out of our lives.

Frequently at the root of not being able to receive is a sense of unworthiness or a lack of self-love. We must find and create our self-worth from within through self-love. Our true sense of worth can never come from another person. When a person seeks to find their validation and worth externally, it becomes a fickle, futile, and never-ending battle. Know with every fibre of your being that you are valuable, lovable, and worthy. You are created by a loving God for a unique purpose, and the God of the universe declares that you are worthy and you are loved.

We may have some barriers and thought patterns that we need to change in order to become great receivers. Many times we view receiving as selfish (except when we want others to receive from us!) It is important to remember that there are tremendous benefits and blessings that the giver obtains through giving. We may find shame in receiving or that it will cause us to be a weight to other people. However, when we do not receive, we are depriving others of the joy of giving. When we receive, we also open ourselves up to be vulnerable, which is *vital* for intimacy in relationships. Another important thing to keep in mind is that when you are only in a giving position, you will attract those who are only in a taking position. Total takers usually come in the form of narcissists, abusers, sociopaths, and predators.

People who are regular receivers won't end up with narcissists. Healthy receivers will know that there is a big component missing from the relationship. (Or they will notice the shift after the love-bombing phase is over.) Great receivers (who are balanced by being great givers), also know that they are worthy of receiving and have a healthy sense of self. It is good for us to give and it is good to allow others to give to us. This is what makes a healthy relationship. We need to learn to become gracious, appreciative, and open receivers in order to have vibrant relationships and get the very best out of life.

8. Stay in Your Realm of Responsibility

Those of us who have attracted narcissists into our lives often want to take responsibility in areas that are not ours to take. We tend to be fixers and pleasers of sorts. We truly want to help, and we often seek to bring healing to another's wounded past. Although we can give support and compassion for a person's trauma and difficulties, we must realize that their healing is ultimately not in our realm of responsibility. It is not up to us to fix them or to right the wrongs that were done to them.

Many times we can take on other areas of responsibility for our partners that we should allow them to own. It could be their financial responsibilities, their work problems, or their relational messes. These are not our areas to pick up. Another area of responsibility to avoid owning is another person's emotions. We may think it's up to us to make another person happy, or we can fall prey to the ploy that we "made them angry." In truth, each person is responsible for their own feelings and how they deal with them, including their anger. You can never be responsible for another person's choices, actions, emotions, or past, so don't take ownership of any of these areas.

> *The addict does not take responsibility for his life, and the codependent feels responsible to take care of people who are not taking responsibility for themselves. So the addict and the codependent will be drawn to people who fill their needs.*[10]
>
> —Henry Cloud

We need to make sure that we do not get on the addict-and-codependent merry-go-round. Narcissists are addicts. They are addicted to getting attention and praise from people, maintaining a false image of themselves, and controlling others. All addicts need a codependent to enable them to stay addicted. Part of being a codependent is taking responsibility for other people, whether for their actions, emotions, successes, or failures. We can stop our own crazy cycle in life when we cease taking on the responsibilities of others, which are never ours to take on.

Want to repel a narcissist? Don't accept responsibility for their choices, actions, or emotions. Do not allow their victim mentality to manipulate you. Know your realm of responsibility and do not pick up something that is not yours to own.

9. Listen to Your Inner Voice and Intuition on a Regular Basis

After being with a narcissist, most likely you've lost touch with your inner voice and your intuition. These vital parts of our being have been confused, negated, belittled, coerced, downgraded, and manipulated the entire time you have been with a narcissist. The good news is that your inner voice and your intuition are still there. You have a voice and it matters. It matters tremendously. It is time to start listening to it and honouring it.

> *Your mind knows only some things. Your inner voice, your instinct, knows everything. If you listen to what you know instinctively, it will always lead you down the right path.*

Throughout your entire life you have had an inner voice offering you guidance. At times it is very quiet and gentle. Other times our voice speaks to us undeniably, powerfully, and urgently. Sometimes we have listened to it and heeded it. Other times we've brushed it aside and thought nothing of it. Our inner voice can be a sense, a hunch, a fleeting feeling, an image, or an impression. It speaks to us in many ways and it is worthy of our time and attention.

> *Always listen to your inner voice.*

Listening is a skill that everyone needs to get better at—both with ourselves and with other people. Learn to listen for the things that give you inner peace, true joy, and ease. Learn to also listen for what makes you feel uneasy, and for any unpleasantness or incongruences that you see in others (such as when it seems like a person's actions do not line up with their words). Pay VERY close attention to when something "feels off" with another person. This is one of the telltale signs that you are with a narcissist, a sociopath, or a psychopath. It all appears right, *and* deep down, something feels … off.

Listen to your own voice, your own soul. If something doesn't feel right, it probably isn't.

Journaling is one of the best tools to reconnect with your inner voice. When Wanda started dating again after her divorce, she would write down everything that she was feeling, both the wonderful things and the things that seemed a bit strange or simply "off." Usually a day or two later, Wanda would get a "reasonable explanation" for the somewhat peculiar behaviour from the person she was dating. She continued to notice that although there were good things in the relationship, including grand gestures of romance, there were some things that were off or made her feel uneasy. Wanda continued to keep her eyes open and to check into things.

This time she was not ignoring, but rather trusting, honouring, and believing her intuition and inner voice more than the words being spoken by the other person. Somehow, things didn't seem to line up, including the "too much too soon." Was this love bombing? Later Wanda discovered that her gut knew the truth the entire time. After she caught the man in his lies, she got out of the relationship very early and very quickly. Wanda realized that she had dodged another narcissistic landmine. Her intuition and inner voice were speaking to her all along and they proved to be right in the end.

Developing sharp inner listening skills will save you. You can learn to tune in to your inner voice. It is a skill to be practised and sharpened on a regular basis.

You have permission to walk away from anything that doesn't feel right. Trust your instincts and listen to your inner-voice—it's trying to protect you.

Before you can improve the access to your inner voice and intuition, it is essential to still the noise of your busy life. Slowing down and listening often requires solitude. Take the time to listen, whether it be to your inner voice or to the voice of God. It is in the stillness that we can hear the whispers of truth.

When you are still, it is also a good time to check in with your body. How do different parts of your body feel? Identify any aches, pains, or tension. When something is "off" in our lives, it usually creates physical sensations in our bodies. As we tune in further, we can discern within our bodies when something is wrong in our lives.

"Listen to your gut" has a legitimate basis, as your GI tract is very much in tune with your true emotions. When things are not right emotionally, you may experience a physical manifestation in your gut with symptoms such as constipation, diarrhea, or a stomach ache. When you veer off course or into harm's way, your body can act as a powerful and trustworthy warning light. After all, the body doesn't lie. Begin to pay attention to your emotional impressions and your body's responses to them.

When things are not right, physical symptoms you may experience include tension in the neck muscles, in the upper trapezius muscle (between the neck and shoulders), and also in the gluteal muscles. When your voice has been squelched, you may feel it physically by having a sore throat or, in severe circumstances, pneumonia. When there is a need to release emotions, you may have watery eyes, a cold, or a runny nose. If things feel out of control, you may be challenged with shallow breathing, having feelings of dread or anxiety, or bouts of insomnia. Chronic headaches and/or migraines are also signs of severe stress. In traumatic times (such as when you are with a narcissist), it is likely you will be more prone to injuries and accidents. You may also feel the physical weight of having constant roadblocks and insurmountable challenges. Our body's physical manifestations are ways that our intuition speaks to us when we can't hear, aren't listening, or won't listen to our inner voice. It doesn't matter if the pain is emotional or physical. Alan Fogel, PhD, demonstrates the connection between emotional and physical pain when he cites how economical the body is as it uses a single neural system to detect and feel pain.[11]

Masterfully listening to your inner voice is comparable to training a new muscle. It takes time and it won't happen overnight. However, when you make a consistent effort to hone your listening skills, your inner voice will become stronger and louder. The more you listen to your inner voice, the more empowered, genuine, and peaceful you will feel. Your body will feel a lack of tension and you will have healthy digestion. You will also notice that good people and positive experiences are drawn to you with ease. By listening to your inner voice, you become the creator of your life rather than the bystander who watches your life slip by. Learning to honour and respond to your inner voice is a life changer.

> *Listen to your own voice, your own soul; too many people listen to the noise of the world instead of to themselves.*

Our intuition has often been referred to as our sixth sense. We can recognize it as our inner guidance, a hunch, a kind of knowing, or our internal compass. It is more of a sense or a feeling, rather than logic *per se*. Our intuition shows up when we feel a sneaking suspicion that something is not right but we can't put our finger on what it is. Intuition is our ability to sense things before they happen or before knowing all the facts.

Our intuition comes from the entirety of our knowledge and from our past experiences. Whenever we encounter something new, the unconscious side of our brain is continuously making assessments. It takes in certain cues, matches them with something similar in our memory database, and makes a conclusion. Our intuition connects our body, mind, and spirit together and works in conjunction with how these three have absorbed everything from our past. When our intuition feels right, it makes us feel expansive, excited, and nervous (in a good way, such as with a new challenge). However, when something feels wrong or off, we may have a sense of trepidation, of dread, of feeling deflated, or even of being terrified.

Intuition doesn't tell you what you want to hear; it tells you what you need to hear.

Your intuition is connected with each of the nerve cells in your body. The gut is lined with around a hundred million neurons and is often referred to as the "second brain." It is known as the enteric nervous system. It contains more neurons than the spinal cord and peripheral nervous system but fewer than the brain.[12] The responsibility of having this sacred gift of intuition is to learn to listen to it. The more attention we give our intuition, the more powerful and accurate it will become.

The more you trust your intuition, the more empowered, the stronger, and the happier you become.

Another avenue along which we can access our intuition is by paying attention to our dreams. Our dreams provide subconscious information that we may not have conscious access to when we are awake. When you want solutions to a certain area of your life, before going to sleep, direct your thoughts to any unresolved issues and be open to all possible options as you fall asleep. Your subconscious may provide you with the answers during your dreams.

At first glance, our dreams may seem to be quite random. However, our subconscious often speaks to us in pictures. It can be helpful to uncover the meaning as to what certain objects, characters, or circumstances represent in our dreams. As each person has unique experiences, the meanings of your dreams will be personal to you.

Pay attention to your dreams. They could be telling you things that you need to know.

10. Take Ownership of Everything in Your Life

When we are completely honest with ourselves, we can admit that we played a role in continuing to be with a narcissist. The point of this section is not to blame or condemn *anyone* who's been in a relationship with a narcissist. You deserve the deepest compassion and sympathy. You were selected by them because you are a beautiful person inside and out. You have a kind heart, a generous spirit, and you are the cream of the crop. This is why they chose *you*.

This section is designed to shed light on some of the blind spots that you may have (we all have them), and to equip you to make better decisions in the future so that this *never* happens to you again. It is a very true statement that you can never change another person, you can only change yourself. When you gain insight as to how you got into a relationship with a narcissist and what made you stay with the narcissist, this awareness and wisdom will transform your life. Now is the time to take ownership of your thoughts and actions and to make some changes.

Most people who were in a close relationship with a narcissist are naturally highly self-reflective people. You are the kind of person who will take the steps to learn about what happened and will continue to discover how you can be different so that this will never happen again. Take the attitude to LEARN from this situation and find out how you will specifically and intentionally grow in order to improve your life.

Below are some of the transformations that I and others have experienced. These were the things that we needed to take ownership of and change within ourselves as we got out of our narcissistic relationships and to a better place in life.

I now pay attention to all of my relationships. I no longer live in unbalanced relationships where I do a majority of the work. I have learned to lessen or eliminate my exposure to people who drain me of my energy, time, and money. I have learned to receive from others and I'm even asking for help! I am also allowing the good things to come into my life as part of setting healthy boundaries.

I realized that I was the first one who stopped listening to myself. I failed to listen to my gut. I slowly quieted my own inner voice in favour of listening to someone else's voice. I am now taking some time for daily stillness, so that I can journal and listen to my inner voice, my gut, and my intuition. Over the past two years I have seen how learning to heed my inner voice early on in the process has already saved me countless times of getting into toxic romantic relationships.

I now recognize that I made too many sacrifices in the relationship and did not stand up for my own needs. Actually, I was not even aware of my own needs. Through working with a life coach, I have discovered what my needs are. I now acknowledge them and seek to fill my needs in healthy ways.

I had some unconscious and unhealthy patterns of "normal" that I learned from my family of origin. My unconscious life patterns included restricting my feelings, suppressing my needs, and staying in relationships where I was not treated well. Now, I am actually grateful that I had this narcissistic relationship. It made me aware of my own blind spots and it has helped me to heal my childhood.

I currently have a strong ability to detect safe and unsafe people. I do not let unsafe people (liars are at the top of this list) into the space of my life.

I am learning to be more self-ish without guilt. Not "selfish" in the fact that I am only looking out for myself and I don't care about others or what my actions do to them. Rather, self-ish as a way of having healthy self-care. I recognize how important it is that I live out self-care on a regular basis, not only for myself but also for the sake of all my relationships. Now I give to others out of the overflow of my full cup, rather than draining myself dry by only serving others. I realize that when I take care of myself, I actually have more to give!

I have stronger boundaries than ever before! I actually never knew how poor my boundaries were! In my narcissistic relationship, I thought my boundaries were strong because I actually did communicate what was wrong and hurtful. However, I never put actual consequences in place. Then when he would cross my "boundaries," I felt so powerless! Since putting consequences in place, I feel that both people in the relationship (myself and the other person) have a choice. They can make a choice to do A or B and I will go ahead with what I need. We both get to choose what we will do. I feel so much more empowered! Through having strong boundaries, I've also stopped being friends with many disrespectful people in my life!

My people pleasing is at an all-time low! I learned that in trying to avoid rejection from others, I ended up rejecting myself. I have now realized that my needs, wants, feelings, and thoughts are just as valid as the people I had been sacrificing myself for. It is up to us to take care of ourselves. We set the standard as to how others will treat us by how we treat ourselves.

Each person here has recognized that they needed to do some work. They took ownership to change. In order to continue down the healthy path, it is essential to take full responsibility for our lives and for learning through every difficult circumstance. Taking responsibility for every area of your life will empower you and cause you to come out of this situation healed, growing, and thriving. If we constantly choose to blame other people (including the narcissist) for what has happened in our life and for where we are, we will fall prey to the toxic victim mentality. The victim mentality is a huge de-motivator whereby you end up surrendering all your power. Blame always disempowers, because it strengthens the belief that your life is shaped and created by the people outside yourself and, therefore, you are powerless to change anything.

By playing the victim we give up the ownership of our life and our choices. While you may have been a victim in the beginning, you do not have to remain a victim or a prisoner to this experience. Now is the time to take back your power. James Belasco wrote in, *Flight of the Buffalo*, "In most situations, I am the problem. My mentalities, my pictures, my expectations, form the biggest obstacle to my success."[13] The shift of power happens when we say, "I am the problem," because this is when we can also become the solution.

You are as empowered as you choose to be. You own as much of your life and your future as you choose. The more ownership you take in your life, the more happiness, fulfillment, and success you will have.

11. Evaluate: What Red Flags Did I Miss in the Past?

Now that you are out of the relationship with a narcissist, it's time to evaluate what happened. What are some of the red flags you missed in the early stages of the game? What will you do differently so that this will never happen again?

In retrospect, we can often see the red flags we ignored in our relationships more clearly after the fact. The following section involves the red flags that we missed, some wisdom as to how to proceed differently in the future, and the areas of needed growth.

Too Much Too Soon

Looking back, the relationship was too much too soon. It was an instant relationship and I was swept away by his charm. I romanticized both the relationship and who he was. I filled in the gaps in positive ways and saw what I wanted to see, not what was actually there.

Wisdom

Move at a slower pace so you can keep your eyes wide open. That will increase your odds for long-term success. Don't get sucked into the honeymoon period or give your heart away too easily. Love bombing is extremely powerful. If you feel like you are losing your head in a relationship, slow down and let reality catch up. If it seems that things are too good to be true, they likely are. Only time will let you know, so allow things to play out without the mad dash. Remember: "Charm is *deceptive.*"

Needed Growth Area

Become a person who is full of love for yourself. Then you won't be taken in so easily and you won't need others to fill a void of love. Take your time! Love bombing is powerful and blinding! Relationships are meant to be an endurance event and not a sprint.

Irresponsible

He did not take any responsibility for his divorces or past relationships. He was ONLY the victim.

Wisdom

Find out what they *learned* from their past relationships. What were *their* blind spots, weaknesses, or life lessons? How did they come out as a better person from their relationships? Healthy and growing people look at their own weaknesses and intentionally find areas to grow in. If they feel they did not contribute in any way to the demise of the relationship and you only hear them blaming the other person, walk away.

Needed Growth Area

Take an honest look at how people take responsibility for their life and circumstances. Fully own your own weaknesses and take responsibility for every area of your life. Raise your standards of ownership and expect others to do the same.

Unable to Acknowledge My Feelings

He dismissed and disregarded my feelings and concerns. In the beginning it was just a light brushing over. It grew. He did not ever truly acknowledge me, my feelings, or concerns.

Wisdom

Never disregard *your own* feelings and concerns. If you confront anyone you are in a relationship with about their disrespect, and they *continue* to disregard or disrespect you, your feelings or your concerns, it's time to say goodbye.

Needed Growth Area

Be fully in tune with your own needs and emotions. Honour and protect yourself by not having people in your life who disrespect or dishonour you. Set clear and healthy boundaries. Don't settle. Go out and find amazing people!

Just Being Sorry Doesn't Last

> *I caught him lying and took him back because he said he was sorry. However, he did not create a proven track record before I trusted him again.*

Wisdom

Don't take someone back after a betrayal just because they are "sorry." Make sure that their sorrow proves itself in actual deeds and not just in words. There must not merely be words spoken, but also a proven change in their actions and character.

Needed Growth Area

Where does your acceptance come from that enables people to lie to you? Is it from your own family of origin? Notice at what point in your life it became tolerable to you when a person chronically lied to you. Decide to only have honest people in your life. If someone has betrayed you and you would like to give them a second chance, take your time to build trust and allow them to prove themself trustworthy. Listen to a person's actions much more than their words. Have they actually changed? Don't give your trust away lightly.

A Lack of Remorse

> *There was a lack of remorse when he treated me badly and there was never an authentic apology. He skirted around the subject and made many faux-pologies that neither dealt directly with nor changed the destructive behaviour.*

Wisdom

A person who is truly on the road to change will acknowledge the real wrongs that were done. Pay attention to see if they are remorseful for their *behaviour* or merely for the *consequences* that they might be experiencing.

Needed Growth Area

Only allow respectful people into your life. It is not acceptable for people to treat you badly. Know your worth!

History

He had a history of cheating.

Wisdom

Do cheaters change? We often want to believe that this is possible. After knowing many cheaters (including women who cheat), the odds are EXTREMELY rare that cheaters will genuinely change, although it can happen. Cheaters make choices. They put themselves first. They choose deception and selfish fulfillment over integrity, trust, and their relationships. Their belief system is entitlement. Rather than ending a relationship before starting a new one, they will choose to betray another person. Cheating is a serious character flaw, never to be overlooked or taken lightly. If you dare, proceed with EXTREME CAUTION! Know that if you choose a cheater (even if they have not cheated on you), they will most likely *eventually* cheat on you. It has to do with their character or lack thereof. Do not be deceived that you are the exception in their world. Yes, there can be the *rare* exception; however, it is *rare*. It is likely best to cut your ties and run!

Needed Growth Area

Recognize that those who engage in this type of deceptive and selfish behaviour are NOT safe people. Your task is to only allow safe people into your life.

Entitlement

I couldn't believe the entitlement! After we married, although he was making a mid-six-figure income, he was content to live off me! I was paying for the mortgage, for all of our living expenses, and for the groceries, all while my own business was struggling. I finally had to demand that he step up and contribute something to the household. I never thought that anyone could be like that!

Wisdom

Money can be a tricky subject. It is good to go into a relationship with clear and communicated expectations. Pay attention to entitlement issues. When you get married every character issue and attitude magnifies.

Needed Growth Area

Set clear boundaries and standards at the beginning of a relationship. Avoid intimate relationships with those who use others. Never allow a person to drain you dry.

Genuineness

He never said "I love you" at any point in our relationship unless I said it first. When he would say, "I love you," he parroted it back to me in the exact same tone that I'd said. Looking back, it never felt genuine.

Wisdom

Pay attention to the absence of spontaneous and authentic confessions of love. Words from your mate or significant other should reach the soul level. There should be some initiation and authenticity of their expressions of love to you. When this doesn't exist in a relationship, something is off or it needs rekindling.

Needed Growth Area

Wait for the type of person who is completely in love with you. You deserve it! Expect to receive. One cannot be in a healthy relationship without learning and exercising this ability. Also, your gut is a good guide if something is not right or not genuine.

My Friends

> *He didn't want to be around my friends. This was not something that happened at first. It changed gradually like the colours in a sunset. In the end he really did not care about my friends. Then he started bad-mouthing them and was negative toward me every time I was with them. This is how the isolation started.*

Wisdom

Pay attention to how your partner interacts with your friends and family. Are they supportive of you and your relationships with them? Make sure that it stays consistent over time.

Needed Growth Area

Do not allow another person (no matter who they are in your life), to downgrade or discourage you from spending time with the people you love. Really pay attention if the heat turns up against you in this area. You never want to be isolated and cut off from the people that you love and who love you back.

A Lack of Appreciation

There was a lack of appreciation and gratitude for all the things I was doing. I actually discovered that this can be an early sign of an affair developing ... which is what it ended up being.

Wisdom

Narcissists are often incapable of feeling gratitude. They won't believe that anything you've done for them deserves appreciation as they are entitled to everything that you give them. Pay attention though, because it does *not* go both ways. In some weird way, they will actually expect you to be grateful for things that they selfishly did for themselves.

Needed Growth Area

People who are never grateful are usually disrespectful as well. Choose to be around people who *appreciate* you. There are *plenty* out there.

Ignoring My Voice

I ignored my voice when it was screaming, "DEAL BREAKER!" at me.

Wisdom

Your gut knows! Having a feeling that something is off is *NEVER* to be ignored. You owe it to yourself to protect yourself and look out for your best interests. Many times you are the only one who ever will.

Needed Growth Area

Learn to prioritize and listen to your voice on a regular and daily basis. Pay attention to it and honour it in all areas of your life.

Outside Sources

I never found out about his past relationships from any outside source. We met online and had no mutual friends. Of course his ex-wife was "crazy" and had "ruined his reputation." Perhaps if I had heard a bit of the other side of the story, I would not have married him. It turns out my marriage mirrored his other two marriages to a T. After I was divorced and started dating again, I did some things differently. This time I verified the guy's character with some mutual friends. My one friend told me quite frankly to "RUN!" I later understood why. Her sage advice saved me from making another mistake. I've learned the importance of getting verification from outside sources.

Wisdom

It is good to confirm a person's character. Pay attention to how others have related to this person in the past and whether this person has a history of broken relationships. If you have mutual friends, it can't hurt to know their experience with this person.

Needed Growth Area

If you've had difficulty discerning a person's character in the past and/ or are a naturally trusting person who seems to get burned, surround yourself with discerning and straightforward friends. They can teach you what to look out for until you sharpen your own skills of discernment.

PART VI

Your Bright Future

What will you do with this experience? Living in empowerment and carving out a new path for your life will involve a positive perspective from this relationship, returning to your authentic and best self, and intentionally creating proactive, healthy habits.

CHAPTER 14

MOVING FORWARD IN YOUR LIFE

The good news is that you can have a wonderful life after a narcissistic relationship! Your healing journey will take time, effort, and intention. You will get there! You can be whole again, and it's possible that you will become even better than you were before this trauma. With your newfound insights and experiences, you have gained more wisdom, you can better appreciate the genuine people in your life, and you can walk in a lasting empowerment that you've never had before.

In coming out of this experience, perspective is *everything*. You have a choice as to how you view this situation and how you would like to move forward. While it is possible to wallow in victim and self-pity modes, to stay trapped, and to continually attract more narcissists in your life, it is *also* possible to gain incredible wisdom from this experience, to make some changes, and to live in greater freedom, empowerment, and fulfillment. May you choose the latter for yourself.

Let's get to *how* you move forward after such a horrific experience.

After the healing has come, you can look in the rear-view mirror to understand why things have not worked out, AND see how these things have actually served you.

1. Acknowledge Yourself

First of all, I would like to acknowledge you. You are a survivor. You are strong. You are resilient. You have lived through hellish abuse and you have come out the other side. You are a beautiful person with real emotions. You demonstrate kindness and empathy. You serve others well, you are genuine, open, kind, and generous. You do a lot of wonderful things for the people you are in relationship with. You *do* deserve better. You will love life again and you will thrive.

The narcissist was pretty hard on you and, most likely, especially toward the end. They likely didn't acknowledge any of the good in you but were determined to tear you down and destroy you in every way possible. Remember, that the voice of abuse (complete with gaslighting and all of its twisted blaming) does not come from a kind person but from a master manipulator and abuser. It is important to get rid of the echoes of gaslighting and blaming that will creep into your head from time to time. Now is your time to validate what you went through, your own feelings, your worth, and your voice. It is time to start recognizing, acknowledging, and appreciating everything about yourself.

- What did you do well in this relationship?
- What are your greatest successes from this experience that you want to continue to move forward with?
- What feelings do you have that still need to be acknowledged?
- What do others love and appreciate about you?
- What do you love and appreciate about yourself?

It is also important to give yourself some compassion for being in this situation instead of continuing to heap the blame, guilt, and condemnation upon yourself. Give yourself the same compassion and understanding as you would to a good friend who has just gone through a horrific trauma. Narcissists are controlling manipulators whose false charm is crafted to strike where it will be the most effective—against kind, empathetic people. You must come to realize that falling for a narcissist doesn't make you weak. It wasn't your weaknesses that they exploited, but rather your strengths of empathy, kindness, and compassion.

Don't be ashamed of your story. It will inspire others.

2. Get Back in Touch with Your Authentic Self

I have yet to meet a person who has been in a relationship with a narcissist and who, after exiting that relationship, feels like they were able to be their true, authentic, and best self in that relationship. Most people experience a slow build-up of making unnecessary sacrifices combined with the gradual erosion of who they really are. To get back in touch with your authentic self, start listening to your emotions, needs, and wants, and get back to doing activities that bring you joy.

Listen to that inner voice that allows you to be you!

After getting out of my own relationship, I realized that one of my self-destructive flaws was that I stopped listening to my own voice. When my voice was no longer clear, I gave into the voice of the narcissist. Until you truly love, honour, and respect your own emotions, opinions, and needs, you will never attract others into your life who will deeply love, honour, and respect you.

At the centre of your being you have the answer: you know who you are and you know what you want.

Perhaps this is also true of you. As with most families, in the time and place that we grew up, feelings were not discussed. Independence, self-sufficiency, and not "being a burden" to others were strong values. Negating, suppressing, numbing, and disregarding feelings, emotions, and hurts were normal parts of life. Trauma was never discussed. Because of learning how to have a "tough skin," many of us unconsciously (and falsely) learned that our feelings didn't matter and that they were irrelevant. You may now be aware that some of the "normal" (yet unhealthy) ways that you learned to operate in your life did not serve you. However at the time, you didn't know what you didn't know. When something is completely normal to you, you may not know that there is another way.

However, if you want different results in your life, you need to function in a new way. Rediscover your inner voice. Speak your preferences and vulnerabilities. Become more concerned about speaking your truth and honouring your values than about pleasing others.

> *Don't let the noise of others' opinions drown out your own inner voice.*[1]
>
> —Steve Jobs

Get back to doing the activities you've always loved to do and that have given you fulfillment in the past. After the devaluation and discard phase with a narcissist, your joy has been smothered and the life has been sucked out of you. You probably unnecessarily sacrificed many of the things you loved in order to put all your energy into attempting to please your narcissist or trying to make the relationship work. *Now* is the time to return to what you love to do. What are the activities and passions that really give you joy in life? What are some things that you have always wanted to do but have not done yet? Invest in your passions, your goals, your dreams, and yourself.

> *When you start doing things that are truly in alignment with what your true self wants, what your soul wants, you flourish and life becomes a lot easier.*

3. Choose to Be Empowered—Not a Victim

A victim can be described as a person who has been fooled, hurt, or harmed, due to his or her own emotions or ignorance; an unfortunate event; or the actions of another person who has deceived, cheated, injured, or killed him or her. Although you have been deceived, hurt, fooled, and harmed by a narcissist, you no longer need to remain a victim. You can choose the path of empowerment. You are no longer fooled by who they are. You are now armed with wisdom so as not to be deceived again. Hopefully by now you have no or little contact with the narcissist and you are out of harm's way. Healing the hurt does take time and intention. It is possible to be healed and to walk freely forever.

When you remain in victim mode, not only do you continue to be wounded but also you are actually giving up your power to the narcissist. A victim is someone who is helpless in the face of adversity. A victim chooses to see that someone else or some circumstance outside their control is responsible for what they do or do not get in life and there is nothing that can be done about it. The truth is that you are not helpless or powerless. You can take action. It is never good to put the responsibility for your circumstances or your life outside yourself, as something that is beyond your power to change. You can always control your *response* to your circumstances and you can create a path forward. You can get your power back.

Never be a victim of your past. It was just a lesson, not a life sentence.

It is both healthy and empowering to get rid of the blame, both for yourself and for the narcissist. Do not fall prey to the blame game! Write a new story for yourself. The stories we speak in our minds become the stories we live out in our lives. What story do you want to live out for yourself? How do you need to change the story that is playing in your mind so that it matches the life you want?

A victim's story may sound something like this: "I am powerless. The narcissist has taken everything from me. I can't help being where I'm at. There is nothing I can do. I sacrificed everything and nothing was appreciated. I put up with so much crap. I wasted my life and it's all the fault of the narcissist. I will be scarred from this experience for the rest of my life." As you can see, this is oppressive and limiting. This story does not serve you.

In contrast, a survivor's story sounds more like this: "I have learned so much! This relationship was actually good for me because I have become a better person for it. It exposed my blind spots and weaknesses so that I am now aware of them and can change. Now I set firm and effective boundaries. ALL the people in my life now treat me with deep respect. I now have healthy relationships of give and take and I treat myself with incredible self-care. I listen to and honour my voice on a consistent basis. My needs are taken care of and I make sure that my own cup is full. My past wounds are healed. I let the good things into my life and I ask for help on a regular basis. I communicate my feelings freely to the people in my life. I have more energy now because I only take responsibility for what is mine. I do not take responsibility for others' feelings or actions. This experience has made me stronger and has enriched my life. I completely own and take responsibility for absolutely every area of my life. I look forward to my bright and beautiful future!"

Making changes in our life after this experience is essential to our recovery and our wellbeing. You have the power to make any and all of the changes you want and need to make. It is possible to undo any damage that was inflicted upon you. Ask for help from the professionals. A counsellor or therapist who understands personality disorders can give you great insights and understanding about yourself and what you went through. Get all the support you need from your friends and those who have been with narcissists and are now living on the other side. Do everything you can to become more empowered.

Arming yourself with information about narcissists and narcissistic abuse will help you to heal faster. The more you discover, it will seem as if all narcissists attended the same boot camp training. There are classic, textbook moves that all narcissists do and say. By learning their tactics and through understanding what they are doing, you can often accurately predict their next moves. Your knowledge will also help you begin to understand that this was never about you. The abuse was, and is, all about who they are. You will also see clearly that you are not the only one who fell into their trap.

Taking responsibility for the individual part you played in this tango is also empowering. You can only change yourself and no one else. When people begin to treat you in unacceptable ways, it is up to you to lay down a clear boundary. If they choose not to respect the boundary, it is up you to remove yourself from that person or situation. Or, if you choose to remain with them, to completely own your choice of staying. Just know that there is absolutely no way that you can change a narcissist.

It is up to you not only to keep abusive and destructive behaviours out of your life but to also ask for help and let the good things into your life. The onus is on you to start healing your heart and your past. It's up to you to fill your unmet needs in healthy ways. By taking complete ownership and responsibility for your life and your choices, you will be well on your path to a wonderful new and empowered life.

4. Determine Your Own Self-Worth

Your inner world creates your outer world. How you see yourself and how you treat yourself will be reflected in your relationships. Take ownership of creating your own self-worth. Let your self-worth come from within rather than basing it on what others say or might think of you. Looking to others to obtain your self-worth is extremely detrimental and meaningless. Codependency is the state of trying to get your self-worth from something or someone outside yourself. When we fully receive the unconditional love (from God or another source) and we extend it to ourselves, we no longer have to "prove" our worth. We can simply be. In the state of being in unconditional love, we can be fully at peace with every part of who we are. We determine that we are worthy. No matter what the people or circumstances outside us are saying.

Celebrate your uniqueness! Acknowledge all the good and wonderful things about yourself. Accept and admit your weaknesses with grace and compassion. No one is exempt from having weaknesses. Everybody has them. Learn to love and accept *all* parts of yourself. To have full acceptance of yourself is part of being an authentic person. You accept the good and the bad, the strengths and the weaknesses. This will also help you to be more accepting and loving of other people's flaws.

Your self-worth will also increase when you stop comparing yourself with others. The comparison game can make us feel insecure when we aren't "as good" as someone in a certain area. Or we can have an elevated, yet fragile sense of pride when we compare ourselves with others and we decide that we score "better" than another person. Keeping up such performances is exhausting. When you constantly live by comparison, someone will inevitably be smarter, richer, more talented, or prettier than you. Don't measure your worth by what you do or by how you perform compared to others. You are worthy because you *are*.

Know that you are special, irreplaceable, and a treasure. There is no one in the world quite like you. You are the only one who embodies the exclusive mixture of your personality, experiences, ways of relating, your quirks, sense of humour, strengths, skills, and perspectives. You have something truly amazing to offer the world. You have a destiny to fulfill that no one else can. Get out there and be fully yourself!

5. Decide This Experience Made You Better

Perspective is *everything*. How you choose to view your experiences, especially your former relationship with a narcissist, can alter the course of your existence. There are two paths you can take. A person can either slowly die on the inside from a poisonous bitterness; or they can grow, get stronger, be grateful, develop resilience, and live in unshakeable freedom. Decide that *you* are a person who is resilient and strong and will come out of this experience richer than ever before. You are now wiser, more compassionate, and very discerning. *Decide* to find all the ways that you are grateful for this experience. You can choose to be a much better person because of what you have lived through.

Healing exists alongside challenge in every trial. As Shahida Arabi says, what seem like obstacles can become portals. Choosing this perspective is not intended to downgrade or minimize the horrors that you experienced while you were with a narcissist. Having a mindset of deciding this situation made you better is designed to empower you. You can use this experience as a springboard for better things in life, and to move you forward into the bright and wonderful future that *IS* possible. I would like to encourage you to find the gifts and lessons that this experience has brought you. Discern how your life will be healthier, more thriving, different, and better in the future because of the lessons you have learned.

Maybe this experience caused you to draw a line in the sand, stating you will no longer put up with the impossible task of pleasing everyone. You have now decided to focus on only being around people who love you for your *true self* and not because you do countless things for them, add to their ego, or live to please them. People can now know you and love you for who you are and not for what you do.

Perhaps through this experience you have learned to set firm boundaries. You no longer attract disrespectful or abusive people into your life. These dark characters don't even bother to try to be in your life because your boundaries are so clear. You no longer allow bad things or harmful people to enter your life. At the same time, you also keep a healthy surge of good things and supportive people in your life.

You have now decided to listen to and respect your inner voice and your intuition. You truly honour yourself for who you really are. You have rediscovered the importance of your own life, your specific interests, and your needs both within and outside your relationships. You have learned, or are learning, to be more vulnerable about your true feelings because you are now aware of them and honour them.

> *I need to forget what's gone, appreciate what remains, and look forward to what's coming.*

Perhaps because of this experience you have healed some of your past hurts, unconscious wounds, and childhood trauma. Many have become aware of unconscious patterns they developed that were their "normal" ways of operating, yet which were also unhealthy. Others discover their blind spots so that they can be fixed and real growth can take place.

Think of how you have gained incredible new insights as to how certain people operate, particularly narcissistic predators. You are no longer naive to the fact that there are truly evil people in this world. You know how to spot them and you know how to protect yourself. You can now see past empty flattery and false promises, and are not caught up in whirlwind romances or love bombing. You no longer enter relationships when something feels off or your gut is telling you to "get out!" You have gained wisdom and insights that you never would have gotten, had you not gone through this experience.

> *Everything I thought was a tragedy, I now know is a gift.*

6. Give Yourself Incredible Self-Care

Self-care is any activity that we do deliberately in order to take care of our mental, emotional, and physical health. Self-care is not being selfish; it is about intentionally taking care of your needs so that you can be your very best self.

Self-care is something that refuels us rather than takes from us.

As was previously stated, we all know that in an emergency situation it is vital to put the oxygen mask on ourself first, before we take care of other people. After all, even with the best intentions, we will be of no use to anyone else if we are unable to breathe ourself. We cannot give what we do not have. We can never give to people when we are entirely depleted. In coaching, we say that your cup must be always be full in order to be truly effective. You then give to others from the *overflow* of your cup, rather than diminishing and draining your own cup. By taking care of your own needs and keeping your cup full, you are actually in a more effective place to serve others.

If I don't take enough care of myself, I won't be able to give to my loved ones.

After getting out of a narcissistic relationship, you need oxygen immediately. It is time to prioritize your own self-care. Focus on what you need. Trim down your normal schedule to include the time and resources you need to get back to being YOU. Self-care isn't something you do once and check it off your list. It is the constant repetition of many tiny habits, which not only soothe you when you need healing but also make sure you are at your optimum at all times.

Self-care is how you take your power back.

Think of someone who takes impeccable care of him or herself. This person probably gets a good night's sleep, eats healthy foods, dresses well, and exercises daily. They may get massages on a regular basis, travel often, and do the things that we might consider "extras." These people also balance their time well and take the time for friends, family, their interests, and solitude. They seem to glow from the inside out and they possess an attractive, irresistible energy because they truly honour themselves. There is a sense of deep peace and abundance about them. Their cup is consistently full and they are attracting people, resources, and opportunities into their lives. Such results start with healthy habits of self-care.

On a regular basis these people are engaged with doing things that are truly good for them in the long run rather than choosing instant gratification. While the quick fix may feel good in the short run, it is usually self-destructive in the end. Consider what you do or have done when you are in pain. Here's a test: in the *long run*, is what you are doing something that is healthy or self-destructive? Consider some of our typical pain-numbing behaviours: eating a gallon of ice-cream, downing a bottle of wine, going on an out-of-control spending spree, staying in bed for three days, or other such behaviours. I'm sure we've all done something like this at one time or another. In the end, these things neither help us to heal nor serve us in the long run. Don't confuse quality self-care that serves you in the long run with quick-fix, numbing coping mechanisms.

People with solid self-care find many healthy outlets such as running or walking in nature, getting a massage, doing a major spring clean, journaling, giving themselves a facial or pedicure, getting together with friends, or going out of town to do something fun. Ask yourself, *Will doing this activity be productive for my healing and will I be happier in the future because I did this? Is this behaviour in line with who I am and also the person that I want to become?*

Self-worth is about valuing, respecting, and knowing your worth. It's you valuing yourself. It's about you respecting yourself, knowing who you are, and what you are worth.

Here are some ideas for self-care:

- **A hot bath:** Go all out! Have the candles, bubbles, and soothing music to boot!

- **Affirmations:** Create affirmations to conquer any limiting beliefs. With enough repetition, your positive thoughts and beliefs will stick, which will change the way you think and ultimately how you live your life.

- **Aromatherapy:** Choose from the variety of scents available to change your moods and improve your mental health. Some scents can help you feel calmer and less stressed. On the flip side, others can make you feel more energized and invigorated!

- **Being in nature:** A wonderful way to experience both serenity and aliveness!

- **Clothing:** Buy a new outfit that expresses your style. Reconfigure your wardrobe. Let your clothing make you look and feel great!

- **Cooking a fun meal:** Try something new. Put on some music, invite friends over (or do it solo), and have a cultural fiesta. Enjoy the culinary process and of course the food!

- **Creative artistic endeavours:** Small acts of creativity in our everyday life increase our overall sense of wellbeing. There are many avenues that stimulate creativity, such as painting, pottery, colouring books, gardening, and creating photobooks.

- **Dancing:** Take some lessons or classes. You can do ballroom dancing, salsa, swing, ballet, tap, hip-hop, or just simply moving to the music. It's amazing how dancing can transform your mood!

- **Declutter:** Treat yourself to a good Marie Kondo purge. Get rid of everything that doesn't "spark joy."

- **Exercise:** Whether you are running, walking, hiking, swimming, cycling, doing Tai Chi, or pumping iron, you will feel amazing from getting the blood flowing and kicking your endorphins (the feel-good hormones) into high gear.

- **Explore:** Go somewhere new! Try a new restaurant or a different beach, drive through your dream neighbourhood, or explore a whole new area.

- **Future you:** Envision what your ideal future self is like. Create the vision and fill in the details of what life will be like for your best future self.

- **Gratitude:** You can keep a gratitude journal and take the time to reflect on being thankful for specific things. Appreciating everything that you have will make you more content and joyful in life.

- **Invite others out:** Some activities are best when others join in with us. Take the initiative to invite others to go to concerts, festivals, the theatre, or picnics at the park with you. Host a game night.

- **Make other people happy:** Get out of your own head and your own life; go out there and serve others. Do some random acts of kindness for strangers or for your friends and family.

- **Massage:** An amazing massage not only heals sore muscles but also the soothing power of touch enhances our wellbeing.

- **Meditation:** Meditate and spend some quiet time following your meditation to simply be aware of what is coming to you in still moments.

- **Nutrition:** Treat your body with the care and respect it deserves by eating whole foods, including plenty of fresh fruits and vegetables.

- **Online Communities:** Find people you have things in common with, either with regard to your interests, goals, or similar life circumstances.

- **Organizing:** Give yourself a fresh organizational reset that will add to your mental clarity, self-esteem, and motivation.

- **Self-Compassion:** Recognize and acknowledge your feelings. Speak as kindly to yourself as you would to your best friend.

- **Simple things:** Be sure to include plenty of simple pleasures in your life: enjoy a cup of tea or coffee; have fresh flowers in your home, scented candles, fresh sheets; do puzzles; or curl up with a great book and a weighted blanket.

- **Sleep:** Getting seven to nine hours of quality sleep each night not only helps you to feel refreshed but it also heals your body.

- **Spa Day:** You can go to a spa or even create a home spa day complete with facials, scrubs, manicures, and pedicures.

- **Sports:** Sports engage the brain and body and are wonderful social outlets. You can enjoy golf, tennis, pickleball, volleyball, soccer, basketball, softball, kayaking, rowing, paddle boarding, swimming, snowboarding, skiing, and countless other activities.

- **Travelling and Day Trips:** Getting away on a vacation boosts creativity, relieves stress, and helps you to reinvent yourself. Travelling (especially internationally) is a personal favourite of mine!

By being intentional to give yourself amazing self-care, not only will you heal and become more whole but your joy will increase. You will feel better about yourself and will attract greater relationships, opportunities, and circumstances into your life! Take impeccable care of yourself. You deserve it!

7. Return to Yourself: Step into Your Bright and Wonderful Future!

Congratulations! Not only have you survived an incredible situation, you are now THRIVING! You have real friends who are there for you already and/or are waiting to be discovered. Friends you can trust, who love you, who won't prey upon you, and who truly have your back. You now have a fresh start! New goals, successes, travels, opportunities, and relationships are waiting for you. Be thankful that you are truly free! The best is yet to come!

May the next few months and years be a period of magnificent transformation.

AUTHOR BIO

Author Freya Strom has lived through the nightmare of a narcissistic marriage. After immersing herself in extensive research, counselling, and personal development, she has come out the other side empowered, healed, and thriving. It is her passion to see women and men transformed after this brutal experience, to walk in wholeness, and to live out their best self.

Freya Strom is an Associate Certified Life Coach with the International Coaching Federation. Freya is currently working with fellow life coach, Anita Reimer (CoachReimer.biz), to cocreate the coaching program, "Return to You - After the Narcissist." This strategic program is designed to dive deeper and to bring further healing and empowerment to those who have left a narcissistic relationship and who desire to create a bright future for themselves.

Freya is also an avid world traveler. Her love for the air, sea, and land has led to skydiving, kayaking, cycling, and hiking ventures around the globe. She loves sports, road cycling, and anything in the great outdoors. Freya has lived in four different countries and currently resides in Canada.

Learn more at SoYouMarriedANarcissist.com

ACKNOWLEDGEMENTS

My heartfelt gratitude goes out to all those who contributed their stories in this book! Thank you for being willing to share your struggles, victories, and vulnerabilities.

Special thanks go out all my friends, my family, my counsellor, my coach, and my special 911 friend whom I was able to call at all hours of the night. Thank you for your listening ears, your support, your kindness, and your willingness to ride this rollercoaster with me.

Thank you, Dr. Henry Cloud, Dr. John Townsend, FBI Special Agent Joe Navarro, Shahida Arabi, the Spartan Life Coach, and countless others whom I've yet to meet who offered me such wisdom and insight on my journey. You are all a huge part in my ongoing transformation.

Thank you to self-publishing guru, Geoff Affleck, who wore many hats and patiently coached me through the process of getting my first book across the publishing line.

Thank you to my editor, Nina Shoroplova, for your excellent work and attention to detail.

Many thanks to all of my clients and my readers who courageously press on through the healing process and transformational growth.

SELECTED BIBLIOGRAPHY

Arabi, Shahida. *Becoming the Narcissist's Nightmare: How to Devalue and Discard the Narcissist While Supplying Yourself.* New York: SCW Archer, 2016.

Brown, Brené. *I Thought It Was Just Me (But It Isn't): Making the Journey from "What Will People Think?" to "I Am Enough."* New York: Penguin Random House, 2007.

Cloud, Henry. *Never Go Back: 10 Things You'll Never Do Again.* New York: Howard Books, 2014.

Cloud, Henry, and John Townsend. *Safe People: How to Find Relationships that Are Good for You and Avoid Those that Aren't.* Grand Rapids: Zondervan, 1995.

———. *Boundaries in Dating: How Healthy Choices Grow Healthy Relationships.* New York: Prelude Press, 2000.

———. *Boundaries: When to Say Yes, How to Say No to Take Control of Your Life.* Grand Rapids, MI: Zondervan Pub. House, 1992.

Gottman, John. "The Four Horsemen: Criticism, Contempt, Defensiveness, and Stonewalling," www.gottman.com/blog/the-four-horsemen-recognizing-criticism-contempt-defensiveness-and-stonewalling/ accessed February 28, 2022.

Jantz, Gregory L. *Hope and Healing from Emotional Abuse.* Grand Rapids, MI: Baker Publishing Group, 2009.

Navarro, Joe. *Dangerous Personalities: An FBI Profiler Shows You How to Identify and Protect Yourself from Harmful People.* New York: Rodale, Inc., 2014.

O'Hara, Frank. *Early Writing.* Berkley, CA: Bookpeople, 1977.

Paramahansa Yogananda, *Autobiography of a Yogi*, www.gutenberg.org

Stevenson, Robert Louis. *The Strange Case of Dr. Jekyll and Mr. Hyde.* London: New English Library, 1974.

NOTES

Introduction

1. Navarro, *Dangerous Personalities*, 91.

2. *Psychology Today*, "Narcissistic Personality Disorder," www.psychologytoday.com/ca/conditions/narcissistic-personality-disorder, accessed May 24, 2022.

3. *Wikipedia*, en.wikipedia.org/wiki/Narcissistic_personality_disorder, accessed May 5, 2022.

4. Gail Meyers, m.facebook.com/GailMeyersNPDM/photos/a.1523162277940892/1535930616664058, accessed June 23, 2022.

5. Narcissist Meme, me.me/i/narcissist-n-a-more-polite-term-for-a-self-serving-manipulative-fddbf1711894484abae3dc7b1f0dc171, accessed June 28, 2022.

6. *World History Encyclopedia*, www.ancient.eu/Narcissus, accessed May 14, 2022.

7. *Greek Mythology*, www.greekmythology.com/Myths/Mortals/Narcissus/narcissus.html, accessed May 14, 2022.

8. O'Hara, *Early Writing*, 27.

Chapter 1

1. Steve Maraboli, www.goodreads.com/quotes/7647508-be-careful-not-all-are-what-they-seem-some-people, accessed June 25, 2022.

2. Arabi, *Becoming the Narcissist's Nightmare*, 37.

3. Melanie Tonia Evans, "The Narcissist and Co-dependent: Two Sides of the Same Coin," blog.melanietoniaevans.com/the-narcissist-and-co-dependent-two-sides-of-the-same-coin, accessed May 30, 2022.

4. *Lexico*, www.lexico.com/definition/fraud, accessed June 3, 2022.

5. *Stevenson, The Strange Case of Dr. Jekyll and Mr. Hyde.*

6. *Dorian Grey*, London: Fragile Films Production Company, 2009.

7. Shannon Thomas, neonplasticlotus.files.wordpress.com/2014/06/img_1984.jpg, accessed June 5, 2022.

8. Paramahansa Yogananda, *Autobiography of a Yogi*, chapter 12.

9. *Merriam-Webster*, www.merriam-webster.com/dictionary/victim, accessed June 8, 2022.

10. Karla Grimes, iheartintelligence.com/narcissists-never-take-the-blame-for-their-actions-instead-they-turn-it-on-you, accessed May 25, 2022.

Chapter 2

1. Zari Ballard, me.me/i/dont-ever-forget-that-a-narcissist-is-first-and-foremost-17455911, accessed April 10, 2022.

2. Navarro, *Dangerous Personalities*, 18.

3. Jeffery Kluger, www.goodreads.com/quotes/6773426-there-s-a-reason-narcissists-don-t-learn-from-mistakes-and-that-s, accessed March 18, 2022.

Chapter 3

1. Arabi, *Becoming the Narcissist's Nightmare*, 41.

2. Ibid., 265.

3. Danu Morrigan, www.happierhuman.com/narcissist-quotes, accessed March 16, 2022.

4. Gottman, "The Four Horsemen."

5. James Baldwin, www.goodreads.com/quotes/6596659-the-way-to-be-really-despicable-is-to-be-contemptuous, accessed May 9, 2022.

6. Brendon Burchard, www.facebook.com/Quotlr/photos/when-someone-disrespects-you-beware-the-impulse-to-win-their-respect-for-disresp/1101371373362815/, accessed April 27, 2022.

7. Steve Stosny, "How to Ruin a Perfectly Good Relationship," *Psychology Today*, December 21, 2012, www.psychologytoday.com/ca/blog/anger-in-the-age-entitlement/201212/how-ruin-perfectly-good-relationship-0.

8. Gottman, "The Four Horsemen."

Chapter 4

1. *PsychCentral*, "What is Narcissistic Abuse?" psychcentral.com/lib/what-is-narcissistic-abuse#1, accessed June 28, 2022.

2. *Oxford English Dictionary*, "Gaslight," www.oed.com/viewdictionaryentry/Entry/255554, accessed May 7, 2022.

3. *Gaslight*, Culver City; Metro-Goldwyn-Mayer, 1944.

4. Rokelle Lerner, twitter.com/lilyguilder, accessed May 8, 2022.

5. *The Life Doctor*, "The Narcissist's Prayer," www.thelifedoctor.org/the-narcissist-s-prayer, accessed June 2, 2022.

6. Arabi, *Becoming the Narcissist's Nightmare*, 42.

7. Jill Blakeway, www.pinterest.ca/pin/714805772090256239, accessed May 8, 2022.

8. Sophia Mitrokostas, "People with This Personality Trait," *Insider*, July 16, 2018, www.insider.com/narcissism-makes-more-likely-to-be-unfaithful-2018-7.

9. Julie Klausner, *Goodreads*, www.goodreads.com/quotes/1163560-if-anybody-studying-psychology-wants-a-concrete-example-of-what, accessed May 20, 2022.

10. Arabi, *Becoming the Narcissist's Nightmare*, 27.

11. Y. Clerebout, *LiveBoldandBloom*, www.liveboldandbloom.com/06/quotes/narcissistic-quotes, accessed April 18, 2022.

12. Jantz, *Healing the Scars of Emotional Abuse*, 37.

Chapter 5

1. Arabi, *Becoming the Narcissist's Nightmare*, 77.

2. Ibid., 74.

3. Cloud and Townsend, *Safe People*, 96.

4. Sharie Stines, "Abuse Amnesia: Why We Stay with Our Abusive Partners," *GoodTherapy*, October 3, 2017, www.goodtherapy.org/blog/abuse-amnesia-why-we-stay-with-our-abusive-partners-1003175.

5. Saul McLeod, "Cognitive Dissonance," *SimplyPsychology*, February 5, 2018, www.simplypsychology.org/cognitive-dissonance.html.

6. Jamie Eske, "What is Stockholm Syndrome?" *MedicalNewsToday*, October 1, 2020, www.medicalnewstoday.com/articles/stockholm-syndrome.

7. *AMFM,* "Trauma Bonding: What Is It and Why Do We Do It?" amfmtreatment.com/trauma-bonding-what-is-it-and-why-do-we-do-it, accessed May 28, 2022.

Chapter 6

1. Anne Brown, twitter.com/scienceofno/status/10954993110 75463168, accessed June 7, 2022.

2. Lindsay Dodgson, "Empaths and narcissists make a 'toxic' partnership: here's why they're attracted to each other," *Insider,* January 23, 2018, www.businessinsider.com/why-empaths-and-narcissists-are-attracted-to-each-other-2018-1.

3. Richard Grannon, "15 Traits of People Pleaser Syndrome," YouTube, March 3, 2014, www.youtube.com/watch?v=mPmv9_UYpxo.

4. John Townsend, "In relationships, you get what you tolerate," *Facebook,* February 18, 2021, www.facebook.com/203707726314451/posts/in-relationships-you-get-what-you-tol erateboundaries/4002272019791317/.

5. Cloud and Townsend, *Boundaries: When to Say Yes,* 209.

6. Richard Grannon: "15 Traits of People Pleaser Syndrome," YouTube, March 3, 2014, www.youtube.com/watch?v=mPm v9_UYpxo.

7. Cloud and Townsend, *Safe People,* 103.

8. Linda Esposito, "6 Signs of a Codependent Relationship," *Psychology Today,* September 19, 2016, www.psychologytoday.com/ca/blog/anxiety-zen/201609/6-signs-codependent-relationship.

9. R. Skip Johnson, "Codependency and Codependent Relationships," *BPD Family,* bpdfamily.com/content/codependency-codependent-relationships, accessed June 21, 2022.

10. *Mental Health America,* "Codependency," www.mhanational.
    org/co-dependency, accessed June 21, 2022.

Chapter 7

1. Mark Twain, *Goodreads,* www.goodreads.com/quotes/8209079-
   the-only-way-to-win-a-toxic-person-is-not, accessed June 18,
   2022.

2. *Posthood,* "40 R.H. Sin Quotes the Guarantee You'll Feel
   Strength After Breakup," posthood.com/r-h-sin-quotes-
   about-strength, accessed. June 30, 2022.

3. *Bible Gateway,* Proverbs 25:18, www.biblegateway.com/
   passage/?search=   Proverbs%2025%3A18&version=NIV,
   accessed May 11, 2022.

4. Lionel Richie, *Quote Fancy,* quotefancy.com/quote/1383764/
   Lionel-Richie-When-your-past-calls-don-t-answer-It-has-
   nothing-new-to-say, accessed, June 28, 2022.

Chapter 8

1. Brown, *I Thought It Was Just Me,* 37.

2. Rhonda Freeman, "Guilt and Shame: A Message to Survivors
   'New' to the Aftermath," *Neuroinstincts,* neuroinstincts.com/
   self-care-narcissistic-psychopathic-relationship, accessed June
   11, 2022.

3. Navarro, *Dangerous Personalities,* 56.

4. Tigress Luv, "Are Narcissists Evil?" Narcissistic MIL,
   March 16, 2017, narcissisticmil.wordpress.com/2017/03/16/
   are-narcissists-evil.

5. Arabi, *Becoming the Narcissist's Nightmare,* 80.

Chapter 9

1. Drew, *Pinterest*, www.pinterest.ca/pin/571675746421660984/, accessed June 29, 2022.

2. Narcissistic Mother, *Pinterest*, gr.pinterest.com/pin/34262548 4157397618, accessed July 9, 2022.

3. Mary Perren, *Pinterest*, www.pinterest.ca/maryperren/i-will-survive/, accessed May 30, 2022.

4. Narcissist Meme, me.me/i/narcissists-play-dumb-when-they re-caught-you-should-never-feel-10434775, accessed June 8, 2022.

5. Destiny Schull, *Pinterest*, www.pinterest.ca/pin/530439662 341083711, accessed July 9, 2022.

6. *Reddit*, www.reddit.com/r/quotes/comments/2yqeej/dont_ make_excuses_for_nasty_people_you_cant_put_a/, accessed June 8, 2022.

7. *Today We Date*, "31 Sad Heartbreak Quotes That Understand Your Pain" todaywedate.com/heartbreak-quotes, accessed June 8, 2022.

8. *Narcissistic Meme*, me.me/i/narcissist-n-a-more-polite-term-for-a-self-serving-manipulative-fddbf1711894484abae3dc7b 1f0dc171, accessed June 8, 2022.

9. Shannon Thomas, *Narcissistic Meme*, me.me/i/narcissistic-per sonalities-are-created-and-sustained-no-one-is-born-5084 899, accessed June 8, 2022.

10. *Narcissistic Meme*, me.me/i/did-you-know-that-narcissist-spelled-backwards-is-asshole-hey-2276982, accessed June 8, 2022.

11. Love This Pic, www.lovethispic.com/image/396106/a-narcissist-is-someone-who-demands-you-to-give-up-

everything-in-order-to-be-their-nothing, accessed June 8, 2022.

12. Eddie Corbano, "21 Narcissistic Quotes That Will Make You Leave," *LovesAGame*, lovesagame.com/quotes-about-narcissists, accessed June 8, 2022.

13. Norman Mailer, *Goodreads*, www.goodreads.com/quotes/5474 22-the-paradox-is-that-no-love-can-prove-so-intense, accessed June 8, 2022.

14. Cynthia French, *Pinterest*, www.pinterest.ca/pin/567453621 806841637, accessed June 8, 2022.

15. *Pinterest*, Parental Narcissistic Abuse, www.pinterest.ca/pin/ 12314598961747793, accessed June 8, 2022.

16. *Finding Your Feet*, London: Eclipse Films, 2017.

17. *Gaslight*, Culver City: Metro-Goldwyn-Mayer, 1944.

18. *The Other Woman*, New Providence: LBI Productions, 2014.

19. *Big Eyes*, Los Angeles: The Weinstein Company, 2014.

20. *Dirty John*, Los Angeles: Nutmegger Universal Cable Productions, 2018.

21. *The Women*, New York City: New Line Cinema, 2008.

22. *The Other Boleyn Girl*, London: Columbia Pictures, 2008.

Chapter 11

1. Lee Jordan and Beth Jordan, "The Healing Benefits of Forgiveness," *Idea Fit*, May 10, 2021, www.ideafit.com/ mind-body-recovery/the-healing-benefits-of-forgiveness.

2. Joyce Meyer, *Quote Fancy*, quotefancy.com/quote/845988/ Joyce-Meyer-Harboring-unforgiveness-is-like-drinking-poison-and-hoping-your-enemy-will, accessed May 1, 2022.

3. Lewis B. Smedes, *Quote Fancy*, quotefancy.com/quote/758944/Lewis-B-Smedes-To-forgive-is-to-set-a-prisoner-free-and-discover-that-the-prisoner-was, accessed April 30, 2022.

4. Ryan Howes, "Forgiveness vs. Reconciliation," *Psychology Today*, March 31, 2013, www.psychologytoday.com/intl/blog/in-therapy/201303/forgiveness-vs-reconciliation, accessed April 30, 2022.

5. Merriam-Webster, www.merriam-webster.com/dictionary/victim, accessed June 12, 2022.

Chapter 12

1. R. H. Sin, *The Mind Journal*, themindsjournal.com/theres-a-message-in-the-way-a-person-treats-you-just-listen, accessed June 25, 2022.

2. Richard V. Reeves, *Quote Fancy*, quotefancy.com/quote/2445728/Richard-V-Reeves-Disagreement-is-one-thing-disrespect-is-quite-another, accessed June 25, 2022.

3. Cloud and Townsend, *Boundaries in Dating*, 37.

4. Amreet, *Pinterest*, www.pinterest.ca/pin/366480488426099887, accessed June 25, 2022.

Chapter 13

1. Cloud and Townsend, *Boundaries: When to Say Yes*, 165.

2. Ibid., 55.

3. Cloud and Townsend, *Safe People*, 35.

4. Ibid., 32.

5. Ibid., 36.

6. Ibid., 37.

7. Ibid., 38.

8. Fyodor Dostoevsky, *AZ Quotes,* www.azquotes.com/quote/43 5249, accessed July 5, 2022.

9. Cloud, *Never Go Back,* 17.

10. Ibid., 158-159.

11. www.psychologytoday.com/ca/blog/body-sense/201204/ emotional-and-physical-pain-activate-similar-brain-regions

12. Adam Hadhazy, "Think Twice: How the Guts 'Second Brain' Influences Mood and Wellbeing," *Scientific American,* February 12, 2010, www.scientificamerican.com/article/gut-second-brain, accessed July 5, 2022.

13. *O'Reilly,* "Try Becoming the Problem," www.oreilly.com/ library/view/100-ways-to/9781601632449/xhtml/ch92.html, accessed July 5, 2022.

Chapter 14

1. Steve Jobs, *Goodreads,* www.goodreads.com/quotes/445287-don-t-let-the-noise-of-others-opinions-drown-out-your, accessed July 5, 2022.

Made in the USA
Columbia, SC
21 February 2023

12773401R00200